"There are tens of billions of dollars being spent on construction of new healthcare facilities in the U.S. today. Before spending another dime, healthcare executives should read this book and learn how it's possible to take as much as 40% of the building cost out before a shovel ever goes in the ground. This result has now been proven over and over by many healthcare organizations on the Lean transformation journey. As a bonus, but even more importantly, we can improve staff satisfaction and clinical quality at the same time as the cost goes down. Naida Grunden and Charles Hagood beautifully document these outcomes by the use of real case studies in addition to her own extensive experience as a careful observer of Lean healthcare."

John Toussaint, MD, CEO
ThedaCare Center for Healthcare Value

"Leading Lean hospitals have learned they need more than ongoing continuous process improvements. Given the chance to build new or expanded facilities and space is a unique opportunity to build in efficiency and patient-centered care from the start. *Lean-Led Hospital Design* is a fantastic book that shows the reader exactly how to incorporate process design with space design in a collaborative and iterative manner. The vivid examples shared by Naida Grunden and Charles Hagood bring these principles and practices to life. This book will help your organization immensely, whether you are just starting to plan for a new facility or whether you are ready to move in."

Mark Graban
Author, Lean Hospitals: Improving Quality, Patient Safety, and Employee Engagement, 2nd Edition and Healthcare Kaizen: Engaging Front-Line Staff in Sustainable Continuous Improvement

"Naida Grunden, author of *The Pittsburgh Way,* and Charles Hagood have nailed an important oversight in Lean and other industrial engineering applications in healthcare. Too little attention is focused on the role of the environment and physical plant in making exceptional performance possible. Would a world-class symphony perform in a substandard hall with poor acoustics, uncomfortable seats, audible distractions and visual impediments? Excellent case studies demonstrate how health facilities can be designed to advance safety, clinical quality and efficiency. This book argues effectively that performance excellence must be aligned with a supportive physical environment."

Karen Wolk Feinstein
President, Jewish Healthcare Foundation of Pittsburgh
Founding co-Chair of the Pittsburgh Regional Health Initiative

"Hagood and Grunden have engaged one of the most complex and important subjects facing our great nation. This generation's place in American history is taking shape and in no small part will be valued on how we responded to the healthcare cost crisis. This book provides useful insight as to how we can design care that fulfills its obligation 'to do no harm' and yet provide it in a cost effective manner."

John Bardis
Chairman, President and Chief Executive Officer
MedAssets

"Lean techniques and tools have been transformative in our organization as a means of systematically analyzing processes and office design to eliminate waste. However, the beauty of Lean principles is that the goal is not simply to eliminate waste or increase efficiency but to ensure that change is always patient centered and driven by the front-line workers who interact with these patients every day. Lean principles help us to keep our patients at front and center whenever we are contemplating changes. In Naida Grunden's *Lean-Led Hospital Design,* she writes with great clarity and wisdom about how Lean principles can be used to create the ideal Hospital of the future."

Eileen Boyle, MD
Executive Director
East Liberty Family Health Care Center
Pittsburgh, PA

"Grunden and Hagood have produced an authoritative, compelling argument for adopting the principles of Lean management integrated through all aspects of hospital management from architectural design, construction through delivery of clinical care. In several examples they document the gains to be enjoyed in more functional design, construction cost savings, operational efficiencies, and more satisfying work conditions for healthcare professionals, and—most important—for the safety, satisfaction, and improved outcomes for patients. The unifying vision for building design and healthcare operation is 'what is best for the patient.'"

Robert W. Mason
Managing Partner
CC-M Productions

Lean-Led Hospital Design

Creating the Efficient Hospital of the Future

Naida Grunden and Charles Hagood

Foreword by Richard P. Shannon, MD

CRC Press
Taylor & Francis Group
Boca Raton London New York

CRC Press is an imprint of the
Taylor & Francis Group, an **informa** business

A PRODUCTIVITY PRESS BOOK

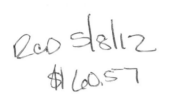

CRC Press
Taylor & Francis Group
6000 Broken Sound Parkway NW, Suite 300
Boca Raton, FL 33487-2742

Printed in the United States of America on acid-free paper
Version Date: 20111117

International Standard Book Number: 978-1-4398-6828-7 (Hardback)

Library of Congress Cataloging-in-Publication Data

Grunden, Naida.
    Lean-led hospital design : creating the efficient hospital of the future / Naida Grunden and Charles Hagood.
        p. ; cm.
    Includes bibliographical references and index.
    Summary: "The constrained atmosphere of rising costs and falling reimbursement threatening the efficiency and safety of the American hospital is practically screaming for Lean-led design and planning. Addressing years of process workarounds and poor space utilization, this book takes readers through the various stages of the Lean design development philosophy, including Lean architectural design and Lean work design. It provides a simplified timeline of architectural planning, using examples from eight real healthcare facility design and construction projects, and interviews with hospital leaders and architects"--Provided by publisher.
    ISBN 978-1-4398-6828-7 (hardcover : alk. paper)
    I. Hagood, Charles. II. Title.
    [DNLM: 1. Hospital Design and Construction--United States. 2. Efficiency, Organizational--United States. 3. Hospital Administration--United States. 4. Quality of Health Care--United States. WX 140 AA1]

    725'.51--dc23   2011046208

Visit the Taylor & Francis Web site at
http://www.taylorandfrancis.com

and the CRC Press Web site at
http://www.crcpress.com

Dedication

This book is dedicated to my late father, James Hagood, whose illness and extended hospital stay inspired me to apply my talents and resources toward making the right work easier to do for all the dedicated and overburdened caregivers in the healthcare industry.

—Charles Hagood

Contents

Foreword

Form Follows Function:
Designing the New Healthcare Delivery System

Never in U.S. history has the subject of healthcare costs been so visible or
so contentious. While few Americans can truly appreciate what $2.6 tril-
lion dollars or 18% of the GDP really means, more and more perceive the
double-digit increases in premiums and their attendant social costs. Stop for
a moment to consider how much money $2.6 trillion represents: spending
at a rate of $1000 every 5 seconds, it would take 412 years to consume. Not
only does the rising cost of healthcare deprive working Americans of wage
increases and the associated social mobility that once was the American
dream, it also has driven unacceptable social tradeoffs. School and library
closings in local communities are attributed directly and appropriately to
rising healthcare costs. While these impacts are real and increasingly recognized, another variable in the healthcare cost equation—the *value* of
the services rendered—should command at least equal attention. Most
Americans might pay more for healthcare if assured of associated value and,
increasingly, a demand for greater value is driving a focus on quality that
actually should make health care cost less.

Value in the U.S. healthcare system has been diluted by visible waste like
over-utilization, lack of price transparency, and failures both in delivery of
care and care transitions. Estimates suggest as much as half of all healthcare
spending brings little or no value to patients. Over the last decade, and long
before the recent debate over the Patient Protection and Affordable Care
Act, a series of pioneers embarked on a precarious journey to transform
the delivery system using principles borrowed from other, more reliable

American industries. The application of these improvement principles has brought remarkable benefits and lower costs to medical care. The concepts are empirically simple. High-performance health care requires continuous improvement. Continuous improvement requires continuous learning. Continuous learning means identifying and solving problems in the course of work. Solving problems requires disciplined skills and a common language for communicating new learning.

Surprisingly, these rational and inarguable reforms, cloaked in the guise of work redesigns and applied at the point of care, have not been widely embraced or adopted, leading to islands of excellence, amid a sea of prolific opportunities for improvement. Most of this success has eluded the medical literature as medical scholars debate the merits and legitimacy of the science of continuous quality improvement. This intransigence and skepticism has led to insufficient and ineffective communication of these lessons to the medical community as a whole.

These stories—many of them personal sagas—are both compelling and inspirational in conveying what is humanly possible through disciplined problem solving. The new knowledge is sowing seeds of transformation in American healthcare. Naida Grunden, a consummate storyteller, has faithfully and reliably recounted the pioneering journeys of the agents behind these changes. In a previous volume titled, *The Pittsburgh Way to Efficient Healthcare*, Grunden chronicled a regional Lean effort in southwestern Pennsylvania that aimed to provide patients with only the care they need, at the optimum time, in the most appropriate setting and with the highest possible quality. The accounts are at once personal yet highly professional, simultaneously capturing case histories and human emotion. The improvement processes and work redesigns are elegant in their simplicity; they underscore the transformative power of human capital and demonstrate the importance of tapping the knowledge and experience of all healthcare workers in the pursuit of habitual excellence.

On the heels of this important work comes another contribution from Grunden focusing on the importance of both work and space redesign in the healthcare delivery system. In *Lean-Led Hospital Design* she and co-author Charles Hagood illustrate why the application of Lean thinking to the design of healthcare facilities is a critical complement to delivery-system redesign. Their work brings new meaning to the nineteenth century American architect Louis Sullivan's heuristic that *form must follow function*. Just as Sullivan applied this thinking to skyscrapers, Grunden and Hagood describe the critical reasons for permitting function to govern structure in the design of hospitals and clinics. In this natural extension of Grunden's decade-long study of applications of Lean principles to healthcare delivery, she and Hagood show that transformation of health care and perfection of its processes often requires transformation of the space in which care is given. They guide us through the ways Lean is contributing to both.

To those of us who aspire to better, higher quality health care, the authors also create innovative music to accompany and advance the cause of defect-free delivery. Even as we have applied Lean principles to medical practice as a means of improving the care we deliver, we often have been constrained by the walls and fixtures in the spaces where we work. That work redesign and elimination of waste now informs space redesign is a truly hopeful sign that our first principles are taking hold.

Wonderful examples abound throughout this book and the underlying Lean concepts are articulated in ways both highly readable and readily absorbed. Some of the most telling examples come in the attention given to waiting areas and lobbies, which for all their modern splendor, sentence patients and families to countless wasted hours and offer grand, if mute testimony to healthcare's yawning inefficiency. What if patients never waited? What savings could be realized in building costs if healthcare facilities didn't require these space-hogging rooms? Grunden and Hagood offer ways to supplant endless waits. They give us ideas about work redesign and complementary space redesign that are the essential ingredients for that seemingly elusive state of patient-centeredness in health care.

The book is a must read for all healthcare CEOs and board members whose hospitals and clinics are contemplating building campaigns. Before borrowing for construction, these executives should pledge adherence to the brilliant, to-the-point concepts the book describes. These ideas are the moral equivalent of the legal debt covenants bond issues require. No project should be considered "shovel ready" without embracing and applying them.

Richard P. Shannon, MD
Chair, Department of Medicine, Hospital of the University of Pennsylvania and Frank Wister Thomas Professor of Medicine at the University of Pennsylvania's Perelman School of Medicine

Preface

When it comes to people's health, we have to set competition aside.

—Hon. Paul H. O'Neill
former secretary of the U.S. Treasury

This book is the result of unparalleled collaboration among hospitals, leaders, staff members, architects, planners, Lean practitioners, and others who, on other days of the week, might consider one another competitors. A recognition has arisen that American healthcare in its current state is *unsustainable,* with notoriously high costs, uneven care, imperfect outcomes, worker dissatisfaction, and lack of access. A recognition has also arisen that we must collaborate in the interest of fixing healthcare for ourselves and our fellow citizens.

Unsustainable is an apt word, with its environmental or "green" connotation as well. But the hospital environment, the built facility itself, can be more than earth-friendly. It can help or hinder the delivery of care and efforts at improvement. When we build new hospitals without adequate collaboration among every affected person, right from the start, we literally cast in concrete certain forms of waste and inefficiency that will have to be worked around until the next big remodeling project, which may only make things worse. That waste, too, is *unsustainable.*

Rather than building a beautiful new hospital that imports the old systems and problems, it may be time to reexamine the hospital. How can a building foster continuous improvement? How can we design it to be flexible and useful well into the future? How can we do more with less?

This book explores the intriguing question of how hospitals could be built to increase patient safety while eliminating waste, reducing travel and waiting, lowering cost, and generally easing some of healthcare's most persistent problems. The solutions are not "plug and play." You will see each institution grapple with common questions and come to rational, if different, solutions. The real insight comes from watching how these institutions learned the improvement process, which will guide their decisions into the future. The following describes how this book is organized.

Section 1: Lean Background and Model

- Chapter 1: "The Two Faces of Lean: Process Design and Facility Design." New healthcare policies will force change to the way in which healthcare is delivered in the United States. Hospitals will no longer be paid for certain hospital-acquired conditions. For the past decade, hospitals have had some success using Toyota-based Lean concepts to make work processes more efficient, and that can have a dramatic impact on hospital design.
- Chapter 2: "Traditional versus Lean-Led Hospital Design." Every stage of the typical "design–bid–build" process is ripe with opportunities to reduce, change, and shorten time lines while dramatically improving the quality of the building. This chapter outlines the difference between the traditional methods and Lean-led design. It also shows that, no matter what the stage of design and construction is, Lean-led design can help maximize efficiency.
- Chapter 3: "A Model for Lean-Led Design." This chapter offers a more detailed look at Lean-led hospital design and presents a model for consideration. The model relies heavily upon the Toyota discipline of 3P—product, process, and preparation—used in industry to design a new item quickly and break through old thinking.

Section 2: Lean Design at Every Stage

- Chapter 4: "Are We Too Late?" Spotsylvania Regional Medical Center in Fredericksburg, Virginia, had already been built and was ready for occupancy when the owner learned about Lean design. It was too late to change the building, but it was the perfect time to introduce the organizing concept of 5S (sort, set in order, shine, standardize, and sustain) during the chaotic time of move-in. It also provided an opportune time to train the all-new staff in Lean concepts.
- Chapter 5: "Are We Too Early?" At Lee's Summit Medical Center in Lee's Summit, Missouri, process improvements made such a dramatic

improvement in space utilization that the hospital scrapped its plans to expand. Regional Medical Center of Acadiana (Lafayette, Louisiana) conducted its own predesign for its new hybrid operating room (OR) before ever hiring the architect. As a result, they knew what they wanted right from the start.

■ Chapter 6: "Standardization Supports Flexibility." Against some objections, staff at Monroe Clinic in Monroe, Wisconsin, decided that all patient rooms should be standardized. In looking at their processes of care first, they discovered that a standardized environment was safer. They also built a smaller hospital.

Section 3: Broadening Collaboration

■ Chapter 7: "When to Break the Rules." Follow a very complex new hospital program in Boulder Community Hospital (Boulder, Colorado) as departments in the Invasive Services cluster decide to share expertise and space. Perhaps most revealing, as team members become more cohesive, they gain the confidence to break a rule of 3P to come up with the best design.

■ Chapter 8: "At the Tipping Point." At Seattle Children's Hospital in Seattle, Washington, supply chain improvements at the main hospital, along with experience building a new clinic, inform the design of the new cancer center. ThedaCare (Appleton, Wisconsin) chooses creativity before capital. The team creates an experimental "collaborative care" unit and then the ultimate mock-up before design and construction begin. California's Sutter Health undertakes retrofitting on a massive scale. Rebuilding or reinforcing half of its 28 hospitals to seismic code, Sutter Health faces design and construction decisions on a massive scale and turns to Lean design concepts to help deliver.

Section 4: Extended Applications

■ Chapter 9: "Cultural Context for Lean-Led Design." At the Abu Dhabi Health Service foreign worker Disease Prevention and Screening Center (United Arab Emirates), a facility is designed that can efficiently screen 5,000 immigrant workers daily, according to their cultural and religious beliefs, in an atmosphere that is dignified, respectful, and welcoming.

■ Chapter 10: "Lean Technology." The new Swedish Hospital in Issaquah, Washington, has found a way to share a nerve center among critical technology areas—not only the building function, but also telemetry, staffing, and disaster preparation. In Pittsburgh, Pennsylvania, the University of Pittsburgh Medical Center found that technology is *not* always the answer. But used correctly, it can save time and lives. How can technology be rationally designed and built into the patient–caregiver experience?

Section 5: Conclusion and Resources

■ Chapter 11: "Looking to the Future." What might the hospital of the future look like and how will we change to accommodate it? When a new building opens that supports Lean process improvements, sustaining the gains still involves leadership.

Appendices

Many Lean thinkers have contributed to these appendices. Each one is a value-added piece of work that can stand alone as well as be used with the Lean-led design model.

■ Appendix A: "A Little History." This appendix sketches hospital care from ancient times through the Nightingale movement. From that point, the focus shifts to the United States, summarizing the decades of the twentieth and twenty-first centuries in terms of legislation, social backdrop, and medical breakthroughs and their effects on hospital design.
■ Appendix B: "Nine Questions to Assess Your Organization's Lean State." This appendix includes a tool for hospital leaders and others who would like to see where they are on their "Lean journey." This short-form scoring matrix is based on the comprehensive Lean organizational developmental matrix developed by Healthcare Performance Partners and is shared here for the first time.
■ Appendix C: "Selecting the Right Design and Construction Team." This appendix provides a helpful matrix for selecting an architect with genuine Lean experience. It includes key questions to ask, what you need to know, and why.

■ Appendix D: "Voices from the Field: The Lean Practitioners Speak." This must-read section is for those interested in the observations of people working at the front lines of Lean healthcare. This section is a compilation of essays by Lean expert Mark Graban; architect David Chambers; David Munch, MD; Gary Bergmiller, PhD; Teresa Carpenter, RN; and Maureen Sullivan, RN.

Acknowledgments

This book would not have been possible without the generous and eager participation of the organizations and people who shared their stories. Thanks for informing and inspiring others with your stories of struggles and triumphs on the road to creating better hospitals. Even the appendices in this book add value because of you.

Thanks especially to the people who have helped shape the book along the way:

Teresa Carpenter, RN, who understands how architects, clinicians, and Lean practitioners work together today and how they can do it even better in the future; Tania Lyon, PhD, for her fearless and insightful editing of the work; Jason Baldwin for multitudes of vital tasks flawlessly performed; Dr. David Munch for his patient analysis; and Lean touchstones Marshall Leslie, Richard Tucker, Alex Maldonado, Ken Lowe, Ronnie Daughtry, Jeff Wilson, Maureen Sullivan, Dave Pickens, Gary Bergmiller, and Dave Krebs.

Author Mark Graban graciously contributed a wonderful essay to kick off Appendix D: "Voices from the Field: The Lean Practitioners Speak." He was also instrumental behind the scenes, directing us to some wonderful Lean initiatives. Thanks to him and to Pat Hagan at Seattle Children's, as well as to Kathryn Correia and Albert Park at ThedaCare. Thanks to Mimi Falbo, DNP, and David Sharbaugh for their insights.

Hats off to the librarians at Western Washington University, who took to the stacks with flashlights during a power failure to locate the works of architect/professor Steven Verderber of Clemson University.

Also, thanks to architect David F. Chambers for a glimpse of the future.

Special thanks to our spouses, Larry Grunden and Terri Hagood, for their sacrifices of our time and attention, and for allowing us to pursue the work we love to do.

Authors

Naida L. Grunden has been a professional writer for over 20 years. Naida has spent the past decade documenting the increasing acceptance of Toyota-based processes (Lean) in healthcare. Her book, *The Pittsburgh Way to Efficient Healthcare,* captured the seminal work of the Pittsburgh Regional Health Initiative (PRHI) during the introduction of Lean in competing hospitals across southwestern Pennsylvania. She received the American College of Clinical Engineering challenge award for her contribution to the clinical engineering profession.

Naida continues to write, teach, and speak nationally and internationally on the topic of Toyota-based principles in healthcare. The wife of a pilot, she also shares an interest in applying aviation safety and reliability concepts to healthcare. She holds a BA in English from California State University, East Bay, and a California secondary English teaching credential from California State University, San Francisco.

Charles V. Hagood, MBA, is the founder and president of Healthcare Performance Partners, Inc., a Lean healthcare consulting firm based in Nashville, Tennessee, that works with the largest for-profit and not-for-profit hospital systems in the United States. He was also the cofounder and former managing principal of The Access Group, LLC, an international manufacturing services and Lean enterprise consulting firm whose clients included such companies as GE, Tyco, Cessna, and Ford, as well as many other automotive, aerospace, and consumer goods manufacturers. He is the creator and editor of the popular LeanHealthcareExchange.com website and founding faculty member of the Belmont University Lean Healthcare Certificate Program.

Charles received his MBA from the Belmont University Massey School of Business in Nashville, Tennessee. He is also an adjunct faculty member of the Massey School of Business.

LEAN BACKGROUND AND MODEL

1

The Two Faces of Lean: Process Design and Facility Design

There is no such thing as an architect or construction firm that can build you a Lean hospital. Lean is not a building. It comes from within.

> **—Kathryn Correia**
> *Senior Vice President, ThedaCare*

This chapter describes the difference between Lean process improvements and Lean hospital design. Although synergistic, they are different.

Introduction

The American healthcare landscape is changing again. As the nation faces increasing fiscal pressure, there is less tolerance for limitless financing of our healthcare system—the world's most expensive,[1] which consumes over 17% of the gross domestic product (GDP)[2] while leaving one in six Americans uninsured.[3] This same system, which routinely performs medical miracles, is also responsible for the deaths of about 90,000 people annually due to medical error[4] and another 99,000 due to hospital-acquired infections.[5] Other nations do far better with far less.

The case for improving quality and safety while reducing cost has never been clearer, and the stakes have never been higher. Although manufacturers have long known that improving quality reduces cost, that understanding has been slow to dawn in healthcare. There is growing acceptance that safety and cost reduction are all of a piece. Now the hard part begins—learning *how* to make dramatic quality improvement.

New Healthcare Policies May Force the Issue

The American healthcare system has some of the most advanced health remedies and technologies in the world, as well as competent and compassionate healthcare practitioners. But our combined technology, science, facilities, equipment, and compassion are only as good as our ability to deliver them. Delivering healthcare requires a completely integrated system that fosters respect for patients and workers, provides the best known care efficiently every time, and improves continuously. Such a system delivers value to each patient. We do not deliver care perfectly—yet.

New healthcare policies and reimbursement experiments at national and state levels are pushing healthcare toward a more integrated, collaborative model of care, in an effort to improve delivery and reduce cost. Tucked into the 2010 Patient Protection and Affordable Care Act is the attention-getting provision for voluntary participation in accountable care organizations (ACOs). In general, ACOs "create incentives for healthcare providers to work together to treat an individual patient across care settings—including doctor's offices, hospitals, and long-term care facilities."[6] The idea is to reduce Medicare and Medicaid costs by paying for integrated, rather than fragmented, care.

Currently, Medicare and Medicaid pay for individual transactions—each doctor's visit, x-ray, hospitalization, test, and so on. When it is paid for like piecework, the care itself becomes piecemeal, rather than one coherent event. Furthermore, paying for piecework encourages more pieces, meaning overuse and higher cost.

New emphasis will be on paying for "episodes of care." That is, Medicare and Medicaid will provide a lump sum for the treatment of a person's illness—from the initial diagnosis in a doctor's office through flawless hospitalization and discharge, rehabilitation, and follow-up—all in an effort to avoid acute problems that result in hospitalization and readmission. Health systems providing the highest quality and most efficient care should find the reimbursement adequate (in other words, they will not lose money on Medicare payments[7]).

One clinician explained the shift in approach this way: We have been paying for, and receiving, a bag full of knurled wheels, pinions, levers, and screws, when what we really needed was a watch. In the new scheme, doctors and hospitals will be paid to provide watches. Their pay will be based on patient outcomes, with bonuses for reaching quality benchmarks, instead of being paid for the number of tests and procedures they conduct. They will also be subject to new transparency requirements, divulging the error and infection rates and other safety measures on which they will be ranked.

The idea behind the legislation is to encourage hospitals to compete on quality. To operate in this demanding new healthcare environment, the hospital itself must change, giving far more consideration to the patient's experience and less to the individual power structures, often called silos, that have existed in hospital departments. Departmentalism, top-down management, command-and-control leadership, and the hospital hierarchy itself must now respond to the demand to collaborate across long-perceived boundaries. To meet the new demands for improved quality and safety and reduced cost, hospitals will have to provide consistently efficient and excellent care to every patient.

These demands will change how hospitals are run. They will also change how hospitals are built. Using Lean as (1) the operating system of the hospital and (2) the guiding philosophy behind facility design is the most enduring way to meet these new demands.

What Is Lean?

Lean is a management philosophy based on two tenets: continuous process improvement, and respect for people. It is a strategy backed by process improvement techniques that were introduced at the Toyota Motor Company shortly after World War II. Decimated by war, the Japanese firm knew that if it were to compete on the world stage, it would have to do much more with much less. Stockpiling inventory, for example, was out of the question. Using techniques promoted by the American quality expert, W. Edwards Deming, Toyota began a cycle of continuous improvement that continues today.[8]

In the 1990s, in Seattle, and in the early 2000s, in Pittsburgh, hospitals began experimenting with the tenets of the Toyota Production System (TPS) as a way to improve healthcare delivery systems by reducing waste and improving quality. They discovered that, in addition to measurably improved performance, impressive cost savings also resulted.

What is Lean? Simply stated, Lean is a structured way of continuously exposing and solving problems to eliminate waste in systems. The objective is to deliver value to patients (customers).[9] The components are, in order:

1. *People.* Lean, first and foremost, values and respects people—*patients* as the recipients of services (customers), partners in care, and the reason for the hospital's existence; frontline *workers* as precious resources and the source of limitless creativity; and leaders as the hands-on visionaries who move the organization toward the goal.
2. *Process.* Lean provides a commonsense, practical approach to transforming processes, which is rooted in the scientific method (the way things get done). The objective is the elimination of waste.
3. *Design.* Process transformation can be supported and accelerated through efficient design (of buildings, facilities, equipment, and technology).

To build a Lean hospital, Lean *process* improvement as a leadership strategy and frontline reality must precede Lean architectural *design.*

It is possible to begin Lean process transformation at the same time that an architecture project begins. In fact, Chapter 4 describes a Lean organizational system introduced in a brand-new hospital that was just hiring staff. But Lean-led architectural design proceeds farther and faster and produces better results when the hospital has already made significant progress with Lean process improvements—especially when everyone, including executive leadership, is active in those improvements.[10]

Leadership: The Key to the Kingdom

Hospital A decides to start a Lean transformation. Leaders engage engineers and consultants steeped in Lean knowledge from other industries to help spread this philosophy and management system, initially as a way to solve problems. The consultants work closely with the people in the quality department. They help train teams of frontline workers and middle managers in solving the real problems that frustrate them every day. This "learning by doing" begins to break down perceived barriers between departments and hierarchies and to foster teamwork for future problem solving. The concepts are simple, but the work is hard.

Liker's 14 Management Rules

In his book, *The Toyota Way,* Jeffrey Liker (2004) outlines the 14 management principles that Toyota uses to achieve world-class results. Leaders of lean hospitals apply these rules, first and foremost, to themselves.

Philosophy

1. Base management decisions on long-term philosophy, even at the expense of short-term financial goals.

Process: eliminate waste

2. Create process "flow" to surface problems. (Smooth flow makes it easier to spot something amiss.)
3. Use pull systems (respond to the demand; do not stock anticipatory inventory) to avoid overproduction.
4. Level out the workload (so that one person or department does not have too much).
5. Stop when there is a problem.
6. Standardize tasks for continuous improvement. (Standardization makes it easier to spot the outlier.)
7. Use visual control so that no problems are hidden.
8. Use only reliable, thoroughly tested technology.

People and partners: respect, challenge and grow

9. Grow leaders who live the philosophy.
10. Respect, develop, and challenge your people and teams.
11. Respect, develop, and challenge your suppliers.

Problem solving

12. Go see for yourself to understand the situation thoroughly.
13. Make decisions slowly by consensus, considering all options; implement rapidly.
14. Continue organizational learning through rapid improvement workshops (kaizen).

Teams analyze individual processes or "value streams," looking at how the patient encounters the siloed organization. For instance, a patient coming in for day surgery must register, wait, get labs, wait, get to pre-op, wait, talk to the anesthesiologist, wait, and so on. By focusing solely on improving the patient experience, teams find ways to cut down useless steps, reduce departmental barriers, increase the time that caregivers spend with patients, and improve patient flow. They repeat the cycle over and over, continuously improving with each pass.

But soon the work reaches a critical point. One of two things happens:

The performance improvement, which had been measurable, tapers off or backslides. Executive leadership begins to complain that Lean is not sustainable and raises the pressure on the quality department. Frontline workers lose enthusiasm because they do not feel supported in the difficult work of continuous improvement. The consultants pack up. The Lean effort falters. The heady days of big improvements are remembered fondly.

or

The executive team by now is rounding two or three times a week—and participation is mandatory. They walk a patient journey (or value stream), watching how information, supplies, and people flow through the system. Rather than meet in a conference room, leaders "go see; ask why; and show respect."[11] Board members practice Lean and now have fewer, shorter meetings and more time in the hospital. Lean work not only ties in with the strategic plan, but informs it. Managers at all levels continue to monitor progress and quickly sweep away barriers identified by the frontline staff. Ongoing Lean classes are taught by in-house staff members, and it is part of staff orientation. The consultants pack up. Patient and worker satisfaction scores continue to rise, quality measures improve, and cost savings continue to accrue. Leadership no longer worries about "sustaining" the effort because it is, simply, the way they do business.

Why would one Lean effort fail and another succeed? The answer almost always comes down to leadership. (See sidebar, Liker's 14 Management Rules.) Lean is not a problem-solving "project" to be delegated to folks in the quality department. (Please see Mark Graban's fine essay in Appendix D.) Consultants and teachers can be helpful, especially in jump-starting the effort and offering more information as efforts advance. But a Lean transformation cannot be outsourced. It must be led, and lived, from executive management through the ranks.

The disk operating system (DOS) in a computer remains the background force at all times, a part of everything that runs on-screen. It helps to think of Lean as a "leadership operating system," running in the background of the hospital at all times. This leadership operating system creates a collaborative culture where everyone, from the executive suite to the front line, works together continuously to improve the care that patients receive.

David Munch, MD, a former hospital executive and current Lean practitioner, notes that leaders have long been taught to manage by objective: just get the results. The problem with this, he says, is that if you have good results but rely on poor processes to achieve them, then you are also relying on heroic efforts by your employees to overcome the bad processes. Lean is focused relentlessly on both objectives *and* means. Reliable processes designed to minimize waste, making it easier to do the right things every time, will bring the organization to its objectives.

The American Society for Quality conducted a study of 77 hospitals and found that 53% of them have some type of Lean initiative, but that only 4% have full deployment, from management to the front line.[12] In other words, in all but that 4%, Lean is starting or growing or may yet be seen as a "project" or a "set of tools" rather than an operating system.

In the 4%, leaders learn to shift roles, from remote-control supervisor to on-site coach and facilitator. They allocate their time differently, reducing the number of meetings and increasing the amount of time in the units with the frontline workers. They plan for the long term.

Take, for example, the experience of physician CEO John Toussaint at Wisconsin's ThedaCare hospital. In his book about ThedaCare's Lean journey, *On the Mend,* Toussaint relates how he and other leaders became frustrated with backsliding and failure to sustain the gains:

> Finally, some brave soul said to a senior executive, "How are we supposed to change when you keep managing the same way?" The truth can be a sharp sting…[The executive team acknowledged that] [L]ean cannot be delegated to a few. It is a discipline that requires a new way of seeing by everyone in every role.[13]

Lean Process Improvement: Rules and Tools

Establishing Lean as the leadership operating system for the entire hospital is as essential as it is rare. But the second big ingredient is frontline engagement, which simply means giving everyone the opportunity to identify and fix problems in their own sphere and giving cross-departmental teams the tools and guidance they need to solve bigger problems themselves. It is important to remember that these "rules and tools," while extremely effective, are just artifacts: An entire system underlies their use.

Rules

Spear and Bowen's Rules in Use[14] remain a useful way to think about Lean process improvement. These four rules describe how people work and interact with each other, how services flow, and how problems come to light and are addressed. Table 1.1 describes these rules.

The objective of this kind of problem solving is to root out waste—redundant activities, useless steps—in every corner of the system. Why? The waste of time and talent dramatically increases frustration and expense, as well as something even more significant: error. For example, any airline pilot will tell you that each needless handoff or wasteful steps in the cockpit only increase the chance for human error. In any high-stakes endeavor, making operations smooth and efficient also makes them safer.

In healthcare, it is instructive to look at how nurses spend their time. The observational study[15] described in Figure 1.1 shows that about 63% of a nurse's time is wasted. Nurses routinely must spend more time in extraneous activities than in patient care.[16] But nurses do not deliberately waste their time; rather, the system wastes it for them. Lean is all about removing the things nurses do that do not add value and that take them away from bedside care—the wrong size blood pressure cuff, slow computer systems, missed communication, and so forth. Ultimately, removing waste helps put the emphasis where it belongs: on the patient.

Table 1.2 describes the eight wastes of healthcare, which key off the acronym DOWNTIME (defects, overproduction, waiting, not using talent, transporting, inventory, motion, and excess processing). Figure 1.2 gives pictorial examples of certain types of waste.

Tools

Of the dozens of Lean tools, three emerge from the start: observation, A3 thinking, and rapid improvement events (or kaizen).

Table 1.1 Ideal and the Four Rules in Use

	Lean is a structured way of continuously exposing and solving problems to eliminate waste in systems. The objective is to deliver value to patients (customers)[9]		
Rule[a]	*What is it about?*	*What does it mean?[b]*	*What might a failure look like?[c]*
Direction	Always aim toward the ideal	Defect free; one by one, customized for each patient; on demand; immediate; without waste or error; in a safe environment for patients and workers	Repeating blood tests because of defective blood draw Prepping patients at 8 a.m. for 3 p.m. schedule
Rule 1	Activities or steps involved in the work (*Note:* Standard work is necessary before processes can be stabilized and improved sustainably.)	Highly specified (standardized) as to: • Content • Sequence • Timing • Location • Expected outcome	Work done differently Beware of these words: "should," "usually," "sometimes," "I do it this way…" Caveat: must retain flexibility to address specific patient needs (~80% same/20% different)
Rule 2	Connections between customer and supplier	Highly specified—requests and responses made the same way every time • Direct—no ambiguity • Yes/no—ensure understanding • Clear and unambiguous	"The patient is ready," means different things to nurses, transporters, physicians. CT ordered without specifying whether contrast is needed

Table 1.1 (Continued)   Ideal and the Four Rules in Use

Rule[a]	What is it about?	What does it mean?[b]	What might a failure look like?[c]
Rule 3	Pathways connect activities in the path of care	• Highly specified • Predefined • Simple and direct • No loops or forks	Patients must go through four or five prompts in a phone tree to schedule an appointment. Medical imaging far from ED
Rule 4	Improvements	Direct response to single problem As close as possible to the problem in TIME and PLACE Using the scientific method (observe, gather data, generate hypothesis, test, measure results) Designed by those doing the work Under guidance of a teacher/coach Always aimed in the right direction: toward ideal	Reporting in May for first quarter's quality metrics Blaming people Guessing causes No follow-up, action plans, or problem resolution

[a] Rules 1, 2, and 3 govern the way work is *designed*. Rule 4 deals with how work is *improved*.

[b] Based on Spear, S., and Bowen, K. 1999. *Harvard Business Review* September–October: 97–106.

[c] Examples of failures supplied by Healthcare Performance Partners.

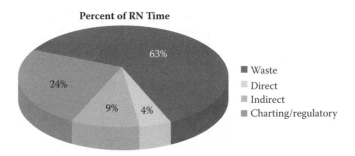

Percent of RN Time

Figure 1.1 Lean practitioners observed and assessed the time spent by nurses on a patient unit following their daily routines. They observed work flow, interviewed floor staff members, and observed discharge procedures and shift handoff processes. They found an alarming 63% of nursing time was spent on tasks classified as waste. Significant drivers were motion (travel), staff interruptions, and waiting for physician response (delay). (Courtesy Healthcare Performance Partners.)

Table 1.2 DOWNTIME: The Eight Wastes of Healthcare

Waste is any step in a process that does not directly provide better care to the patient/client			
Waste	*Definition*	*Example*	*Ways to address*
Defects	Work that contains errors or something unnecessary	Batching case cart assembly, often the day before needed; fax arrives on the pharmacy screen upside down Patient injured in a fall	Goal of zero sentinel events; find root causes of common "glitches" before they become sentinel events; institute checklists
Overproduction	Producing more than what the patient needs now; batching	Reports that autoprint when nobody needs them; supplies sent on a schedule instead of on demand; patients pushed into holding areas before processes are ready to receive them	Improve communication between customers and suppliers; install on-demand "pull" systems
Waiting	Idle time created when something or someone is not ready	Staff wait while OR is cleaned; patients wait in ER for bed on the floor; batched pathology slides wait to be read	Remove unnecessary steps from work pathway

Table 1.2 *(Continued)* DOWNTIME: The Eight Wastes of Healthcare

Waste	Definition	Example	Ways to address
Not using talent	People are not confident about the best way to do a task	Nurse has one definition of the patient being "ready"; doctor has another	Simplify IT interactions; standardize rooms and equipment; standardize definitions of common terms
Transporting	Unnecessary transporting of people, medications, specimens, or supplies	Pharmacy is a quarter of a mile from the ER and ambulatory surgery—the units that use it most	Look at distance, number of trips for access to people, information, supplies; reduce handoffs
Inventory	More materials are on hand than are needed to do the work	Crates of expired alcohol wipes are donated to Doctors Without Borders; yet, "We need more storage!"	Decrease excess inventory (kanban or similar "pull" system that replenishes only as necessary)
Motion	Looking, searching, rearranging of people, product, and supplies	Nurse must travel to three automated dispensing devices (like Omnicells) to gather materials to start an IV	Look at time, distance traveled, and how much time it takes to complete a milestone task (cycle time)
Excess processing	Ambiguous, redundant work; unessential paperwork that adds no value from patient perspective; providing a higher level of care than the patient needs	At 10 a.m., Mrs. Smith was repositioned to avoid bedsores. The nurse notes it (1) on the paper record, (2) in the EMR, and (3) on the white board. (Yet the aide still feels the need to ask, "Did you turn Mrs. Smith at 10 a.m.?")	Eliminate redundancies; standardize procedures, roles, communication; focus on actual needs of patients

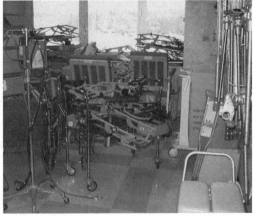

Figure 1.2   Examples of waste: *Defects* **as staff has no clear way to order or retrieve;** *Overproduction* **and** *Inventory* **problems with the equipment room (photos by Healthcare Performance Partners); and** *Waiting* **in the waiting room (Getty Images).**

■ *Observation.* Formal, firsthand observation at the point of care provides an invaluable look at the way in which work is actually (not theoretically) conducted. When done properly, observation is a way to honor the person whose work is being observed. Observation is the only way to understand the complexity, waste, and cost of processes, as well as how those things may be frustrating workers while impeding the flow of value to the patient.

■ *A3 thinking.* The discipline of the A3 (named for the 11 × 17 in. sized paper on which it is drawn) is that it helps frontline teams quickly analyze problems to their root causes, envision a better way to work, and devise countermeasures and experiments to get there. It's a one-page, hand-drawn document that relies on observation and teamwork to devise experiments and make improvements. Some think of it as the scientific method writ small.

■ *Kaizen.* In Japanese, kaizen is typically translated as "change for the good" and implies continuous improvement. This is a team-based, usually multiday rapid improvement event designed to analyze particularly complex problems that flow across departments. Together, members of the interdepartmental team analyze the current state, find the root causes of problems, develop a vision of the future state, and experiment with new ways to work, implement, and evaluate the new method and sustain it over time. Take a peek ahead at Figure 8.15 in Chapter 8, which shows a current state and future state (before and after kaizen). Notice how many unnecessary process steps (opportunities for error) have been removed.

Kaizen can also be a tool to cross (and eventually dismantle) departmental barriers. Some have argued that Lean optimizes pieces of processes, and that does happen. In terms of Lean strategy and work design, the focus should be on optimizing the whole patient experience, integrating care, and "pulling value to the patient."[17]

What is "value" for the patient? Value is created when a good or service delivered to the patient is something for which the patient and/or customer (i.e., insurance company) would be willing to pay.

Patients are willing to pay for the correct medicines, delivered correctly and on time; for the correct diagnosis and medical services delivered without waste or error; for proper treatment, timely discharge, and so on.

Anything that does not add value—such as nurses hunting for supplies or calling the lab repeatedly for results, or patients waiting on gurneys in the hallway or contracting hospital-acquired infections—is to be designed out of work. In Lean-led design, the objective is, as much as possible, to design a facility that paves the way for non-value-added activities to be removed from the processes and systems and hence out of the building.

When Lean Succeeds

Lean thinking can consolidate processes and travel, increase workplace organization, and lead to another unexpected benefit: decrease in the number of square feet required. For example, using Lean tenets, a Boeing plant in Auburn, Washington, improved productivity while reducing the space required from 650,000 to 450,000 square feet.[18] This paradox—less space leading to greater productivity—flies in the face of typical demands in healthcare facilities for "more space," "more personnel," and "more equipment." Those cries are usually expressions of frustration emanating from inefficient systems; in fact, adding more of everything often only increases the chaos and makes matters worse.[19]

In perhaps the most famous example of Lean hospital improvements published in recent literature,[20] Virginia Mason Hospital of Seattle noted that after 2 years of Lean improvements, it saved millions of dollars, without resorting to layoffs, solely by eliminating waste from its system.

While many fine hospitals have likewise begun finding major savings using Lean tenets, the Virginia Mason example is worth studying (Table 1.3) because, among the things that it found as it ironed out process after process, was a great deal of unrealized space. It saved on capital expenses by not adding a hyperbaric chamber, not relocating an endoscopy suite, and not adding new surgery suites that, it was discovered, were no longer necessary. Of the gains shown in Table 1.3, imagine how many affect the physical use of hospital space.

Table 1.3 Success Summary: Pilot Unit, Virginia Mason Hospital[20]

Category	Change
Inventory	Down 53%
Floor space	Down 41%
People travel distance	Down 44%

Lean-Led Architectural Design

> In most people's vocabularies, design means veneer. But to me, nothing could be further from the meaning of design. Design is the fundamental soul of a man-made creation that ends up expressing itself in successive outer layers.
>
> **—Steve Jobs**
> *"Apple's One-Dollar-a-Year Man,"* Fortune, *January 2000.*

Lean can be more than a way to remove waste from processes inside hospital walls. When a construction opportunity arises, the leadership operating system and rules and tools can apply directly to the design of a new facility. Applying Lean thinking in a structured way to hospital design can result in an environment that promotes continuous improvement, efficiency, safety,[21] and better flow of information, supplies, and service to patients. Lean-led design can help reinforce a Lean culture within the new building.

The same traits that lead to successful Lean process improvement will lead to successful Lean architectural design: hands-on executive leadership participation, a commitment to operating the entire facility as a learning organization, and enthusiastic participation at the front line of care.

> What is lean-led design? It is a systematic approach to healthcare architectural design that focuses on defining, developing, and integrating safe, efficient, waste-free operational processes in order to create the most supportive, patient-focused physical environment possible.

"Lean process transformation is about continuous improvement," said Charles Hagood, CEO of a Lean healthcare consultancy. "Can we create an environment that can continuously improve too? That's the idea behind Lean-led design."

Dr. Munch notes, "Again, one must manage to the means instead of the objective. Before design ever begins, the people in the organization must determine how they want to design their work. We have to constantly ask ourselves: 'How can we make the right work easier to do?'" He notes that, although the terms have almost become clichés, it is the learning organizations, the high-velocity organizations, the knowledge-sharing organizations that speed ahead with Lean process transformation and Lean design. He says:

> The paradigm shift with Lean-led design is this: We no longer rely on experts or architects to tell us how to design the building. Instead, we deeply engage the frontline in codifying their ideal work flows. Architects are design team participants who take the process information and transform it into a design. They are not the project leads: They are team members.

The presumption, then, is that Lean as a management philosophy and frontline strategy is already deployed in the hospital, even if in the early stages. Against that backdrop, Lean-led architectural design can begin as a way to remove physical barriers in the work flow. But what should the hospital consider before embarking on Lean facility design? The following three points are worth considering.

1. The Building Is Not an Excuse

Dr. Gary Kaplan, former CEO of Virginia Mason Hospital in Seattle, noted at a 2011 Lean healthcare conference that not every hospital that needs to rebuild or remodel has the budget to do so. But a dysfunctional building is no excuse not to strive for continuous process improvement within the existing walls.

At Monroe Clinic (Chapter 6) in Wisconsin, workers mocked up a new registration arrangement in their existing clinic building. Rather than waiting for the new building to be completed, they began using the new process in their improvised space, and noted a dramatic improvement in patient flow.

In a starker international example, consider the contrast between the health outcomes and cost in the United States and in Cuba. According to the World Health Organization's 2000 world health report,[22] the United States and Cuba rank neck and neck in quality (37 and 39, respectively). Life expectancy in both nations is nearly identical; infant mortality in Cuba is significantly lower.[23]

The differences are that the United States has the world's most expensive health system and Cuba's costs are among the lowest (118 in the world).[23] Per-capita income in the United States in 2008 was $45,000 to Cuba's $5,500.[24]

Figure 1.3 is a photograph of a newly renovated maternity unit in a provincial hospital in the Cuban countryside. The photo demonstrates that for

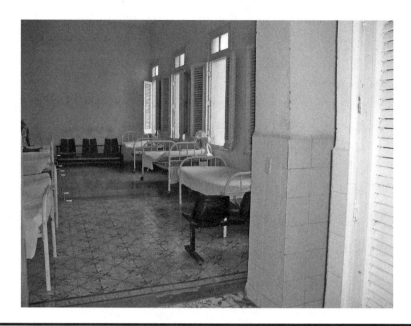

Figure 1.3 An example of "not using the facility as an excuse": a newly renovated maternity ward in a rural Cuban provincial hospital. Despite the simplest of facilities, health outcomes in Cuba are on par with those in US hospitals. Cuba's infant mortality rate is significantly lower than that of the United States, which ranked number 41 in the world in a 2011 WHO study. (Photo by Mimi Falbo, LLC, with permission.)

a poor country to achieve health results nearly on par with the world's most expensive system, it cannot let buildings become excuses that keep it from striving for perfection.

2. Build Only If It Creates Value

The heyday of hospital building, described in Appendix A, is over. Every dollar and every resource that goes into a new hospital building must be justified. Often, leaders believe that more space will solve their process problems, but only a systematic and deliberate approach, using Lean thinking, will do it. Process improvements will produce results that have implications for use of space, facilities, and equipment.

When do you build? Build when process improvements cannot take you any further. Here are two examples:

A. *Equipment use.* A large Midwestern hospital planned to expand its heart program, adding several surgical suites. The sticking point came in the central sterile area, where surgical instruments were cleaned and repacked. The machines there did not keep pace cleaning and drying surgical instruments as quickly as they were needed. The obvious answer was that plans for the new central sterile area should call for more space and more machines. Fortunately, the hospital did not accept the "obvious" answer.

A small Lean team looked at the way the machinery was currently used. It noticed that the dryer was at the lowest setting. The racks were 8 in. apart instead of the recommended 6 in., which reduced capacity by almost a third. Furthermore, the sophisticated dryer was able to read bar codes and adjust drying times to match, but the bar codes on incoming trays were missing, faded, or had just fallen off.

By adjusting the machines to their optimal settings and adjusting the way in which workers loaded them and bar-coded incoming items, the hospital increased capacity by 67%. In reality, it would have plenty of capacity to handle equipment from all of the new surgery suites *without adding equipment or space to the new central sterile area at all.*

When do you build? Build when process improvements cannot take you any further.

B. *Process improvement creates virtual space.* At a medical center in the South, process improvements in the Endoscopy Department improved patient flow, which created enough additional capacity that the hospital decided to forgo a $6 million renovation and even cancelled plans to move the department, which would have cost $1 million.[25]

3. If You Build or Remodel, Be Prepared to Invest Up Front

Applying continuous improvement to both process design and facility design means a significant investment in people, especially on the front end of the project.

Investing in People

Speaking of the difference between a traditional approach and a Lean-led approach to facility design, Pat Hagan, COO of Seattle Children's Hospital, said, "The traditional way of designing a building yields a nice even cash and expense flow that finance and operating officers like to see. With Lean design, there's a big bolus of expense at the very start that looks kind of threatening, because you wonder, will there be a return?"

When the team at Seattle Children's Hospital built a suburban outpatient facility in Bellevue, Washington,[26] traditional programming told them that they would need 110,000 square feet to accommodate all the functions they needed: estimated price, $100 million.

The initial Lean investment meant assembling not just doctors, nurses, executive officers, and an array of frontline workers, but also families, architects, the general contractor, and members of the construction team for several days of brainstorming. Together, they mapped out how various processes were done in the existing space and how they could be done even better and more efficiently in the future.

"This multidisciplinary workshop was a big investment of human resources, but it really paid off in the end, in improvements in safety, quality, less waste, and, ultimately, less cost," said Hagan. "We didn't have an even cash flow, but a heavy cash flow at the beginning to get all the parties together. From then on, the cash flow tapered off dramatically."

The investment in people paid off at Seattle Children's Bellevue Clinic and Surgery Center. Patient and staff satisfaction scores are higher than ever. Yet the new facility, with all envisioned functions, was 25,000 square feet smaller than estimated and came in at $40 million below the $100 million budget, because the design and construction were integrated (more on integrated project delivery in Chapters 3 and 8). "This was not such a big building that you would expect to save $40 million," said Hagan. "There is a linear connection between investing on the front end in an integrated facilities design, and savings at the end. We won't design a building any other way."

Taking the Long View, Even at the Expense of the Short Term

Albert Park is a construction manager and architect in the facility development department of ThedaCare in Wisconsin. To him, using Lean in facilities design is a way to use Liker's first principle of management: Base your decisions on a long-term philosophy, even at the expense of short-term goals.

"The life cycle cost of operating a hospital dwarfs the cost of the physical plant," says Park. "Over time, you will spend more on supplies and labor than you ever spent on the building....Looking long-term, the cost of the facility is minor. Any money you can spend that will make the process more effective and efficient, which will pay for itself many times over the life of the hospital."

For these reasons, Park says, he believes that well intentioned facilities managers who base decisions on the lowest fee and cheapest construction are missing the point. The architect and builder need to work collaboratively to support the operational model devised, in detail, by the staff.

The initial investment also extends to things that will make the building agile in the future. Says Park, "While things like modular storage, OR equipment on booms, customized bins, and visual management systems may present up-front costs, they will pay off later when the facility needs to change. Leaders need to be enlightened enough to know that nonrecurring costs pay off when design enables better work flow." In the end, architects cannot "give" hospital leaders a Lean hospital.

The life cycle cost of operating a hospital dwarfs the cost of the physical plant. Over time, you will spend more on supplies and labor than you ever spent on the building. Looking long-term, the cost of the facility is minor. Any money you can spend that will make the process more effective and efficient will pay for itself many times over the life of the hospital.

—Albert Park, architect and construction manager
Facility Development, ThedaCare

"Architects design the building and are gone, leaving hospital leaders and staff to live with the result," said Park. "Hospital leaders and staff must lead the effort, with architects as members of the team."

Summary

This chapter explains the interaction between process design and building design. Before hospital design can begin, the entire design team needs to develop a thorough understanding of (a) the way things are currently done and (b) how they could be done better, more safely, and more efficiently. In these circumstances, with process and architectural design coexisting, Lean-led design can proceed.

Discussion

- When we speak of "process" in a hospital setting, what kinds of things are we talking about?
  - What are the four Rules in Use, and why would they help to look at processes?
- Why should process mapping precede architectural drawing?
- What role does leadership play?
  - Discuss Liker's 14 points for leaders. Would hospital leadership find it challenging to put long-term plans ahead of short-term expenses? Why?
- Why can leaders not "outsource" Lean process improvement like any other program?

Suggested Reading

Graban, M. 2011. *Lean hospitals: Improving quality, patient safety, and employee engagement,* 2nd ed. New York: Taylor & Francis.

Grunden, N. 2007. *The Pittsburgh way to efficient healthcare: Improving patient care using Toyota-based methods.* New York: Productivity Press.

Institute for Healthcare Improvement Innovation Series. 2005. Going lean in health care.

Liker, J. 2004. *The Toyota way: 14 Management principles from the world's greatest manufacturer.* New York: McGraw–Hill.

Liker, J., and Hoseus, M. 2008. *Toyota culture: The heart and soul of the Toyota way.* New York: McGraw–Hill.

Ohno, T. 1988. *Toyota production system: Beyond large-scale production.* Portland, OR: Productivity, Inc.

Spear, S. 2009. *The high-velocity edge: How market leaders leverage operational excellence to beat the competition.* New York: McGraw–Hill.

Spear, S., and Bowen, K. 1999. Decoding the DNA of the Toyota production system. *Harvard Business Review* September–October: 97–106.

Notes

1. Organization for Economic Co-operation and Development (OECD). 2005. Health data sheet, 2005. http://www.oecd.org/dataoecd/15/0/35000577.pdf (accessed June 12, 2011).
2. Centers for Medicare and Medicaid Services (CMS). National health expenditure fact sheet. www.cms.gov/NationalHealthExpendData/25_NHE_Fact_Sheet.asp

3. Kaiser Family Foundation Report, cited in Wolf, R. 2010. Number of uninsured Americans rises to 50.7 million. *USA Today,* September 17, 2010.
4. Kohn, L., Corrigan, J., and Donaldson, M. (eds.). 1999. *To err is human: Building a safer health system.* Committee on Quality of Health Care in America, Institute of Medicine. Washington, DC: National Academy Press.
5. Klevens, R. M., Edwards, J., Richards, C., et al. 2007. Estimating health care–associated infections and deaths in US hospitals, 2002. *Public Health Reports* March–April 2007, vol. 122. Centers for Disease Control and Prevention.
6. U.S. Department of Health and Human Services. 2011. Accountable care organizations: Improving care coordination for people with Medicare: Proposal for accountable care organizations will help better coordinate care, lower costs. News release, March 31, 2011. http://www.hhs.gov/news/press/2011pres/03/20110331a.html (accessed June 12, 2011).
7. Minich-Pourshadi, K. 2011. How to break even on Medicare reimbursements for health leaders media, February 28, 2011. http://www.healthleadersmedia.com/content/FIN-263122/How-to-Break-Even-on-Medicare-Reimbursements.html## (accessed June 14, 2011).
8. Ohno, T. 1988. *Toyota production system: Beyond large-scale production.* Portland, OR: Productivity, Inc.
9. Healthcare Performance Partners presentation, Lean Healthcare Certificate Program Series, Jack Massey Graduate School of Business, Belmont University, Nashville, TN (http://www.buleancourse.com/).
10. Appendix B in this book describes how to assess where your hospital is on the lean continuum.
11. Womack, J. 2011. *Gemba walks.* Cambridge, MA: Lean Enterprise Institute.
12. ASQ Lean Six Sigma Hospital Study Advisory Committee. 2009. Get your checkup: ASQ study looks at hospital deployment of lean and six sigma. http://asq.org/perl/search-Google-Mini.pl?q=cache:8nXEL4Er1Hg:http://asq.org/quality-progress/2009/08/six-sigma/get-your-checkup.pdf+lean+hospital&site=my_collection&output=xml_no_dtd&client=my_collection&access=p&proxystylesheet=my_collection&oe=UTF-8 (accessed June 12, 2011).
13. Toussaint, J., Gerard, R., and Adams, E. 2010. *On the mend: Revolutionizing healthcare to save lives and transform the industry.* Cambridge, MA: Lean Enterprise Institute.
14. Spear, S., and Bowen, K. 1999. Decoding the DNA of the Toyota production system. *Harvard Business Review* September–October: 97–106.
15. Observational study conducted over 40 hours by Healthcare Performance Partners at a client hospital.
16. Thompson, D., Wolf, G., and Spear, S. 2003. Driving improvement in patient care: Lessons from Toyota. *Journal of Nursing Administration* 33:585–595.
17. Chambers, D. 2009. *Efficient healthcare: Overcoming broken paradigms.* © David Chambers.
18. US Environmental Protection Agency. Lean manufacturing and the environment. http://www.epa.gov/lean/studies/auburn.htm (accessed October 30, 2009).

19. Silvester, K., Lendon, R., Bevan, H., et al. 2004. Reducing waiting times in the NHS: Is lack of capacity the problem? *Clinician in Management* 12:1–8.
20. Institute for Healthcare Improvement Innovation series. 2005. Going lean in health care.
21. Reiling, J. 2007. *Safe by design: Designing safety in health care facilities, processes, and culture.* © 2007 Joint Commission on Accreditation of Healthcare Organizations. Author interview with Dr. Reiling was conducted September 29, 2010.
22. World Health Organization World Health Report. 2000. http://www.photius.com/rankings/healthranks.html
23. Oestergaard, M. Z., Inoue, M., Yoshida, S., et al. 2011. Neonatal mortality levels for 193 countries in 2009 with trends since 1990: A systematic analysis of progress, projections, and priorities. *PLoS Medicine* 8 (8): e1001080.
24. *World statistics pocketbook,* United Nations Statistics Division. www.data.un.org
25. Data from Healthcare Performance Partners.
26. Wellman, J., Hagan, P., and Jeffries, H. 2011. *Leading the lean healthcare journey: Driving culture change to increase value.* Boca Raton, FL: CRC Press.

Chapter 2

Traditional versus Lean-Led Hospital Design

Architecture today is not seen as an important part of the health care delivery system...But architecture is an unexpected point of leverage for intervening in the current situation...and can play a pivotal role in the strategy for breaking free from the present mess.

Architect David F. Chambers
Efficient Healthcare: Overcoming Broken Paradigms[1]

This chapter compares and contrasts the traditional and Lean-led approaches to hospital design. The following chapter goes into more detail on Lean-led design and presents a model.

Introduction

During early design of their new hospital, clinicians at Owensboro Medical Health System (OMHS) in Kentucky became convinced they needed to buy two new CT scanners and plan large, additional spaces to accommodate them. They based this assumption on the best data they had—that, currently, with two CT scanners, they were turning away outpatient business and were barely keeping up with inpatient demand. But other data showed that the community was adequately served by the number of CT scanners it had. The forecast increase in demand did not seem to justify a 100% increase in the number of scanners at the new OMHS.

Owensboro Medical Health System (OMHS)

This 442-bed, full-service, acute-care hospital is located in Owensboro, Kentucky. The new hospital opened in 2010, replacing the one that opened in 1938. Lean process improvement has been introduced at the facility and has been considered part of the work for about 2 years. As planning progressed, Lean process improvements played a significant role in certain decisions, saving space and money.

Lean practitioners at OMHS were working to help introduce continuous process improvement. Lean practitioner Richard Tucker took Lisa Jones, vice president of clinical services, to the imaging area, where the two of them stood between the two CT scanners for 45 minutes during prime time one Tuesday afternoon. The scanners should have been humming. But during their observation, not a single patient came through. People were working hard, but the upstream processes were so broken that patients could not be delivered to the CT scanner reliably. For example, patients who needed contrast ahead of the procedure had not received it due to communication gaps between the patient care unit and the pharmacy. Delays then cascaded from the pharmacy back to the unit and on to transport and the CT scanner. Since the root causes of the delays were never addressed, they had become an expected part of the system.

Once the Lean team streamlined those internal processes—a difficult but rewarding exercise—all inpatients were easily accommodated. In fact, volume promptly increased by 120 procedures per month due to improved access; the bottom line improved by $100,000 per month, and the hospital has not turned away any outpatients. Said Jeremy Handley, CT supervisor, "We would not have believed that we could handle this kind of volume, and yet the staff's stress level is perceptibly lower."

Had OMHS based square-footage calculations on historical data without first understanding the waste in the value stream, it would have created more square footage and far more expense than necessary. Furthermore, the expanded capacity would not have addressed the process problems, and it is likely that outpatients would still have been turned away.[2]

More Is Not Necessarily Better

The leaders at OMHS learned firsthand the importance of basing decisions on real-time observation of the front line instead of assumptions based on historical, aggregated data. This case exemplifies the difference between Lean-led design and traditional design.

Traditionally, an architect leads the design process, starting out right away to draw up some general options based on the perspectives, preferences, and experiences of a handful of hospital leaders. Strong departmental identities and reliance on the status quo discourage outside-the-box thinking that might yield unimagined efficiencies. Without a careful look at process first, as almost happened with OMHS, assumptions about the work will not match what is actually happening. The result of casting these suppositions in concrete is a suboptimal building.

With Lean-led design, the emphasis is on processes that add value for the patient. The hospital, not the architect, is in the lead. Through a series of disciplined exercises, multifunctional teams look at how work is done today and how it could be done better in the future, and then they design for that future target. They scrutinize the connections and pathways throughout the facility; in other words, they learn to view the facility itself as a system. Far more planning and process development go into the first stages of Lean-led design; drawing comes later.

With Lean-led design, changes include:

■ The amount of time spent in each phase (more in the early phases, less later on): Liker's first management principle speaks to planning for the long term, even at the expense of the short term. Spending this time up front saves time later.

■ A completely different perspective comes from looking at each step as an opportunity to design more value for the patient into each process (optimizing the parts).

■ The opportunity is available to ask audacious questions and upend prevailing notions about how the hospital can deliver value to the patient (optimizing the whole).

The following discussion describes the steps in the architectural design process, examining the differences between traditional architectural design and Lean-led design (summarized in Table 2.1).

Traditional Design

Master Planning

How will this hospital continue to renew itself over the next 20 years? This is the question at the heart of master planning, a facility-level strategic plan.[3]

Table 2.1 Traditional versus Lean-Led Architectural Design Philosophies

Traditional architectural design	Lean-led design
Focus on design	Focus on adding value for customer/patient
Starts with a functional and space program	Starts with observation at the point of work
User groups (staff leaders within a department or service)	Value-stream-focused teams (key stakeholders involved across the whole process of delivering the service to the patient) used to analyze processes
Each user group provides feedback to designers without benefit of understanding "the bigger picture"; rule 2, connections, not used	Multidisciplinary consensus-based, future-state processes drive the development of the floor plan
Floor plan diagrams are adjusted to accommodate the way the hospital currently works; anticipated process improvements remain unclear, undefined	Floor plan diagrams are used to validate the value stream, optimize future improvements; rules 2 and 3 (connections and pathways) are addressed

Over time, whole sections of the hospital need to be remodeled, removed, or replaced. The outcome of a master plan is a fuller understanding of the overall sequence in which the major work will be done in coming years.

Whenever work is done in one area, the rest of the facility has to keep operating. Planners must identify the first building site—an office, a lab, a block of rooms—and then decide how to accommodate that operation elsewhere in the facility during construction. Before embarking on any major building project, savvy hospital planners revisit their master plan to see how the contemplated improvements fit into the long-term picture and budget.

In traditional master planning, the focus is on architecture, rather than on operations. Architects understand the life expectancy of current building and where the next expansion is most appropriate. They forecast and prepare diagrams and renderings of what the building could look like in the future.

"Traditional master plans don't delve into what you could do to maximize your current operations," said Teresa Carpenter, RN. "For example, does the ED [Emergency Department] really need to be expanded, or could internal process improvements create capacity by improving flow? Those questions—those opportunities—are left on the table in traditional design."

Predesign

The architectural team is firmly in the lead, guiding hospital leaders through the basics, like where to site the building, how tall it may be, and so on. At this stage, major blocks of functional areas and adjacencies emerge, along with a rough time frame and budget.

The project team, led by strategic and clinical operations consultants, guides facility staff through a design process. Its members hone in on their clients' expectations and look at how the new building will function for patients and staff. From the start, the focus is on the future; however, without a detailed examination of the current state, opportunities to remove waste remain largely unexamined.

Programming begins during this phase, and it consists of two component documents:

- *Functional program.* This narrative document describes the basic assumptions—for example, the number of patient visits that the new ED will accommodate and whether it includes a fast track option, for how many hours per day.
- *Space program.* This line-by-line spreadsheet lists all the spaces that will be needed. The proposed ED, for example, may need a waiting room of 2,000 square feet to accommodate 50 people, the restrooms, the registration area, and all of the spaces needed to complete the project.

Planners arrive at the sizes and numbers of rooms and clinical department square footages based on data from historical and projected volumes, operations models, and formulas created over time by experience on other projects. However, those calculations may not be sacrosanct. If processes of care have not been vetted before programming, space allocations may not truly match the need. Space calculations and adjacencies are sometimes weighted more toward the way in which the last few projects were conducted, rather than toward the specific needs of this client.

For example, executives at a Midwestern hospital were shocked to discover the name of another hospital on their plans: The drawings had been hastily recycled and merely adapted to the site, and the title blocks had not been changed.

That is too bad. Although hospital buildings may not need to be reinvented each time, hospital architecture is anything but "plug and play." Each new project offers an opportunity to go through process development to improve the standard every time. Shortcuts hurt.

When traditional programming is completed, the architect begins "bubble diagramming" and "blocking and stacking" departments. This is the point at which the project begins to be "cast in stone." Changes after this are possible, but expensive. Opportunities for standardizing rooms or combining areas—such as pre- and postprocedure areas or preadmission and registration—will be lost if they are not discovered now.

Based on the results of programming, the architectural team usually presents two or three options for the design. Those options are shared with "user groups" that ordinarily consist of department leaders and, occasionally, some frontline workers.

Typically, user group meetings pore over programming spreadsheets line by line, asking questions such as, "How many offices do you need?" Considerations like standardization, movement within each space, processes, and patient flow are not considered as closely as the specifics of the program.

The end of programming marks a key milestone in the project: Hospital executives must sign off on the selected model before schematic design begins because major changes after this will be hard to make. In this traditional model, hospital leaders are asked for this commitment before they have deeply examined how their processes will work in the new space.

"The adage, 'form follows function' is as old as the hills," said Carpenter. "Asking executives to sign off this early, before they know if the space will work for them, means function will have to follow form."

Schematic Design

Schematic design begins a few weeks later, when the architects return with a more differentiated floor plan. The large, generalized blocks of space now show where rooms will go. The major structural pieces—columns, stairwells, elevators, and the like—are finalized. The "onstage" or public areas are differentiated from the "offstage" or service and staff areas.

If the hospital has called for standardized rooms from the beginning, the structural grid with column placement can be created in a way that accommodates it. If not, immovable columns in the wrong spots can reduce the chance for optimal standardization.

If a mock-up is called for, it will be created now. In traditional design, a mock-up is created mainly to see how a single patient room will look and where things might go. Simulations and large-scale or multiunit mock-ups are not ordinarily a part of traditional design.

The hospital sets its goals and budget and identifies which patient floors will be affected. Department managers and selected staff members form user groups and review the plans to give feedback. Unless user group members have been involved in a major hospital renovation before, they may not know what to expect or what is expected of them. Standardized training and data collection are rare.

By the end of schematic design, departments and adjacencies are established and no longer movable, and the design is frozen. Other functions get involved now, such as engineering, site planning, and interior and exterior design. Adequate space for equipment must be allocated now.

Because so many big decisions have been made precipitously, traditional schematic design can be a time of confusion and conflict between staff, leaders, and architects. Concluding this phase of work can take months.

Design Development

During design development, refinements become specific, room by room. Only now, after crucial building elements are "cast in stone," do user groups begin to discuss whether the new space meets their operational needs. For example, in an operating room (OR), the group would consider the placement of table, lighting, and anesthesia machine. The room's internal work flow is only now considered: Where will the circulating nurse be? How will items be unwrapped or prepared for the next patient? Minor problems, like a counter that is across the room from the automated medication dispenser machine, can be changed. It is too late to fix major problems that surface now, such as circulation or placement of major components.

At this stage, the architect produces a floor plan and elevation and section details and takes into consideration things like telecommunications, IT, and electrical and mechanical systems. Interior space is considered, creating that balance of beauty, function, and cost. The general contractor is probably already involved and is analyzing the work for feasibility and cost.

Bidding/Documents/Construction

Whether traditional or Lean-led design has been used to this point, the participation of the user groups is complete. Architects now prepare the construction documents for presentation to the construction manager. The construction documents translate the final decisions into detailed drawings that will determine what kind of facility the general contractor and subcontractors will build.

The project manager, architect, engineers, and perhaps even the sub-contractors may have individual contracts with the hospital. Managing the work among these groups while maintaining the schedule is difficult and can become a source of friction, cost overruns, change orders, and delay. Communication among all parties must be maintained.

Move-in/Postoccupancy

The new building, with its new spaces and new technology, is ready for occupancy. Architects and engineers take key hospital personnel through the exercise of building commissioning, showing them how the new facility operates, how physical plant and HVAC systems work, how the alarm system operates, and so forth.

Moving into a new medical facility requires meticulous planning that starts well before construction ends. The move and the adjustment to the new space are stressful. Adding to the stress is nonstandard work. Without a facility-wide plan and facilitated workplace organization, supplies and equipment are fit into the spaces provided without thought to overall standardization. The result is a lost opportunity to influence hospital culture through the efficient and standardized use of space. This is a loss that will reverberate well into the future.

After about a year, the architect and construction team will check back to see whether the facility is being used as designed, what works well, and what more can be learned. Figure 2.1 shows approximate time lines with traditional vs. Lean design.

Lean-Led Design

Lean-led design begins with Lean process design. The more Lean thinking permeates the work environment and culture, the more committed the leaders are, the more engaged the frontline staff are, and the better the facility design will be. "The key is deep respect for work at bedside," said Carpenter. "Leaders must seek to understand, use systems thinking, and involve others. They need to consider plans for the future and create a plan about how to get there, together."[4]

The rest of this chapter will serve as an introduction to Lean-led design, phase by phase. The following chapter includes a more detailed look at the underlying model.

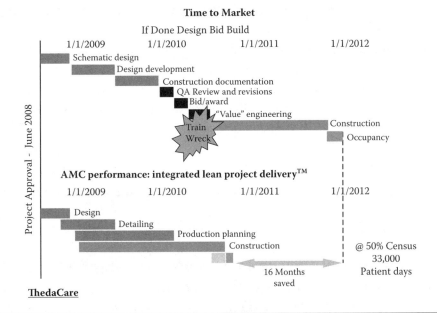

Figure 2.1 The top line shows a traditional design–bid–build project. The bottom line shows the time compression possible when Lean-led design is coupled with Lean construction management with Integrated Project Delivery (IPD). (Courtesy ThedaCare.)

Master Planning

The objective of master planning remains the development of a long view of how construction projects will fit together to create a continuously renewing hospital. Hospitals learning Lean thinking tend to ask bold, paradigm-shifting questions about the way in which healthcare will be delivered in the future, and they continually look at new ways to eliminate departmental barriers and patient handoffs.

Master planning is the time to collect data about the different service areas, observing each one and mapping at a general level the way in which work is currently done. Using data from these current-state value stream maps, hospital leaders can make decisions about how these service lines could work together better in the future.

Now is the time to make the decision to standardize the hospital rooms. The case study in Chapter 6 shows one hospital's struggle to come to terms with standardization, which is safer for patients and better for caregivers. Starting with the agreement to standardize at this early stage makes the design much easier for architects to accommodate. Later decisions may require moving structural columns, which is cost prohibitive. Discoveries made after master planning quickly become impossible to accommodate.

Traditionally, architects start by trying to understand work flow, but not to the detail of the future state. They get a general sense of it, through their conversations with hospital leaders. The difference is, by mapping out value streams and drilling down with 3P, you necessarily have frontline staff at the table. We have a better possibility of getting to the "real" versus the "should."

—Maureen Sullivan
RN, Lean practitioner

Consider the discovery made during master planning by a small community hospital in the South. Its design team, which included personnel from the emergency and ambulatory surgery departments, began looking at process flows at the earliest phase of master planning. Together, the team's members developed an innovative recommendation—creating a patient space that would "flex" from a surgical prep and recovery room to an emergency exam room. The differing peak utilization times during the day, room standardization, and colocation allowed the patient rooms to double as prep and recovery rooms for procedures during the day and as ED exam rooms in the evenings. The design included 12 "flex" patient rooms and 14 ED exam rooms. The arrangement created 86% more capacity without adding square footage, saving the construction of 9,000 square feet that would have been required if two separate areas had been built.

"By the design development stage, drawings are already many layers deep. Waiting quickly compromises what Lean-led design can do," Carpenter said. "Using Lean makes it more likely you'll make sound decisions early and then you don't have to change them."

Had this efficiency been discovered later in the design process, after architects had drafted more and more layers of systems, this opportunity would have been lost. Early opportunities like the "flex" space at this hospital are significant—and perishable.

Toyota's model for efficient development of new items and new designs is called 3P—for product (in this case, service to patients), process, and preparation. The next chapter details the ways in which 3P can be used during facility design, from the broad strokes of master planning to the details of move-in. 3P is indispensable for operationalizing the staff's great ideas about the way in which processes should occur. The master 3P done during master planning examines potential changes to the service lines that will be affected by the project.

Predesign

Hospital leaders start predesign by looking at the way in which current processes are done at the front line and planning how they could best be done in the future. While architects are valued team members at this point, the hospital is still in the lead. In fact, the architect could be viewed as the "customer" at this stage—eager to receive the process information that will inform design. Said architect Dennis Robert:

> Nobody communicates to a nurse like another nurse. Architects are very caring people, but we live in a different world. Nurse leaders with knowledge of architecture help us press beyond the architectural question to the operational question that affects design. We are better architects when we can truly understand clinicians' needs.

Value Stream Mapping

A multifunctional team of staff members looks at how processes are done in the major areas to be renovated. A high-level process map may be a useful first step, providing a flow chart that shows a process from start to finish. But a process map does not necessarily consider the point of view of the patient. The team will soon need more specifics, which are best supplied through value stream mapping.

A value stream map reveals the process from the point of view of the customer (generally the patient). It isolates value-added activities (those for which the patient would be willing to pay, like administering meds, charting, or actual treatment) from non-value-added activities (looking for charts, calling for missing medications). Figure 2.2 shows the difference between a process map and a value stream map.

The first step in value stream mapping is firsthand *observation.* Taking groups of employees on a "waste walk" to observe in their work areas is almost always a revelation. The staff at one mid-Atlantic hospital walked through the outpatient waiting room as part of a formal observation exercise. Although many of these same staff members often walked through that space—maybe even daily—the observation exercise gave them a patient's-eye view of the waiting room. What they saw with their "new eyes" shocked them: torn upholstery, stained carpet, and faded artificial plants with trash tucked into the containers because the trash receptacle was 40 steps away.

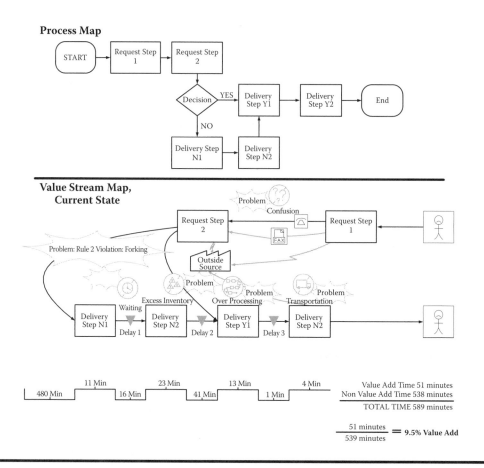

Figure 2.2   A process map (top) provides a useful, general view. A current-state value stream map (bottom) provides more specific information about information and process flows. (Courtesy Healthcare Performance Partners.)

The observation provided enough data to persuade decision makers to upgrade the area. In almost every instance, workers welcome the insight that comes from facilitated observation. They are excited by the prospects for improvement. The usual refrain is, "We can do better than this."

Significantly, the value stream mapping exercise itself is a way to build consensus among team members. One architect, after observing at a hospital, said:

> The thing that stuck out the most was how heroic the staff members are, every day. They work around broken systems, trying to improve them as they go, but all the while they are completely focused on getting patients what they need. I saw how thoughtful design could make things easier for them.

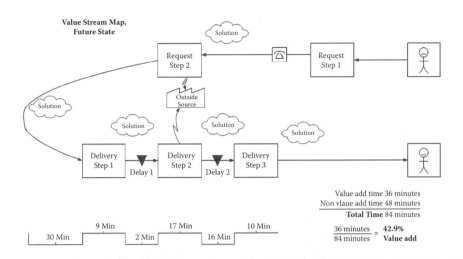

Figure 2.3 Future-state value stream map shows the streamlined process. (Courtesy Healthcare Performance Partners.)

The results are a *current-state value stream map* (the way in which work is done today, as depicted in Figure 2.2) and a *future-state value stream map* (the way in which work could happen in the future, Figure 2.3) for each area under consideration. Creating these value stream maps takes time. Architects who are not yet familiar with Lean-led design may feel nervous at this stage because they are observers rather than directors in the process and because they are used to drawing at this stage; therefore, *not* drawing can feel stressful, as if they are behind schedule.

To complete predesign and conceptual design in a Lean way takes longer up front, but the patience pays off. Not only is more information revealed early, but it is also highly important and useful process information that is unavailable any other way.

With Lean-led design, programming changes too. Traditional design allocates space right away and fits functions into them as time goes by. With Lean-led design, the emphasis is on understanding process. The architect will not call out the number of bathrooms, for example, but rather wait to let the process reveal the appropriate number.

"It's as if you're backing into programming," says Carpenter. "The process tells you how many rooms you'll need, not vice versa. If you do it this way, form will indeed follow function."

Lean-Led Design Principles

Lean-led design is a systematic approach to healthcare architectural design that focuses on defining, developing, and integrating safe, efficient, waste-free operational processes in order to create the most supportive, patient focused physical environment possible. Lean design is about making the right work easier to do. The following list is presented in the order of the Rules in Use (Chapter 1).

Rule 1. Activities

- Think system, not silos. Look for opportunities for sharing spaces between services—for example, prep and recovery rooms that serve all invasive procedures. If possible, colocate exam room spaces between two departments with opposing peak census needs, such as Preadmission Testing and the Emergency Department, to increase capacity for both.
- Standardization in design promotes defect-free, standard work. Standardize configurations to reduce variations in work processes and promote long-term flexibility. In shared work spaces such as medication rooms, a standardized layout permits instant familiarity and reduces the potential for error.

Rule 2. Connections

- Create a visual workplace. Build in visual cues that permit the staff to determine normal from abnormal instantly in their workplace. Designate parking places for frequently used equipment to prevent time spent searching when it is in use.
- Caution! Waiting is waste. Carefully scrutinize waiting rooms beyond the point of entry (public lobby and reception areas). Do not design subwaiting areas to queue patients; rather than shift the wait from one area to the other, strive to move patients through the system with smooth, one-piece flow.

Rule 3. Pathways

- Pathways should be direct. Make way-finding intuitive. Make it easy to visualize the destination from the point of entry. Remember that straight corridors make stretcher travel easy with minimal motion waste.

- Design in smooth flow and motion. Design the layout for smooth flow, where work proceeds in one direction where the start and end are in proximity. Consider how the work starts and ends and the handoffs and travel in between. For example, are the patient and family member arriving for imaging able to enter and exit the same door near their car?
- Make the trip to the toilet a Lean journey. Configure patient rooms with the toilet room on the same wall as the headwall to reduce travel, promote patient autonomy, and reduce the risk of injury to patients and staff through falls.
- Space should be intentional. Design for every square foot needed and no more. The belief that space will solve problems is a myth: Excess space leads to increased travel distance (motion waste) and stockpiling of supplies and equipment (inventory waste). Process redesign solves problems.

Rule 4. Continuous Improvement

- Make the environment easy to change. Consider using standardized modular equipment, casework, and workstations on wheels to provide flexibility for continuous improvement. Make storage accessible, flexible, visual, and temporary. Create long, shallow equipment rooms to keep items from being lost or having to be moved to reach items behind. Designate visible parking spaces for each piece.
- Think quality at every step. Design in inspection (quality checks) before the product/patient/service is passed on to the next level. Incorporate ways to communicate visually real-time progress toward continuous improvement goals.

—Teresa Carpenter, RN
Lean Facilitator

At Wisconsin's Monroe Clinic,[5] for example, process analysis showed that three distinct areas of the hospital—outpatient phlebotomy, preadmission testing, and registration—should all be combined into one area and placed near the main entrance of the hospital. Without value stream mapping, an architect would likely have carved out three distinct spaces in the new building. After all, that's what was in the old one and the architect could only assume that that's what was desired.

How important is it to get things right at this stage? It is very important: Opportunities for consolidation, adjacencies, and new areas are closing. Just a few weeks later, this window of opportunity for efficiency at Monroe would have been closed.

Schematic Design

The advantage of front loading the entire process with the creativity of staff and architect starts to pay off with a much quicker, more efficient schematic design. By this stage, the team will have moved beyond value stream mapping and into even greater detail, completing its master 3P—a disciplined, quick way to start experimenting with designs that will support the future state. The objective is to try different ways to mock up designs quickly, using the humblest of materials (paper clips, Post-its, Legos, masking tape, chairs, etc.; see Figure 2.4). While these 3P mock-ups may not be full size, they allow staff to conduct quick process simulations. In a 3P mock-up, the team uses only what is needed to assess whether or not the idea will work. More detailed information on the hows and whys of 3P is included in the following chapter.

Figure 2.4   Humble materials are quickly mocked up into a three-dimensional model of a unit secretary's station. See Chapter 3 for more detailed information on 3P. (Photo courtesy Healthcare Performance Partners.)

Design Development

The project team convenes its multifunctional work group for each affected area. The OR team might include the circulating nurse, who coordinates many functions; an anesthesiologist; surgical nurses; support workers; and others with key functions. Having already had a hand in creating the value stream maps and 3P mock-ups, this team is now free to look at standardizing and reducing inventory within each OR and customizing space, rather than merely accepting the usual "two walls of storage." "If the hospital decides early to standardize rooms, design development will go very quickly," said Carpenter. (As Chapter 6 will show in more detail, standardization reduces risk and increases patient safety and worker satisfaction.)

With traditional design, participants meet separately (or in one long, exhausting meeting) with the interior designer, the lighting, telecommunications, mechanical, plumbing, and medical equipment experts, and so forth. With Lean design, these experts come in at strategic points in various 3Ps to hear frontline concerns and offer targeted solutions, in context. These subcontractors become, in the language of Lean, both supplier (of the goods or service) and customer (receiving input about true frontline needs).

Bidding/Construction

"Waste in the project delivery process begins with poor problem seeking, but it certainly doesn't stop there," said architect David F. Chambers. "Handoffs, queues, and rework are rampant in project delivery, just as they are in healthcare delivery."

In a hopeful development, new tools and new thinking have begun to address the eight wastes as they occur in project delivery. Powerful new building information model (or BIM) software has started to transform facility planning and to blur the lines between architect, engineer, technician, designer, and construction manager. And the promise of cross-discipline interaction through integrated project delivery (IPD) is picking up steam as well. Both developments promise greater efficiency in large building projects.

Building Information Model

BIM software is the most advanced design technology currently available. The BIM image of one floor or one department is a realistic, three-dimensional model that can layer in every detail and track proposed building changes in real time.

BIM creates these detailed images using parametric modeling, which means that it can manipulate large parameters across all the disciplines of a building project. Parameters include things like sizes and shapes of spaces and their relationships, orientations, whereabouts, natural lighting, quantities, changes in building components, and cost. Parametric modeling tracks all aspects simultaneously. Thus, for example, when the location of a light fixture changes, all infrastructure requirements, manufacturer's details, and even the costs of the change can be tracked in real time.

BIM's chief advantages are coordination among disciplines and "clash detection" (for example, when a heating duct interferes with a structural member). With BIM, such problems can be visualized and called out immediately.

With BIM, "the potential grows to build increasingly sophisticated functional systems for designing, modeling and fabricating buildings."[6] BIM can handle greater levels of detail and complexity than has ever been possible before. The software is designed to handle detailed knowledge up front—exactly the type of information that Lean-led design helps to create.

Integrated Project Delivery

Just as the team approach can work for Lean-led design, the same can be said for coordinating among architect, engineers, and construction managers. Integrated project delivery, also called integrated facility design (IFD), is gaining favor in hospital building programs. IPD grants a single contract for all of the major players in a project: architect, engineer, construction trades, etc. Meeting project deadlines becomes a group effort, and responsibilities are shared.

IPD requires fundamental changes in the traditional model of "design–bid–build," which relies on individual contracts for each discipline and makes coordination a problem. Time and again, design–bid–build has proven adversarial and inefficient. (Note the "train wreck" allusion in Figure 2.1. IPD helps eliminate that.)

Instead, IPD relies on close collaboration among all project stakeholders—owner, architects, engineers, builders, subcontractors, building inspectors, and more—from concept through completion. Because bidding and negotiation are woven into this process all along, they require no additional time at this point in the project.

The case for IPD gained favor when Sutter Health replaced the old and seismically unstable Eden Hospital in Castro Valley, California, with a new facility, Sutter Medical Center Castro Valley (SMCCV)[7]:

> The most remarkable design metric for the SMCCV IPD project is that design time for structural [planning] was reduced from an expected 15 months to 8 months and was informed by far more information from other disciplines than is usually available, which led to better design quality…the cost for design is at or below what was anticipated. Thus, design is proceeding with higher quality, at a faster pace, and with no quantifiable increase in cost.[8,9]

More discussion about IPD (or IFD) at Sutter and other hospitals can be found in Chapter 8.

Move-in/Postoccupancy

Commissioning of the building proceeds as it does with traditional design, when in-house facilities workers learn the infrastructure of their new building. The customers for this round are the caregivers who will be working in the new space.

The meticulous planning that began during construction now culminates with the Toyota disciplines of 5S[10] and visual workspace,[11] collectively called "workplace organization." When implemented (with facilitation) across a facility on move-in, it can help with system-wide standardization. "At move-in, workplace organization helps caregivers figure out how to use the building from a functional standpoint," said one hospital director.

5S stands for:

■ Sort
■ Set in order
■ Shine
■ Standardize
■ Sustain

Planning with 3P means that spaces have been created in the size and configurations needed. A carefully crafted plan uses 5S to organize the move, standardizing the placement and amounts of supplies, medications,

Figure 2.5 Nurses label and place supplies where they know they will need them in a new hospital. (Photo by Naida Grunden.)

and equipment in each room (see Figure 2.5). Modular casework and workstations also increase flexibility in work spaces.

Using workplace organization on move-in gives frontline workers a chance to craft their own work space and to call out problems and safety concerns in a blame-free environment, and it gives them a stake in the outcome. This is much more than a tool to keep things tidy: It is a way to change the culture. Said one physician, "Workplace organization designs storage that 'talks' to everyone who encounters it. The visual workplace means you not only know what is there; you instantly know what is *not* there, and exactly what is needed to replenish it."

To those whose work lives have been transformed through the ability to find exactly what they need quickly and to know that it will be there every time, workplace organization is not only about eliminating guesswork—It is ultimately about patient safety. Chapter 4 describes the use of workplace organization on move-in at a hospital in Virginia.

When to Begin with Lean

Collaborative models drive out waste. Wherever you are in your architectural design or construction project and whether or not you already have robust Lean process improvement catching on across your organization, introducing the concepts of Lean-led design will help save waste from entering the new physical environment. The rule of thumb when it comes to using Lean design is that earlier is better, but that it is never too late.

Summary

This chapter describes each phase of the architectural plan. The differences between the traditional approach and Lean-led design include:

- Frontline involvement at each phase is necessary from the very start.
- Observation concerns how things are actually—not theoretically—done today and how they could be done better in the new space.
- Process redesign is part of Lean-led architectural design. The four "Rules in Use" are built in.
- Lean-led design provides the most value during the initial design phases and then again later, in preparation for move-in. During construction, the IPD model promises to improve results.

Discussion

- In Lean-led design, architects sit side by side with hospital staff from the very start. They begin drawing later in the process. How does this result in a potentially better design?
- By creating a single contract, IPD provides the incentive for teamwork among all contractors. How could such an arrangement align with Lean-led design?
- Why is process improvement (as done with value stream mapping and 3P, for example) an integral part of building design? Once streamlined, does that "better way to work" have to wait for the new space or can it begin to be introduced in the current environment?
- How could Lean-led design improve respect for frontline workers? Architects? Hospital leaders?

Suggested Reading

Chambers, D. 2009. *Efficient healthcare: Overcoming broken paradigms.* © David Chambers.

Notes

1. Chambers, D. 2011. Efficient healthcare: Overcoming broken paradigms. © David Chambers.
2. In one groundbreaking study from England, where the National Health System (NHS) seems to have accepted the inevitability of the queue, British physician Kate Silvester has discovered that certain types of additional capacity "will not increase the overall output from the service or may even make the situation worse...The knowledge exists to design healthcare systems that deal with the variation in demand."
3. See Appendix A for a history of master planning.
4. Appendix B provides a summary tool to help assess your organization's place on the Lean journey.
5. See Chapter 6 for a fuller discussion of this work.
6. Lee, G., Sacks, R., and Eastman, C. M. 2006. Specifying parametric building object behavior (BOB) for a building information modeling system. *Automation in Construction,* 15 (6): 758–776.
7. More on the Sutter seismic transformation, use of lean design, and IPD is located in Chapter 8.
8. Khemlani, Lachmi, AECbytes, SMCCV case study, cited at http://www.aecbytes.com/buildingthefuture/2009/Sutter_IPDCaseStudy.html
9. See Chapter 8 for more discussion of Sutter Health's construction initiative.
10. Some have proposed a sixth "S" for "safety"; however, Lean-led design hard-wires safety into every aspect of work, including each stage of 5S. Safety is ingrained, not added on.
11. Galsworth, G. 2005. *Visual workplace, visual thinking: Creating enterprise excellence through the technologies of the visual workplace.* Portland, OR: Visual-Lean Enterprise Press.

Chapter 3

A Model for Lean-Led Design

We cannot solve our problems with the same thinking we used
when we created them.

—Albert Einstein

*This chapter offers a more detailed look at Lean-led hospital design and
presents a model for consideration.*

Introduction

For the beautiful new south tower, the most recent major construction
project at this Midwestern hospital, designers created centrally staffed front
desks on every floor, where nurses and unit secretaries would work. But
just weeks after the south tower opened, the team found itself scrambling to
redesign not just the front desk, but the entire central core because it did not
function the way that it needed to.

"The supervisors and designers didn't understand the work flow well
enough. They didn't fully realize what unit secretaries and nurses do. The
work flow should have been the key to establishing the design, not vice
versa," said a hospital staff architect, adding:

> We didn't want to repeat a problem like that when we built our
> new north tower. This time, we knew we had to incorporate the
> voice of the staff, the people who use the space, from the very start.
> We needed to take a completely fresh look at everything—even at
> whether to have central nursing stations at all—to make sure the
> space would support the best care for the patient.

Call it the paradox of hospital architecture, but one of the main challenges seems to be "how do we *not* build the same units and import the same problems all over again?"

Human nature demands that we stick with the familiar, so time and again—although frontline workers and managers give voice to the frustrations that make their work hard and envision a better way to work—often, when it comes to talking about how the new unit might actually function, they revert to the familiar.

The clean supply closet must be large and located down the hall. Why? Because that is the way it has always been. The nurse's station must be a large, open central area allowing constant interruption to nurses' work. Why? Because interruption of the nurse is a given. No matter how creative, every worker in every hospital—indeed every worker in every industry—eventually jumps right back "inside the box."

Recognizing this conundrum, Toyota developed a way to break through it: 3P. Like so much about Toyota, 3P is a tool, but it is rooted in the philosophy of respect and dignity for all, and of continuous improvement. And like all things Toyota, 3P is an ongoing experiment.

In industry, the 3Ps refer to product, preparation, and process.[1] 3P offers a way for those involved in design to think up entirely new and better ways of doing things, and to design waste out right from the start.

Lean practitioner Maureen Sullivan, RN, explains the link between industry and healthcare:

> At Toyota, new product design took too long, cost too much, and when it was all done, it didn't match up with the way work was done on the shop floor. When you transfer that problem to the design of a new unit or hospital, you can see the importance of creativity and teamwork to make sure the most efficient design is achieved.

Documentation starts immediately. Each process map, value stream map, and refinement made during 3P is saved and placed with a write-up for context. This stream of documentation, collected "just in time" all along, will become the operational profile or "owner's manual" for the building upon move-in. A typical design-and-build project takes about 2 years, during which time thoughts and processes evolve. Creating the operational profile in real time gives a history of the thought processes used as the project unfolds, so a new staff member could answer the question, "What were they thinking?"

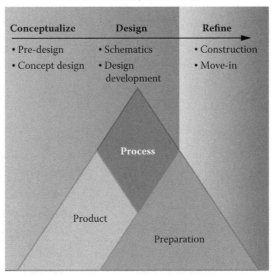

Figure 3.1   Lean-led design model, based on 3P. (© Healthcare Performance Partners.)

This chapter will describe (1) what happens during a typical 3P, and (2) an overall model showing several ways to use 3P during hospital design—whether for an interior remodel or a whole new "green field" hospital.

While no single approach can claim to be "the" model, the one presented in this chapter[2] and shown in Figure 3.1 has proven useful. It reinforces the Lean-led design principles discussed in Chapters 1 and 2. This model also provides a helpful framework for discussion and—always—further refinement.

What Happens during a Typical 3P?

Although rooted in industry, 3P is remarkably adaptable to healthcare. In healthcare, for purposes of this discussion, we will present the components in this slightly different order (with process before preparation; see Table 3.1).

Although it is called 3P, the three components comprise a single process. As it unfolds, teams discover new things about the current state and possibilities for changes and future refinement. The focus is not necessarily on the item itself, but rather on how to make it better and faster so that the customer's request can be filled sooner.[3] The customer (patient)—not the item (component of care)—is the focus of 3P.

Table 3.1   The 3Ps in Industry and Healthcare

Phase	Activity	In industry	In healthcare
Product	Conceptualize	What is the purpose of this item? What is it supposed to do? What is the concept behind it?	What is the purpose of each component of care within the system? (e.g., steps, vendors, suppliers, equipment) How can we best deliver care as a seamless whole to the patient? What are the service lines within the continuum of care?
Process	Design	What is the easiest way to put this thing together? Could we quickly mock up a few designs?	How can we quickly test space configurations to see which will best support continuous process improvement?
Preparation	Refine	What does this thing look like? Where does it fit in the larger piece of equipment? What else is affected by this change?	How could we design space in a way that will avoid unintended consequences elsewhere? How can we make sure patients get what is needed, immediately, every time? How do we operationalize our new design? How can we prepare to move into new space?

How Does 3P Differ from Kaizen?

3P differs from kaizen[4] in important ways. Kaizen looks closely at processes or problems, analyzing how they arose,[5] and uses the wisdom of the team to devise experiments and improve them. Kaizen is done within the existing walls, using as few resources as possible to effect the biggest improvement.

"3P affects the processes, systems and everyday activities that people will improve on an ongoing basis," notes Lean practitioner Teresa Carpenter, RN.

Ten Principles of 3P

After the careful deliberation of value stream mapping, 3P can seem fast and loose. It is intended to be, because it is a way of sparking the most creative ideas that may reside at the periphery of consciousness. The 10 principles of 3P for healthcare are:

1. Make production and preparation lightning fast. "Avoid over-planning; use what you have; act now."
2. Make the process adaptable. "Use many speedboats instead of one tanker."
3. Aim for smooth work flow and motion. "Flow like a river, not like a dam."
4. Build in quick setup and changeover (equipment, shift change).
5. Make everything easy to move. "No roots; no vines. Put everything on wheels!"
6. Use simple machines that perform one function well. Use technology only when needed and only as much technology as needed.
7. Use only the space necessary. "Build townhouses, not ranches."
8. Create small, fast, focused lines, not multipurpose workstations.
9. Remember single-piece (patient) flow: one-piece pull, no batching.
10. Build in first-time quality: Know normal from abnormal and "stop the line."

Adapted from "The 16 Catch Phrases of 3P." Miller, J. *Designing Processes to Fit Lean Manufacturing with the 16 Catch Phrases of 3P*. May 2, 2006. http://www.gembapan-tarei.com/2006/05/designing_processes_to_fit_Lean_manufacturing_with_the_16_catch_phrases_of_3p.html (accessed February 12, 2010).

"We reach for 3P when there is a significant change in the design of the hospital or a new service line to launch."

3P starts where value stream mapping leaves off.[6] After mapping the current and future states, 3P asks participants to imagine the many ways in which the entire value stream could be optimized. If walls could be moved, what sort of process optimization could occur? 3P means dreaming bigger; it is *structured innovation*.

3P accelerates design because it allows cross-disciplinary teams of staff members and physicians to envision the ideal design themselves, with new levels of detail and clarity that emphasize patient service over departmental silos. The value comes from having frontline people delineate their processes and potential spaces, rather than transferring all the decision making to the architect at too early a stage. This increases the chances that the final product will align with the way they work and with what the patients need.

After deliberating through one or two rounds of value stream mapping, 3P can seem fast and loose. It is intended to be, because it is a way of sparking the most creative ideas that may reside at the periphery of consciousness. The 10 principles shown in the box emphasize the compressed nature of this work.

One hospital executive said that she believed that each 3P condensed about a month's worth of design work into a few days and produced exponentially better results.

Evaluation Criteria

In addition to the 10 principles, participants need to consider what they can and cannot change. They need to consider these criteria up front:

- *Key assumptions.* Certain design realities may already exist, such as space and budget, building codes, regulatory requirements, site selection, stairwells, elevators, and so on. Regulatory guidelines, for example, establish minimum sizes for rooms, beds, and hallway widths. During the 3P, these items may not change.
- *Design criteria.* These criteria will be considered, beginning with the "voice of the customer," space utilization, staff work flow, patient accessibility, process and product flow, and scalability and safety (ergonomics). For example, the team may want to work on flows of specimens to the lab, instruments to and from the OR, and information technology.
- *Organizational criteria,* including mission and vision, values, and criteria for the facility plan. Every organization has a performance matrix or balanced scorecard—organizational criteria against which the design must be measured.

Sullivan said:

People get the mission and vision, or the Lean value matrix. But in design criteria, you have to make those principles real in the new environment. You don't just take that high-level quality statement, you have to come up with ways to measure against the criteria, test, and refine again. You create a PDCA[7] cycle, your own test of value. [See Figure 3.4]

Speed is the key as participants brainstorm, test, and refine. To move the exercise from the imagination to the "shop floor," teams quickly build basic models. Because it is not just an intellectual exercise, it is not considered "brainstorming." Rather, it is called "trystorming"—a more hands-on version. Ultimately, these steps connect 3P to PDCA or the scientific model.

Seven Ways

To open the creative phase of the work, each participant receives a paper clip to ponder and is asked to develop seven possibilities for its use.

The exercise at first seems lighthearted and then tedious, until the participants begin to see just how many dozens of different, sometimes unexpected, ideas emerged. Toyota asks workers to look for seven ways to encourage them to look beyond the obvious or the easy. Looking for seven ways in each major step of a process yields a similarly rich vein of ideas from these experienced teams.

The teams then set to work finding seven ways of meeting the design objectives in their areas. A prerequisite for the work is to understand the voice of the customer and the flow of work before creating this future-state design.

Says Sullivan, "The seven ways pushes people beyond what's easy, to what is possible. It keeps them from folding the same problems into their design."

The group comes up with seven ways, mocks up the top three, and then builds a three-dimensional model of the one that most closely matches the evaluation criteria (key requirements, design, and organizational criteria). See Figure 3.2 for an example of such a mock-up.

During the earliest 3P, the architect firm may not yet have been selected. But if it has, the architects should observe as many 3Ps as possible. One architect, after observing 3P for the first time, said, "How can any architect possibly know everything these different staff members know? Watching them mull over these options in the 3P exercise was very helpful."

Figure 3.2 Example of quick 3P mock-up of a floor and nurses' station.

Using 3P as an Overarching Model

3P can be more than a technique for optimizing one unit or service line; it can serve as a lens for viewing the entire project:

- Product: master 3P governs the project (conceptualize)
- Process: multiple cascading 3Ps for each service area (design)
- Preparation: optimization of 3P on move-in (refine)

The first goal is to create a master 3P, a basic Lean road map that synchronizes services across value streams rather than by department. But before the master 3P can be developed, some prerequisites must be attended to: listen to the voice of the customer, arrange basic Lean training for participating staff and medical members, and arrange basic Lean training for the design team.

Listen to the voice of the customer. It is essential to define who the customers are and what they expect and value. In one recent example, Swedish Hospital of Issaquah, that system's first community hospital, had a vibrant and engaged community steering committee from the earliest design phases. Listening to the voice of the customer persuaded the leaders to change the very definition of the hospital, creating more of a town square out front, with a coffee shop, retail fitness-wear shop, child care, and a five-star restaurant featuring cooking classes with local, organic foods (see Figure 3.3). Although the hospital just opened, it is becoming a community destination and gathering spot, as the steering committee envisioned. Not every community desires or can afford such an approach; however, these ideas resonated with the community—the ultimate customers.

But "customer," broadly defined, also includes physicians, executive leaders, and hospital staff members. Serving all customers means designing a

Figure 3.3 The presence of health-related shops makes the hospital entrance feel more like a town square. The voice of the customer was key in decisions at Swedish Hospital's new Issaquah campus. (Photo by Naida Grunden.)

system of providing healthcare that is safe, reliable, and efficient and that gives meaning to their lives. With the advent of healthcare policies like accountable care organizations (ACOs)[8] comes the opportunity to define customer values and expectations in new ways. For example, could focus groups among physicians, caregivers, strategic employers, and community members push the conversation beyond consideration of comfort and amenities? Could the thinking include the requirements of the health system, what it needs to thrive, and what would drive community support for the hospital? The voices of the customers—all of them—are vital to creating a community asset that will promote health well into the future.

Arrange basic Lean training for participating staff and medical members. For many hospitals, Lean is not new. In fact, they may have a Lean department or may have been conducting kaizen or rapid improvement events for years. However, this is not uniformly the case. If hospital participants are not familiar with Lean, they will need training before design begins.

Arrange basic Lean training for the design team. Lean is still new to most architects. Those who will be working on the project will probably need to receive basic Lean design training "just in time" as the project begins. The architects should plan to spend time with the teams during the 3P exercise, while they are still customers themselves, gathering the information they will need to proceed with design.

Product: The Master 3P (Conceptualize)

With the prerequisites complete, work begins on the predesign and concept design. 3P at this stage yields two things: a business case and basic block and stack diagrams.

The team creates a master 3P based on the high-level value stream maps (current and future) prepared for each of the seven general service families:

1. Patient access/intake services–business services
2. Unplanned/emergency services
3. Procedural/invasive services
4. Imaging/diagnostic services
5. Clinical support services
6. Operational support services (materials management, IT, environmental services)
7. Inpatient services

Note that the service families are not defined by departments, but are delineated by service to the customer. In the future, the distinction between outpatient and inpatient services will also continue to blur, so approaching work by service line instead of department is one way to design for that future.

If traditional programming spreadsheets have already been developed, the master 3P will align and synchronize them by service area. Square footage requirements will be viewed in terms of value streams rather than departments.

Once the group delineates the seven service areas, they discuss ways in which a new design will enhance quality, time, and satisfaction of patients, staff, and physician and improve the bottom line. They also know how they will measure these things as the project unfolds. Looking at seven service areas helps the team envision how they articulate with one another and with the site.

Business Case

A strong business case should emerge from the master 3P. In a facilitated discussion, the client is led through each point in the Lean value diamond (Figure 3.4)—a Lean tool to help clarify the impact on the organization, prioritize the work, and strategize the way to quality. Each point on the

Lean Value Diamond: Core Measures, Quality Goals, Service Issues

Figure 3.4   Most Lean organizations have a matrix, mission, or vision against which they assess needs and measure change. Here is a "Lean diamond," a type of plan–do–check–act (PDCA) where each point usually affects the others in some way. Tools like these are excellent conversation starters and idea clarifiers. Lean diamonds or PDCAs help develop the organizational profile in real time, as work proceeds. (Lean value diamond © 2011 Healthcare Performance Partners.)

Lean value diamond affects the others: satisfaction, quality, time, and financial impact. Going over the Lean diamond as part of the master 3P creates consensus about what will be measured during design. It is a kind of quality checklist to be consulted over and over. This analysis also becomes part of the operational profile.

Block and Stack Diagrams

Each issue has already been through a "voice of the customer" exercise and the Lean value diamond. Enough information now exists to begin to evaluate the benefits of standardized rooms and develop adjacencies using basic "block and stack" diagrams.

"This is a big point of approval, the pinnacle of concept design," said Carpenter. "When you put services into the right buckets, you catch things—like whether you really need three separate registration areas with different processes. What could be combined? What needs to move apart? The master 3P will give you the information and a way to measure whether it will work."

Process: Schematic Design and Cascading 3Ps (Design)

As the Master 3P and concept design conclude, the teams drill down into each of the seven service families (see box). They conduct "waste walks" through each service area, looking for ideas to keep and others that need to change as the new design proceeds. Value stream maps in each service area set the groundwork for a series of seven 3Ps, one per service family. (Some service families are so broad that they may need to be broken down further, with each subtopic becoming a 3P.)

Seven Service Families

It helps, from the earliest stages, to categorize the hospital functionally, rather than just by department. One way is to use service families:

1. Patient access/intake services–business services
2. Unplanned/emergency services
3. Procedural/invasive services
4. Imaging/diagnostic services
5. Clinical support services
6. Operational support services (materials management, IT, environmental services)
7. Inpatient services

By now, the architect is part of the discussion, listening for ideas and advising the group on design and "buildability" issues, in an effort to keep construction costs down. For example, two ideas may be close, but one calls for an unusually shaped room, which would be very expensive to build. The architect is keenly aware of these issues, can call them out for the group, and can help them come up with alternatives. (Ideally, as schematic design progresses, the team should also confer with the ultimate arbiters of "buildability"—engineers and construction managers.)

Linking Principles to Design

"During schematic design, we work with the architect and go through the 3Ps. We align everything with the Rules in Use and Lean design principles," said Carpenter:

We peg everything to the organization's mission, vision, and values. We align everything with the business case and check against the Lean value diamond for clarity. We standardize. In other words, the ideas generated may be way out, may be something we've never tried before, but if they are congruent with the values, then we experiment with them.

3P helps link operational ideas with design criteria. For example, one popular idea is for procedural spaces to share prep and recovery space. That is a Lean *operational idea* emanating from the staff and physicians. But how can we be sure that every service line sharing these spaces has good patient flow, minimal travel distance, excellent communication, and direct pathways? Will our new space give us this kind of functionality now and still ensure room for expansion later? Those are *design criteria* that come from the architect.

Table 3.2 shows a design evaluation at one hospital. Four teams came up with ideas about how to arrange the medical/surgical area. To determine which ideas would be mocked up, they scored each idea against the health system's values (safety, quality, delivery, cost, growth) and against the stated goals of the building program. All of the alternatives were scored against the current condition, and all improved it. Scoring this way is objective and tends to tamp down strong emotions. Furthermore, the best ideas from every plan usually migrate into the mock-ups. Everyone is acknowledged.

Mock-ups and Simulations

Mock-ups begin now. Some may be humble tapes on the floor or on a tarp that can be rolled up and moved. Sometimes people use cardboard, chairs and a hospital bed to scale a room. Other hospitals, like Seattle Children's, have taken to creating whole-unit and whole-floor mock-ups in warehouses or parking garages to see how each space and each sight line will actually work. (See Figure 8.2 in Chapter 8.) The most important aspect of the mock-up is the ability to run simulations in it—from routine care to a code. Simulations and mock-ups give everyone a chance to see how the activities, connections, pathways, and potential improvements play out in reality.

Changing Relationships: Hospital, Architect, and Management

Working this way calls for a whole new relationship between hospital and architect. The 3Ps done now are all about laying out the floor plan. With the architect as valued team member at this stage, the usual conflict-ridden

Table 3.2   Design Evaluation

Design alternatives	Design criteria: safety, quality, delivery, cost, growth								Scoring		
	Privacy, prevent harm	Space	Family amenities	Quality of care	Communication	Way-finding	Efficiency, productivity	LOS, capacity	+	–	Total
① Star	+		+			+		+	4	0	4
② Designated	+			+				+	3	0	3
3 Flex							+	+	3	0	2
4 Triangle						+		+	2	0	2
5 Current state	–	–	–	–	–	–	–	–	0	8	–8

Notes: Key: + (plus) = significant positive impact; – (minus) = significant negative impact; shaded = neutral. Circled options achieved the highest scores and will be mocked up. Teams may borrow ideas from other options.

back-and-forth between owner and architect disappears. The architects know what is needed and bring their vast knowledge of code requirements, parking, curb cuts, and how all of the physical spaces and equipment interact. The amount of time for schematic design is greatly reduced with 3P.

"I'm a nurse, not an architect," said one nurse. "And the architect is great at what she does, but she is not a nurse. In these 3P sessions, we learn a lot from each other. I talk about processes and the architect translates that into design."

Working this collaboratively calls for a new management structure within the hospital. There is great efficiency to be gained, for example, by placing the ambulatory surgical center and Emergency Department (ED) next to each other. By evening, the ambulatory care beds are empty—at just the time when the ED is busiest. But this degree of flex requires a new management model. With departmental lines blurred, who governs those flex beds, by day or by night? Who is the manager? Significant cultural barriers need to be addressed. And yet, with everyone sitting in on the 3P and understanding that this configuration could be best for patients and easier for staff, there is motivation to make it work.

Value Engineering

By now, a process of value engineering (cost cutting) may begin (refer to Figure 2.1). After a hospital initially establishes budgets and scope of work, it finds that it needs to reevaluate no later than schematic design. Perhaps a bid comes in high, or the budget is cut. To make sure the budget and service areas align, cuts may need to be made.

Traditionally, cuts to the program come in areas considered extraneous, like the grand piano or soaring atrium. Too often, though, value engineering inflicts cuts that are indiscriminate and harmful—for example, reducing room size by 10%. These decisions are usually made by people who are not involved in day-to-day work or in the 3P process. With Lean-led design, efficiencies and space reductions will suggest themselves. Cutting, if it needs to happen, can be done in a more rational way. In other words, people involved in value engineering need to be part of 3P.

Process: Design Development (Design)

At the conclusion of the 3Ps for service families, the floor plan is now frozen, and design development begins. The overall configuration, walls, and floors are set, and the location of casework and cabinetry are becoming established. The focus shifts now from floor plan development to environmental details. During this phase, four completely different design development 3Ps focus on these vital topics:

- *Global operations management, resource control, and oversight.* This is a chance to create a nerve center, a centralized area that acts as a global resource center. From staffing and bed management to telemetry, a central area enhances communication. (See Chapter 10.)
- *Systems standardization of mechanical and electrical objects, plumbing, and lighting.* Light switches, for example, should always be in the same place. The type of lighting and placement of plugs in the wall, when considered carefully, can result in better pricing. Standardized casework, for example, in addition to being safer, is cheaper. Some components can be assembled off-site (see ThedaCare example in Chapter 8), making installation quicker, cheaper, and more reliable.
- *Systems standardization of information systems.* This includes telecommunications, low-voltage selections, security system, nurse call. These communications are vital to the smooth running of the hospital.
- *Systems standardization of interior finishes.* When chosen well, interior finishes can promote standard work. Modular casework enhances function, as they can be disassembled and moved; because the components can be built off-site and delivered, speed and quality are optimal. Each quadrant of the value diamond is addressed. Function, satisfaction, quality, and safety increase. In more than one hospital, the needs of the housekeepers and infection control practitioners were considered in the decision to have seamless walls around sinks. They were assembled off-site, delivered, and quickly installed. They are easy to clean and reduce the potential for infection.

Design details are standardized now. For example, can all of medical/surgical agree to have the same headwall? How identical can headwalls be from area to area? Involvement by the electrical engineer and construction manager at this phase becomes extremely important. Decisions made now affect future standard work and future-state Lean processes.

FMEA

Humans are fallible. This knowledge is at the root of human factors engineering and it needs to be taken into consideration at each stage of hospital design. One tool for detecting latent errors is the failure modes effects analysis (or FMEA) that Toyota uses. With it, teams look for any vulnerabilities in the design, whether from a human or a tool, that could cause error and harm. (Chapter 6 describes the FMEA conducted at Monroe Clinic.)

Table 3.3 shows an example of the concerns generated in an FMEA during the design of a new labor and delivery area. The idea is to brainstorm about the things that could possibly go wrong and evaluate the frequency of occurrence, severity of effect, and effect on the value diamond. Each potential mishap is scored. The teams determine whether the problem is one of process or design—or both. Items scoring seven or higher must be addressed immediately with a countermeasure because they are considered quality or patient safety issues.

"The FMEA gives us a way to apply objective calculations to the risk and work to eliminate the high-scoring items first," said Lean practitioner Bradley Schultz. "The score is objective. That tones down emotion and gets us working toward the same purpose."

During hospital design, teams will conduct three FMEAs at the conclusion of each of these stages:

- Concept design to test adjacencies (master 3P)
- Schematic design to test departmental flows (seven cascading 3Ps)
- Design development to check overall pathways during extreme circumstances, such as emergency or natural disaster (four design development 3Ps)

The FMEA helps staff, physicians, and architects to achieve alignment among their systems. It is also a way to maintain the integrity of Lean concepts that have been designed in: standardization, pathways, connections, and activities.

Preparation: Optimization on Move-in (Refine)

In terms of design, the plans are complete and the floor plan is frozen. The construction phase begins, one hopes, with Lean construction practices, such as the single-contract integrated project delivery, as described in the prior chapter.

As soon as construction gets under way, plans for move-in, occupancy, and opening can begin. The operational narratives, value stream maps, and standard work instructions that have been developed along the way will

Table 3.3 Example of Failure Modes Effects Analysis in OB Admissions

Potential failure	Frequency (low–med.–high)	Severity (low–med.–high)	Priority score (3–9)	Guiding principles (low–med.–high)	Required change Process/design	Possible change
Delivers on the way to OB	Low	Med	5	High	1. Design 2. Process 3. Process 4. Process	1. Relocate OB 2. Screen patients better 3. Staff, community awareness 4. Delivery pack with transport
Delayed on first floor, lost	High	Med	7	High	1. Design 2. Design 3. Process	1. Provide private route 2. Provide OB ambulance entry 3. Treat patient in ED
Cannot find wheelchair/ stretcher	Med	Low	4	High	1. Design 2. Process 3. Process/ design	1. Provide alcoves for wheelchairs/ stretchers in ED 2. Provide sufficient equipment 3. Create command center to facilitate transport to OB screening

now help guide and optimize move-in. Staff and physicians begin workplace organization, guided by these goals:

- Standardize the workplace.
- Train everyone in standard methodologies of 5S and visual management.
- Standardize the work.

Even at this late stage, three crucial processes usually have yet to be examined fully: (1) laundry, linen, and environmental services; (2) materials management; and (3) chart and patient documentation. These three areas are so significant during move-in and occupancy that separate, detailed value stream maps must be created in preparation.

Standardizing Space

Within each of the seven service families are key repetitive patient and staff work spaces, where the healthcare team shares space and performs tasks crucial to care delivery. These spaces, known as prototypes, will be the basis for developing Lean workplace organization. In a typical community hospital, 40–50 key rooms and work areas can be standardized prototypes.

Prototype spaces will serve as the template for a standard working environment. Each prototype room will provide detailed instructions about how to set up and sustain all the rooms of that configuration and purpose. The spaces targeted for replication are known as clone spaces.

Each prototype is documented, with step-by-step instruction on replicating the standards in other similar work spaces. Workplace organization documentation usually includes:

- Basic instruction regarding the general work flow, use of the space, inventory, replenishment, and auditing routines.
- Graphic plan-o-grams of casework cabinetry and drawers describing supply item locations, along with the number and types of bins, drawer dividers, and other organizational devices.
- Basic floor plan of the area that shows where each piece of equipment or furnishing goes.
- List of unnecessary equipment (red-tag items) that is not needed there and can be returned.
- Photographs depicting each area and specific locations for equipment and other devices.

- List of visual control tools to include labels, signage, and floor marking.
- Standard audit template for sustaining the organizational framework.
- List of any incomplete items, missing equipment or supplies, and additional work required to complete the space.

Solid workplace organization will make move-in much faster, easier, and efficient. The hospital will look great and function well on day one of operation.

But how will the rooms and closets look after a year? Will supplies still be organized, labeled, and sustained?

Most hospitals form a workplace organization steering committee, which has authority over 5S and monitoring tools for the whole hospital—not just for a few departments. Audit tools in each prototype room make it easy to check equipment and supply levels.

Most hospitals find the organization so vital to their functioning that maintaining it simply becomes part of the work. Workplace organization also helps the staff members continue their Lean journey because people tend to protect what they have created.

Summary

This chapter goes into some detail about one proposed model for Lean-led design. Every hospital project faces the same dilemma: how not to design the same shortcomings into the new building. Toyota's 3P process offers a way to snap the adhesions and get teams thinking in new and fruitful directions.

Discussion

- Why does this method call for product–process–preparation, instead of the standard for industry, which is product–preparation–process?
- How does 3P differ from kaizen?
- How do the 10 principles help to spark new ideas?
- Why bother creating seven ways to design something, when you will only use one?
- Why check each major design criterion against something like a Lean value diamond?

■ For the overall model for Lean-led design, describe the importance of the three phases below and tell how they align with each architectural stage:
  – Product. Master 3P governs the project (conceptualize).
  – Process. Multiple cascading 3Ps for each service area (design).
  – Preparation. Optimization of 3P on move-in (refine).
■ Failure mode effects analysis (FMEA) is not ordinarily associated with 3P breakthrough thinking, but rather with human factors engineering. Why is it important to consider both?

Notes

1. As presented in this model adapted for healthcare, we discuss the 3Ps in this order: product, process, and preparation.
2. This model was developed by Nashville-based Healthcare Performance Partners, a Lean healthcare consulting firm.
3. See definition of "ideal" in Table 1.1, Chapter 1.
4. See Chapter 1 for discussion of kaizen.
5. In the A3 document, this research into the root cause is known as the "five whys."
6. Value stream mapping is discussed in Chapter 2.
7. PDCA: plan–do–check–act. This four-step cycle of problem solving was popularized by W. Edwards Deming, "father of modern quality control." Mark Graban uses the term "plan-do-check-adjust" to denote the continuous improvement required with each iteration. See his essay in Appendix D.
8. See Chapter 1 for a discussion of ACOs.

LEAN DESIGN
AT EVERY STAGE

2

Chapter 4

Are We Too Late?

Although we started late with Lean-led design, we still managed to do a lot of streamlining before we opened. Our only regret is that we didn't incorporate it sooner.

—Tim Tobin (FACHE)
CEO, Spotsylvania Regional Medical Center

Case study: Spotsylvania Regional Medical Center, Fredericksburg, Virginia

Introduction

The beautiful new Spotsylvania Regional Medical Center (SRMC), Virginia's newest hospital, was almost complete (Figure 4.1). It would be that rare hospital built strictly to handle growth, rather than to replace an aging facility somewhere else. Along with the new facility would come new leaders, a new staff, and, shortly before opening day, new supplies and equipment.

Establishing the Culture

Once the hospital has already been built, is it not too late to factor in Lean-led design? There are definite points along the construction continuum where the introduction of Lean ideas will bring the most benefit. Move-in is one such point.

Figure 4.1 Beautiful new flagship, Spotsylvania Regional Medical Center, where Lean-led design began at move-in. (Photo by Naida Grunden, with SRMC permission.)

Spotsylvania Regional Medical Center (SRMC)

This 126-bed, $175 million hospital opened June 7, 2010, on a 74-acre campus south of Fredericksburg, Virginia. SRMC is a new hospital, not a replacement for another facility. Staff numbers around 400 people. Few employees had any prior experience with Lean process improvement.

No matter when it is introduced, Lean thinking provides an organization with the chance to introduce workplace efficiencies and a healthy work environment. As staff members learn to confront and solve problems together, they create the foundation for a new work culture that is more open, respectful, and free of blame and in which all suggestions are honored, no matter where they originate in the hierarchy. Instead of higher-ups deciding *who* is at fault, frontline staff decide *what* happened and how to fix the underlying trip wire so that the same thing does not recur.

Changing the work culture from top-down to collaborative is hard, because the current set of values in established institutions has long been cemented in place, and doing things differently will require wrenching (and usually unwelcome) change. One advantage of a brand-new hospital with a brand-new staff is that the culture is being created as the supplies are being put away, from the first hello.

As one Lean practitioner said:

> It is so much easier to teach Lean philosophy to people as they come on board. We aren't undoing anything. As we begin together, we just say, these are the commonsense principles we're going to use to operate this facility. Lean is very rational, and people are excited by its simplicity and sense. And not having to fight the status quo is thrilling.

Here is how it happened at SRMC.

Value Stream Mapping

As construction neared completion at SRMC, or Spotsy, the enormous job of move-in loomed. Leaders realized that they would need help to bring the right equipment and supplies into the new facility in an organized fashion. They thought Lean-led design could help them do that, while introducing members of an entirely new staff to their workplace and fostering teamwork among them.

The first order of business was to conduct frontline observations and value stream mapping[1] for the current and future states—something that would be impossible to do in a hospital that did not yet exist. The Spotsy team, which at this early stage comprised a handful of leaders and employees, conducted a simulation at a sister facility, CJW Medical Center's Chippenham Campus in Richmond, 50 miles away. Observing how work was done there, the Spotsy team drew up current- and future-state value stream maps for their new hospital's service lines.

Value stream maps provide a visual analysis of the flow of information and material during each process—from assessing a patient in the ER to drawing blood. Visualizing each process helps all involved to see and fix glitches, remove steps that do not add value, and move ever closer to ideal care.

Not only did these value stream maps benefit the Spotsy team in its planning, but they also provided insight on process improvements at Chippenham. In fact, the value stream maps were shared widely with the hospitals across that Virginia health system.

"If Lean-led design had not been made available to us, we would not have spent the time examining so many flow processes preopening," said SRMC CEO Tim Tobin, FACHE. "Our only regret is that we didn't do Lean sooner."

The SPOTSY Way

What is in a name? Very few organizations are enamored of the "Lean" name, which unfortunately, conjures up erroneous images of layoffs or worse. Most facilities personalize the name of their improvement system to make it part of their organizational culture. Here is Lean the "SPOTSY Way":

S—smile and acknowledge
P—polite, positive attitude
O—offer assistance
T—take ownership
S—show compassion
Y—you make a difference

Setting the tone for this new hospital, CEO Tim Tobin said, "The key is positive energy. People have to have it to work here."

Ordering supplies was a challenge. Traditionally, department managers would be asked to create their own individual estimates. But at Spotsy, not all department managers had been hired. So, hospital leaders created reasonable estimates by using supply lists from demographically similar hospitals and made a mass purchase. This provided a chance to standardize most items from the start. Still, the numbers were only estimates.

Workplace Organization

The term "workplace organization" is used to denote the wall-to-wall application of two Lean disciplines: *5S* and *visual management:*

5S is the Lean discipline that results in workplace order, cleanliness, and standardization. It consists of these steps: sort, set in order, shine, standardize, and sustain. Many hospitals have discovered that 5S provides a great way to clean out disorganized closets or storage space. Yet the discipline can do much more when applied across an entire institution.
Visual management is a sister discipline to 5S. It provides a way to sustain the gains made in 5S by making it obvious, at a glance, what is there and what is not. As one nurse said, "It's as if the cupboards talk to us now."

Author Gwendolyn Galsworth is quick to point out, "The visual workplace is not a brigade of buckets and brooms or posters and signs. It is a compelling operational imperative, central to your war on waste."[2] Lean philosophy and workplace organization are aligned but not the same. Galsworth explains it this way:

> The correct relationship between visuality and Lean is more in keeping with the way wings work on a bird. Both wings are required if the bird is to fly. One of the bird's wings represents Lean production. The other wing is for workplace visuality. The first wing is about pull, about flow. The second wing is about information, about meaning...The enterprise needs them both—pull and information, flow and meaning—if it is to get off the ground and sustain flight.

At Spotsy, teams of frontline staff members were trained in the tenets of workplace organization. Then, in unit after unit, staff began thoughtfully placing and labeling supplies, establishing par levels, standardizing every room, and red-tagging and returning what they could not use. The idea was to design out as many of the eight wastes as possible (see Chapter 1) as the hospital was being supplied.

"We looked upon this as the hospital's once-in-a-lifetime opportunity to organize the whole place," said Lean practitioner Teresa Carpenter, a nurse with broad experience working with architectural firms. "It's a big win when any hospital can organize, standardize, and maintain standard work, especially from opening day."

"From day one, everyone will know what is where," said CNO Nancy Littlefield. "Documenting how the 5S was done will help us create checklists. The more we simplify and standardize basic tasks, the more we free our creative staff to work on complex problems."

Prototype Rooms

With the hospital already built, equipment and supplies had to be placed before opening day, and the new staff needed to be introduced—to the hospital, to one another, and to a new way of doing things. Introducing standard work and standard placement of supplies would be key.

To do the work in the allotted time required near-military planning and the concentrated efforts of all department leaders, hospital leaders, and seven experienced Lean practitioners.[3] Carpenter stated the challenge this way:

Why can't highly repetitive spaces…be truly standardized so that no matter where you are deployed to work, you are instantly familiar with the environment and you can do standard work without the waste of searching for supplies and equipment?

To answer this challenge, the leadership team identified over 40 room types where highly repetitive tasks made standardization mandatory. These prototype rooms included medication and nourishment rooms, the emergency department (exam and treatment rooms), labor and delivery (OR, recovery, triage, NICU, nursery, workrooms), surgery, cardiac catheterization lab (cath lab), and the medical floors. Once the prototype rooms were

---

What Is Red-Tagging?

The first "S" in 5S is *sort*. The people who do the work sort through items and decide what is needed and what is not. Reducing inventory and restocking frequently become the new norms.

Inevitably, there will be items that are not needed in the workplace. Those items receive a red tag, which includes the date, description, location, and reason for the red tag.

Red-tagged items are moved to a holding area where they are kept for a week. If items are needed during that time, people can retrieve them. If not, the items are moved to a central storage area for a month. From there, they can be redeployed to other areas of the facility where they may be needed. If not, they are disposed of.

What can be red-tagged? Anything in the workplace, including inventory, equipment, furniture, fixtures, clutter, and outdated signs and bulletin board materials.

During the 5S at Spotsy, hundreds of thousands of dollars' worth of equipment was red-tagged. Much of it was redeployed to other areas of the hospital, but most of it was returned to the manufacturer.

"Without 5S and red-tagging, redeployment would have taken a long time to figure out," said CFO Sean Thompson, CPA. "It allowed us to send unneeded items back immediately and receive full credit. The financial benefits have been significant."

---

established to the satisfaction of the frontline staff, the rest would be "cloned" and each room would be a standardized copy of the prototype—at least, as much as possible given the variation in room layouts.

At first, a small cadre of employees came in to receive workplace organization instruction; for most, it was their first introduction to Lean thinking. They learned the basics—that it should be easy for people to find what they needed, when needed, and where expected. Most important, these new employees learned that they would be in charge of setting up their own work areas.

After a few days, more employees came in, were trained in workplace organization, and then joined their colleagues on the floor. Concentric circles of employees filtered in until everyone had training and hands-on experience doing 5S and visual management in their units.

The teams found themselves standardizing equipment and procedures within a new building that had not necessarily been designed for it. The following sections describe how they reconciled function with form and some of the revelations that resulted.

Emergency Department

The opening discussion among employees in the Emergency Department (ED) had nothing to do with supplies, but rather with work flow. It began with a series of questions: When we enter this exam room, where will the patient be? The nurse? The doctor? How about the family?

To make sure that the people in the room would not be in each other's way, the workplace organization team taped three arrows on the floor of the prototype room, making visible the flow of clinicians, patients, and family members (Figure 4.2). After carefully mapping the movements of people, they placed items so that, for example, doctors would not have to reach over a family member to retrieve a piece of equipment.

Teams placed supplies in purchased blue bins inside the cabinets, standardizing placement as much as possible, even though the cabinets varied in configuration from room to room (Figure 4.3). They fabricated bin dividers, assembled drawer dividers, and created labels (with par levels) for every item. The slogan became "If it casts a shadow, it gets a label."[2]

On the job for only a week, Lindsay Rogers, RN, coordinator of emergency services, could already see the value of standardization. "We like to standardize as much as we can, especially given that there are differences in the layout of the rooms," she said, adding, "Nurses love labels!" (Figure 4.4)

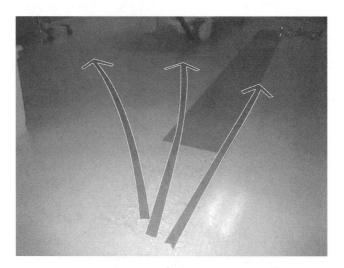

Figure 4.2 Mapping the flow of people in the prototype room. (Photo by Naida Grunden, with SRMC permission.)

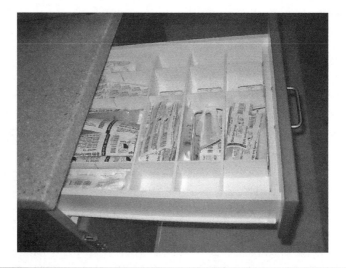

Figure 4.3 Drawers partitioned; labels include par levels. (Photo by Naida Grunden, with SRMC permission.)

Assistant Administrator Ken West appreciated the organization at move-in, but realized that Lean thinking could have helped earlier in hospital design. "With traditional hospital architecture, we've always designed the processes around the physical layout," he said. "But it should be the other way around. For example, this cabinetry looks great, but may not be as functional as it could be because nobody can reach the top shelf. If we'd let process guide the layout, we'd have found a way to avert that."

Figure 4.4 Labeled blue bins in upper cabinets. (Photo by Naida Grunden with SRMC permission.)

Lean practitioner Gary Bergmiller, PhD, challenged the nurses to organize supplies not by "what is there," but by "what you need." To further clarify, what do you need this day? What about this shift? What is a day's worth or a shift's worth of each supply? How many would you need on a bad day or during a bad shift? With this information, nurses began to decide what should be in each bin, how big the bins should be, how many of each thing should be in the bin, and how often it would need to be restocked (Figure 4.5). (In the end, the nurses decided to try restocking at the end of each shift.)

After the "what" comes the "where." What goes above should be seldom used, light, and easy to pull down without injury. What goes below can be heavier, but not frequently used.

Bergmiller recommends grouping things by "tendency." He says:

> If you're doing this certain type of work, these things *tend* to go together. Place them in groups that way. So if you're doing a blood draw, you won't be going over here for the tourniquet, over here for the syringe and so on. Those items *tend* to be used together, so let's store them that way.

Groups of employees conducted simulations in the prototype room based on their own experiences in emergency medicine. They ran through various scenarios, refining placements of items with each pass. One nurse noted that the hand sanitizer dispenser was by the door of the large treatment

Figure 4.5 ED coordinator Lindsay Rogers, RN (second from left), consults with frontline nurses as they create a treatment room that is both standardized and visual. (Photo by Naida Grunden, with SRMC permission.)

room. This is sensible placement, since clinicians must sanitize their hands upon entering and leaving the room. But the nurse thought that they needed another one closer to the table where the patient and doctor would be. It was an easy request to satisfy and one that would save innumerable steps over time.

As the new employees took charge of their environment, the work accelerated. Against the intermittent din of a miter saw cutting bin and drawer dividers, Bergmiller said:

> I expected to see them create the prototype room and then, much later, start cloning the other 20 rooms. But the employees have already finished the prototype checklist and are busy cloning more rooms and designing more spaces. At this point I'm just reinforcing the basics and staying out of their way. There's such enthusiasm for them to set up their own shop. That sound you hear is a nurse running the miter saw.

The nurses looked at the way the nurses' station was set up. They recruited three ED physicians to help them simulate its use; together, on the spot, they redesigned it, drew up a sketch (Figure 4.6), and had the contractor help with the reconfiguration.

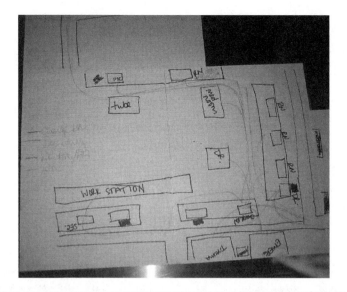

Figure 4.6 ED nurses and doctors redesigned the nurses' station on the spot. (Photo by Naida Grunden, with permission of SRMC.)

Chief Operating Officer Terika Richardson said, "It's hard to overstate the importance of engaging the frontline staff. They are an army of 400 experts. Our job as leaders is to remove barriers to their best work."

Cardiac Catheterization (Cath) and Electrocardiogram (EKG) Labs

Setting up the cath lab presented similar challenges and more revelations.

The cardiovascular physiologist said, "I could have told you where I wanted things, but what's best for me may not be best for the person next to me. We needed the rest of the people here to get all the input before we started placing things." One cath lab nurse said, "Labeling took longer than I thought it would. It requires a lot of thought to customize one prototype nurse server, then make them all exactly alike."

The team mapped out the cabinets in each lab and then began stocking item by item (Figure 4.7). Some items had arrived; many had not.

As she opened another cardboard box full of supplies, one nurse noted, "We found things we didn't need, some things we couldn't identify. So we red-tagged them and sent them all back."

Move-in created opportunities to look at the ways in which supplies and equipment would be ordered and accounted for once the hospital was in full operation. Meanwhile, red-tagging began.

Figure 4.7   After labeling the doors, nurses begin the daunting job of stocking and standardizing the cath lab. (Photo by Naida Grunden, with SRMC permission.)

Red tagging is part of the 5S discipline. As the supplies were thoughtfully placed, labeled, and standardized, with par levels established, frontline workers red-tagged items they could not use. Red-tagging allowed these items to be redeployed quickly to other areas of the hospital or sent back immediately for full credit. During the Spotsy move-in, the value of supplies and equipment that were redeployed or returned in time to receive full credit amounted to hundreds of thousands of dollars.

Medical-Surgical Unit (Med-Surg)

With Ruby Higgins (RN, BSN) leading Critical Care Services, nurses began to create a prototype med-surg room. Of particular interest was the headwall, where the various medical gas outlets and hookups for auxiliary equipment were located.

So engaged was the nursing staff that two nurses in their coats and carrying their purses, who were leaving for home at the end of their shift, stayed to discuss where the sphygmomanometer gauge ought to be placed to make blood pressure reading easiest (Figure 4.8).

The building's own glitches became apparent as teams began standardizing storerooms. Some of them seemed to be architectural afterthoughts, of irregular shape and configuration. Figure 4.9, for example, shows the detail required to place items into the storeroom. As currently staged, the biohazard waste container is too close to the sink. There was not much room to move things around. Had the processes and functions of each storeroom

Figure 4.8 Two med-surg nurses, on their way home at shift's end, cannot resist trying to place one more gauge where they want it on the headwall. (Photo by Naida Grunden, with SRMC permission.)

Figure 4.9 Workroom: physical limitations surface when process is not considered first. (Photo by Naida Grunden, with SRMC permission.)

been considered during design, architects would have had the chance to accommodate them.

Surgery

The surgical suite at Spotsy is second to none. As new surgical equipment, still wrapped in plastic, was wheeled into the suite, staff members became visibly

Figure 4.10   Krystal Atkinson, RN, director of surgical services, shows 5S in drawers in a surgical suite. (Photo by Naida Grunden, with SRMC permission.)

excited. This staff was completely committed to making sure that the operating room (OR) worked perfectly from the very first surgery on the very first day. As in the other areas, staff members collaborated to think about where to put pieces of equipment. Simple post-it notes along the wall were moved from here to there, as a way to experiment quickly with the placement of each piece of equipment. Drawers and cabinets were planned and fitted with dividers or bins, and every item was labeled by name and par level (Figure 4.10).

In the cabinets, the blue plastic bins were retrofitted with angled pieces to tip them upward so that the contents—not just the label—would be visible at all times.

"Everything is standardized in the core," says Krystal Atkinson, RN, director of surgical services. "We're not wasting time looking for anything. Having everything right there has a definite impact on patient care and safety—for example, when we can reduce the time a patient is under anesthetic."

In the months since the hospital opened, Atkinson has come to appreciate more features of workplace organization. She remembers prior work settings where overproduction—hoarding too many supplies—itself became a management problem.

"I don't have to worry about that now," she says. "Deliveries come twice a day. The techs are taking responsibility to cross train, so if somebody is absent, the orders always get here. The system has become very reliable. It's a simple process, well understood, and easier to comply with than not to comply with."

Staff members realize that they can experiment with refinements to make the work easier. Because they own the process, they challenge each other to make sure that things stay organized. Atkinson thinks the level of satisfaction is exemplified through an experience she had never had before: A surgeon walked the halls to seek her out after a particularly difficult surgery. Most of the time, this would be a bad sign. She said:

> He sought me out to make a point of telling me how accommodating the staff had been, and how surprised he was to have had everything he needed without delay. I know how proprietary OR people can be—"this is our area, this is how we've always done it." So it's a pleasure when people recognize that change, when it's done deliberately this way, can make a big, positive difference. Besides being better for patients, it can actually create a competitive advantage for the hospital and the surgeons who work here.

Labor and Delivery

The labor and delivery suite is often the backdrop for some of life's greatest emotions. As it turned out, setting up the labor and delivery area turned into an emotional experience itself.

Several new employees just out of orientation arrived in labor and delivery, reporting to Meredith Scaccia, RN, coordinator of Women and Children's Department. Scaccia introduced them to the concept of Lean and let them know that their unit would be set up according to Lean principles. She showed them the work flow as depicted on the future-state value stream map, and she asked for their feedback. She introduced the basics of workplace organization and let them know that they would be helping to put the rooms together in the way that made the best sense to them. With that, she turned it over to the nurses, whose initial response was shock:

> "Will you tell us where things go?"
> "Will the consultant tell us where to put things?"

The answer to both questions was no. Scaccia restated that the nurses were the people doing the day-to-day work, and they would be setting up and standardizing the rooms according to their best ideas. This was Lean thinking, the way things were done in this new hospital.

One nurse burst into tears. "I can't believe it," she said. "Nobody has ever really listened to us before. Nobody has ever given us the freedom to do what we came into nursing to do. Am I dreaming? I can't believe that I might actually be happy to come to work again."

Labor, Delivery, Recovery, Postpartum

Setting up the labor and delivery area involved creating standard prototype rooms for labor, delivery, recovery, and postpartum (LDRP), the OR, recovery, triage, nurse's desk, nursery, neonatal intensive care unit (NICU), and workrooms.

The 10 LDRP rooms posed some of the biggest challenges. "In these rooms, we serve two patients," said Scaccia. "We have both mother and baby as patients, and the family is present, too. Anything can happen in these rooms, so we need to set it up for the optimal work flow."

Permanently installed casework varied from room to room. For example, three LDRPs had one fewer upper cabinet than the rest. The nurses realized that standardizing the placement of everything in each room would make or break their efforts at streamlining the work, so in the rooms with an extra cabinet, the nurses decided to leave them empty.

"It's like when you come across a blank page in a technical manual," said one participant. "The page will say, 'This page intentionally left blank.' That's what we did with some of the nonstandard storage."

For quick access to less used items that were not stored in every room, nurses created standard "jump bags" and designated a storage area for them. As necessary, the nurse could quickly grab a bag and take it to an LDRP, confident that all the standard items were in it.

The LDRPs were mirror-image rooms, laid out with the same zones. To one side of the laboring mother was the family zone; to the other side, was the obstetrician's zone. Over farther was another zone containing the baby's warming bed and the work area for the pediatrician. One nurse noticed that, as currently configured, the cupboard for the patient's belongings was in the baby zone.

"We don't want the family to have any reason to go to that area," she pointed out. "There's room for the patient cupboard in the family area. Why not move it over there?"

Of ORs and Floors

Not everything had arrived yet and that, it turned out, was a good thing. Before any new facility opens, every square inch of every floor must be sealed, a time-consuming event that can be hard to plan around. Every piece of equipment that rests on the floor must be moved. Work in the wet areas stops.

Scaccia's team noticed something about the floor during their process simulations. A line of embedded red linoleum squares by the front desk provided a no-nonsense visual cue denoting that, beyond this point, people needed to don masks, hats, and booties. But there was a problem. The staff bathroom was behind the red line: Workers at the desk would have to gown up every time they needed to use it. Moving the red line behind the bathroom meant removing and replacing some floor tiles—fortunately, before the floors were sealed.

It seemed as though the architects had thought of everything. There was even a permanently installed desk in the cesarean OR, where a clinician could sit to enter information into the computer in real time. It was near the surgery table, but with plenty of room to walk by.

The surgery table had not yet arrived, but the team determined its exact dimensions and taped out a corresponding area on the floor. They also began taping where the other equipment would be placed around it (Figure 4.11).

One nurse asked, "Where will the doctor's instrument tray go?" As it turned out, the doctor's instrument tray is always at the head of the table to the patient's right side—which, in this case, ran right into the convenient

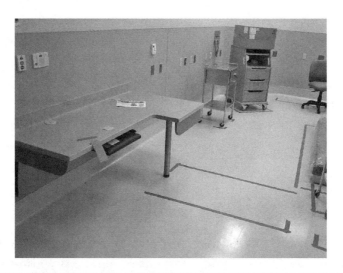

Figure 4.11   The desk was a great idea in the wrong place. Because it interfered with the placement of the doctor's instrument tray (taped on the floor), it was red-tagged and removed. (Photo by Naida Grunden, with SRMC permission.)

new desk. Placement of the instrument tray is non-negotiable. After considerable discussion, the team red-tagged the desk.

Every new facility will have glitches. But in this case, having frontline workers simulate the major processes, right down to the details, allowed them to catch glitches like errant cupboards, lines, and desks, averting considerable trouble on opening day.

Great Expectations: The Nurses Speak

Reaction from employees, especially the nursing staff, has been uniformly positive. Said former Air Force nurse, Janie Lott, RN, MSN, a 20-year veteran of labor and delivery:

> I appreciate being given the opportunity to set things up so they work best for the patient and the staff. So often, processes are set up for nurses by people who are not nurses, so they don't understand the footwork involved. Processes set up that way usually end up taking time away from the patient. Setting it up ourselves has worked well, has made us a team, and it makes me feel acknowledged.

Labor and delivery nurse Amy Frederick, RN, concurred:

> They let us help, rather than having somebody else plan it out, say, 'Look what we've done for you,' when it may not be what we needed at all. I've never been in a hospital where they actually asked your opinion about where you thought things should go, how you thought things could go smoother, and listened and then let it happen your way.

Visual Management Helps That Fifth "S"—Sustain

Once the supplies were put away, plan-o-grams were created to document where each item should go. These visual diagrams help with the fifth "S," which is "sustain." The name plan-o-gram was borrowed from retail, where they are used to create "perfect" displays according to a precise formula. Often posted inside the cabinet door or drawer, plan-o-grams give anyone a

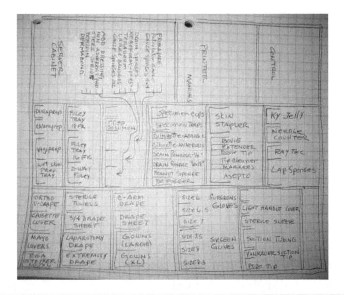

Figure 4.12   In one glance, the plan-o-gram sets the standard and creates a checklist for auditing. It is a tool borrowed from retail. (Photo by Naida Grunden.)

quick way to see if things are in the right place and the right quantity. They are a type of visual checklist—extremely useful not only for restocking, but also for checking to see that nothing has deviated from the plan (Figure 4.12).

"It makes it clear to anyone," said Carpenter, "that this is the standard. These are the four shelves, and here is what's laid out in each one. A good visual management system lets you see at a glance what's there, and maybe even more important, what's *not* there."

Audits may be set weekly or even daily. More important than the frequency is ownership—that somebody or some position is responsible to maintain the supplies. It cannot be left to chance or be "everyone's job."

"People in healthcare are very uncomfortable with this idea," notes Carpenter. "Hospitals are 24-hour-a-day ventures, and restocking isn't as systematic as it is in manufacturing. Assigning it to a position, rather than a person, works better."

Managers are ultimately responsible for making sure that the system is sustained and for identifying vulnerability in the resupply system. This means that managers must come and see the work—in the parlance of Lean, they must "go to *gemba*" to the front line to watch. This improves employee engagement and allows managers to coach and mentor.

Hospitals with vibrant workplace organization programs have steering committees capable of monitoring daily audits and giving measurable feedback. Friendly competition between departments, such as determining which one came closest to 100% compliance for the week or awarding coupons and prizes for winning departments, can keep the effort in the forefront and make sustainment fun.

The Leadership Perspective

In this brand-new hospital, the experienced members of the executive team, the so-called "C-suite," had never worked together before. The same was true for the staff.

CEO Tim Tobin believes that the opportunity to found a new hospital—not build a replacement—is what he calls a "once-in-a-four-or-five-lifetime experience." A veteran of building and remodeling projects in the past, he notes that ordinarily, the culture, practices, and policies from the old building just transfer to the new.

"If we had not had the opportunity to do this Lean work, without a doubt, we would not have spent the time dissecting so many flow processes so early in the preopening period," said Tobin. "We'd likely have gone on the assumption that we know how to run a hospital. But we're bringing in people from other organizations, along with their experiences and expectations. Mapping out value streams gave us a great way to learn from each other."

In fact, new employees were selected for their adaptability and willingness to (a) look without bias at the way things are done, (b) leave behind the things that did not work, and (c) collaborate continually to figure out better ways to work. Tobin says value stream mapping lets everyone visualize how it is going to work and challenge one another: Is that the best way? How shall we do it here?

"Detailing those processes on the front end helps ground everyone's expectations properly. When you have a patient in a wheelchair with a need—that's not the time to be working this out," said Tobin. At the same time, he is sensitive to the responsibility associated with raising people's expectations (Figure 4.13). In orientation, many employees express the hope that this hospital will be the place where they begin to love their careers again.

"That is a serious goal. If we can achieve that together," said Tobin, "it will be best for our employees and their families, our patients and their families, and our organization. In return, we will keep challenging ourselves, striving constantly toward breakthroughs in quality and efficiency."

Figure 4.13   This unusual degree of involvement by employees in setting their own work environment inspires confidence and hope. "I feel acknowledged," said one nurse. Said CEO Tobin, "Leaders bear a lot of responsibility when they raise people's expectations. We are all responsible for providing the highest quality of care while continuing to build a healthy work culture." (Photo by Naida Grunden, with SRMC permission.)

Administrator Ken West confirms that this is a new kind of administration—less authoritarian, more collaborative. They are often seen on the front lines of care, coaching, mentoring, and removing obstacles. "We trust people to do their jobs conscientiously," said West. "In return, we expect their highest level of performance. We believe every employee is capable of great things."

The newness is both challenge and opportunity. West said:

> Leaders may want to pop a kaizen event or do a 5S, but in established institutions, the people may not be ready for major culture change. For us, we've been able to craft the environment, create the team, and start using Lean right away. It's a relief for people. Nurses aren't born knowing where everything is. The system fails the people, not the other way around.

CNO Nancy Littlefield notes that with a brand-new hospital, it is impossible to know with absolute certainty what staff will need or what kinds of patients will show up. "We have to think outside the box, so the value stream mapping has really encouraged that kind of thinking," she said. "Workplace organization is essential. From the first day, everyone will know where things are, rather than having 50 people asking the one or two people who put it away to begin with."

Littlefield notes that as rote tasks are simplified, it will free the minds and the time of staff members so that they can work on the more complex problems that will always arise.

CFO Sean Thomson, CPA, sees an even bigger advantage to the work just completed: "I envision continually using Lean to look for more and more improvements after we open. When individuals are not scared of change, it puts us at a competitive advantage."

Thomson was impressed with the amount of money saved in the red-tagging exercise, but the real gain he sees is in employee engagement. He believes that spending the time and money to do workplace organization on the front end will eliminate an incredible amount of frustration. "Frustrated nurses leave; happy ones stay. You could do an ROI just on that," he said.

Asked what advice he would offer others contemplating a building project, Thomson said that he would urge leaders to start with Lean process improvement work to see if improved throughput can eliminate the need for building. Thomson believes that hospital expansions can cause more problems, create more steps, spread out equipment, and stress already malfunctioning systems. If a building project is absolutely necessary, he advises using Lean-led design from the outset.

"Even though we wish we'd started with Lean-led design earlier, the work we did on move-in still helped us eliminate a lot of stumbling around," said Thomson. "And let's face it: Stumbling around is expensive."

Results

A focused look at one unit gives a good example of the benefits of workplace organization in the units where it was applied. The following results relate to one room, the Emergency Department central supply room, following workplace organization done on move-in. For that room, SRMC reports:

- A 40% reduction in square footage required to house supplies (There are fewer supplies in inventory than in other facilities of similar size.)
- A 75% reduction in the anticipated cost to purchase extra shelves and storage (as compared with other new hospitals in the system).
- A gain of $500,000 in returned capital equipment.

Similar savings were achieved in other units where workplace organization was applied.

Staff satisfaction with the new work environment is very high, and staff orientation to the new Lean environment has taken less time than budgeted. As predicted, the hospital's Lean journey continues.

Summary

The beautiful new Spotsylvania Regional Medical Center (SRMC) was signed, sealed, delivered, and ready for move-in when leaders discovered the potential value of Lean-led design. While unable to reap benefits from early design, SRMC discovered how valuable it could be to team-building and culture establishment to conduct comprehensive workplace organization on move-in.

Discussion

- The hospital was new. The staff were new. The leaders were new. Why was it so important to have a smooth move-in experience? What else besides 5S and visual management was going on?
- Workplace organization ensures that staff have what they need, when and where they need it, and in the quantity in which they need it. What are the psychological benefits of establishing standards around the supply chain? What are the patient safety benefits? What are the financial benefits?
- Why label everything?
- Why did the nurse cry? Discuss respect in the workplace.
- Why did the group not do a workplace organization 3P (Hint: they had no employees. What did they do instead?)
- Rule 2 of the Rules in Use (Chapter 1) states, "*Connections* must be direct, with an unambiguous yes-or-no way to send requests and receive responses." How does the visual workplace support rule 2?
- Rule 3 of the Rules in Use states, "The *pathway* for every product and service is simple and direct." How does 5S support a cleaner pathway?

Suggested Reading

Galsworth, G. 2005. *Visual workplace, visual thinking: Creating enterprise excellence through the technologies of the visual workplace.* Portland, OR: Visual-Lean Enterprise Press.

Notes

1. Also discussed in Chapter 2. See Figures 2.1 and 2.2.
2. Galsworth, G. 2005. *Visual workplace, visual thinking: Creating enterprise excellence through the technologies of the visual workplace.* Portland, OR: Visual-Lean Enterprise Press.
3. Ordinarily, assistance from a few Lean consultants would be augmented with staff members from a hospital's quality department. The heavy reliance on consultants in this case was necessitated by the hospital's lack of staff at this time.

Chapter 5

Are We Too Early?

I'm seeing folks that have been doing this work for 20 to 30 years really show some excitement about the Lean design we are doing.

—Charles Wyatt, MD
Chief Medical Officer
Regional Medical Center of Acadiana, Lafayette, Louisiana

Case studies: Lee's Summit Medical Center, Lee's Summit, Missouri; Regional Medical Center of Acadiana, Lafayette, Louisiana

Introduction

"We've got plenty of time to introduce Lean in our new hospital," said one hospital manager overseeing the construction of a small community hospital in the Pacific Northwest. "But it's too early now. We haven't broken ground yet. The drawings aren't even finished."

This manager holds the common but mistaken belief that Lean is another set of "tools" to factor in later, rather than what it truly is—an underlying operational philosophy affecting every aspect of the hospital enterprise. In an environment as complex and critical as a hospital, Lean thinking begins to add value as soon as it is woven in.

Before embarking on expansion, smart hospitals look at ways to maximize the space at hand through process redesign. They resist the siren song of "more space," relying instead upon careful analysis of the way in which work needs to be done. If building or remodeling proves necessary, they start with Lean design.

Lee's Summit Medical Center: Lean Process Improvements Obviate Expansion

When staff frustration runs high, patient satisfaction dips, and bookend problems like a crowded Emergency Department (ED) and lengthy discharges bog things down, a sweeping solution like "more space" may seem temptingly obvious. But what do bottlenecks really signify?

In 2009, Lee's Summit Medical Center in Lee Summit, Missouri, seemed already to have outgrown its 2-year-old, 64-bed hospital. The overriding assumption was that the facility was too small to serve the population and that expanding it was the only reasonable solution.

Lee's Summit Medical Center

This 64-bed, full-service, acute-care hospital is located in Lee's Summit, Missouri. The facility opened in 2007. The staff includes 500 people and 100 volunteers. Lean process improvement has been introduced at the facility. Crowding in the emergency department constrained hospital capacity. Could they create more capacity without building on?

Rather than charging ahead with construction, however, a forward-thinking leadership team decided to see whether more efficient processes might allow them to care for more people in the same amount of space. In earliest "predesign," the hospital decided to work with Lean practitioners to look anew at how work was done.

The practitioners' initial assessment revealed that the hospital was indeed at capacity. However, it looked like improving the way beds were assigned, increasing communication among departments, and accelerating discharges—in other words, improving throughput—might break the logjam and create more capacity without construction. Lee's cross-functional kaizen rapid improvement team took a closer look.

A kaizen (or rapid improvement event) was set up to look at ways to increase capacity by improving throughput. The group also looked at the supply chain to determine how many materials were needed and how much space to store them.

"The hospital needed a better way to handle fluctuations in demand," said Lean practitioner Alex Maldonado. "One process in obvious need of restructuring was discharge, which routinely took about 5 hours."

Discharge: Untangling Current Practice

The team's current-state value stream map (Figure 5.1) showed vulnerabilities at transfer and at discharge. Patients remained in the ED, unable to move to the floor because discharges took so long.

Problems with transfer and discharge signified other organizational challenges. In the absence of solid communication among departments, teamwork and relationships had suffered—a situation common to many American hospitals. The ED could not understand why discharge took so long, staff on the floor were unhappy with the incomplete documentation that sometimes arrived from the ED, and Case Management was frustrated with its attempts to control the process. Misunderstandings proliferated.

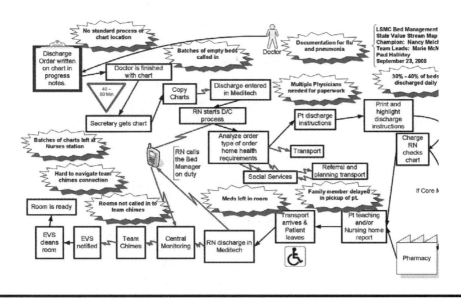

Figure 5.1   A convoluted discharge system plagued Lee's Summit, as it does many hospitals in the country. This shows the "current condition," from which the team started improving. Jagged shapes represent problems. (Courtesy Lee's Summit Medical Center.)

Patient satisfaction scores stagnated at "average," although everyone sensed that they could do much better. They decided to look first at discharge and then streamline the operating room (OR). They looked at their current state to see where the glitches were (Figure 5.1).

Definition of Terms

Details matter. Certain key words were misunderstood, especially at discharge. For example, what does it mean to be "done"? If environmental services is done cleaning the room, does this mean that the room is ready for the next patient? What does "discharge" mean? When a doctor says that a patient is to be discharged, does that mean right now or later, after certain procedures are completed, certain arrangements made, or prescriptions filled?

The Rules in Use state that the activities of work are to be "highly specified as to content, sequence, timing, and outcome."[1] This rule mandates standardized work and highly specified definitions and communications so that each activity is concrete, understood in the same way by everyone, and done the same way every time.

The team agreed on definitions and prepared a checklist so that everyone could see exactly where the patient was in the discharge journey. The patient would be "ready," for example, when the physician, nurse, case manager, pharmacist, and physical therapist had completed and signed off on critical tasks on the checklist. The checklist triggered tasks for several people and helped everyone coordinate and standardize the work.

Redundant forms were another source of confusion and miscommunication, so they were reduced from more than half a dozen to two standardized pages, designed by the people who use them.

Staff on the unit typically waited until several beds were empty and then called environmental services to have them all cleaned. Batching the requests, rather than asking for service one by one, created a logjam for environmental services. Batching actually reduced the number of beds available.

Now, each unit uses a white board to let environmental services know as soon as a room needs to be cleaned. They opted for the low-tech white board to eliminate time searching for a computer terminal, logging on, entering a password, and so on. Lean improvements tend toward low-cost and low-tech solutions for the sake of simplicity.

Yet, there is a place for electronic management. The team decided to use an electronic white board to help with the bed management so that assignments could be made quickly, relieving the bottleneck in the ED.

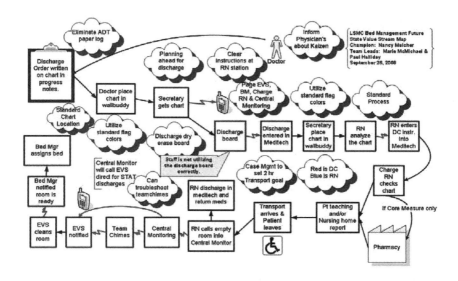

Figure 5.2   The rounded cloud shapes represent problems that have been solved: waste that has been removed from the system so that discharge goes much more smoothly. (Courtesy Lee's Summit Medical Center.)

Engaging Physicians and Leaders

The team engaged physicians, who had not realized, for example, that leaving batches of charts in unspecified locations created problems for others. The physicians agreed to work on patient charts one by one, placing them in a standard location when they finished.

The unit secretary and case manager created discharge checklists. They now work first on patients being discharged to home because these situations are less complicated and go fast. Once those are under way, they turn their attention to more complicated discharges to nursing homes or long-term care facilities. The future state is shown in Figure 5.2.

Leaders got involved. Nancy Melcher (RN, MBA), chief nursing officer, who participated in the Lean sessions, walked the units daily, asking targeted questions, coaching, and helping to remove barriers to improvement. Frontline involvement by top leaders often heralds facility-wide acceptance of Lean methodologies and culture change.

Results: Less Time, Zero Construction

Lee's Summit parent organization, HCA, sets its target of having 25% of patients discharged by 11 a.m. Before Lean improvements began, 5.4% of Lee's patients met that target; within 3 months, it had reached 11.4% and continues to rise. The quality of the discharge—patient information, preparation, safety considerations, and so forth—has also improved. Rework is rare.

The staff defines "discharge time" as the time between the physician's order for discharge to the release of the patient from the hospital. In the beginning, discharges took on average 324 minutes (over 5 hours). The initial round of improvements moved the number to 295 minutes—under 5 hours. Within 2 months after the departure of the Lean consultants, staff's continued improvements reduced discharge time to 172 minutes. As of February 2011, discharge time hovers at just under 80 minutes—not quite an hour and a half.

Perhaps most significantly, after years of stagnant patient satisfaction data, Lee shot to the top 10% among HCA hospitals. That kind of improvement is a staff satisfier, too. Many of the old interdepartmental tensions have eased as everyone has collaborated and succeeded together.

With more patients discharged on time, improved patient flow, and improved communications and processes, the hospital is accommodating more patients without construction.

Outpatient Surgery Improvements

When just 42% of the outpatient OR first cases began on time, several people thought that more prep rooms were needed. But a look at the current-state value stream map revealed that it took 90 minutes to move patients from registration through prep. The multidisciplinary improvement team thought it could increase capacity by using less time, rather than by adding more space. Team members knew they could streamline prep.

First, they standardized registration, creating a process from what had been largely improvised work. Patient prep also needed to be standardized; too often, orders for lab work came as a surprise, causing delay and frustration all around. Now, a purple checklist attached to the front of each patient chart triggers everything and every department required during prep. The physicians, anesthesiologists, nurses, charge nurses, and those in charge of the OR know the order in which things are to be done and where the patient is in the process. The checklist follows the patient through to the end of surgery. At that point, it becomes concise documentation of the entire procedure.

The checklists are aggregated daily into a quality improvement tool. They are put into a simple electronic spreadsheet, which pinpoints where the process may have bogged down. It's a real-time, case-by-case way to see results immediately, and it is more useful than aggregated monthly or quarterly results.

"The lab was awesome," said Maldonado. "They drastically improved their turnaround times and increased the percentage of pre-op labs that were ready and verified by 6 a.m."

According to Quality/Risk Management Director Rod Carbonell, "For the past 2 years, first cases have started on time over 90% of the time. This meant that we were able to add 100 surgical cases per year while reducing overtime by 1,263 hours."

Again, more patients were accommodated without costly rebuilding or remodeling.

Linens and Things

"From the moment the hospital opened in 2007, linens were a problem," said Carbonell. "We were out of compliance, with linen carts in the hallway [because we had] nowhere to put them. It seemed obvious that we needed more space."

Carbonell and laboratory director and co-Lean coordinator Ashlea Servi formed a team to look very closely at underutilized or misused storage in the hospital.

"It was a real eye-opener," said Servi. "Because nurses couldn't rely on always having linens where and when they needed them, they hoarded, and that resulted in over-ordering."

They called in an often overlooked expert to help: the linen supplier. Together, they determined that the hospital was holding about 50% too much linen. They started by removing the linen bins from the hallway, which did two things: (1) immediately brought the hospital into compliance, and (2) removed about 30% of the linen (Figure 5.3).

"We were astonished to remove 30% of the linen and have zero stock outs," said Carbonell. "Nothing else changed. We made no physical alteration. We hadn't even started looking at the system yet; we just removed the excess. We still have plenty of linen and, now, plenty of storage."

Later, concurrent with process improvements, they removed another 40% of the linen and stored smaller amounts at the points of use.

When Carbonell looks back on prior building projects in which he was involved, he now believes that most hospitals overbuild storage. The mind-set is one of dearth, but in truth, he says, "We have an abundance of storage."

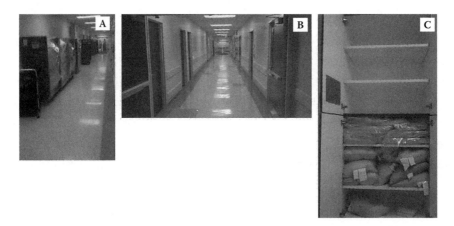

Figure 5.3 **(a) Before: hallway loaded with linen carts creates compliance issue. (b) After: hallway is clear. (c) Storing linens near point of use means that there is *more* than enough storage in the building. Construction was not needed. (Courtesy Lee's Summit Medical Center.)**

Regional Medical Center of Acadiana: Hospital Staff Conducts Its Own Predesign

The marquee service at Regional Medical Center of Acadiana (RMCA) of Lafayette, Louisiana, is its full spectrum of cardiovascular services. It is the only hospital in its region to offer the most current surgery for peripheral vascular disease (PVD). The surgery offers a way to open vessels distant from the brain or heart, alleviating pain and sometimes saving limbs in patients suffering from conditions like atherosclerosis or diabetes. RMCA offers courses for physicians in the latest PVD surgical techniques, drawing cardiologists and experts from cardiac catheterization labs (cath labs) from across the country.

Regional Medical Center of Acadiana (RMCA)

This 142-bed, full-service, acute-care hospital is located in Lafayette, Louisiana. The facility is 25 years old. Lean process improvement has been introduced at the facility and is spreading, although it is not yet fully ingrained in everyday work. RMCA boasts a robust cardiology program, which necessitated a look at reconfiguring current facilities. Without adding square footage, could they find a way to accommodate patients and staff better?

The cardiology program was increasing by 20% per year. The corresponding uptick in cath lab procedures meant that both cath labs were operating at capacity. The hospital already flexed its schedule to meet demand, operating into the evenings. It was time to consider expansion.

The initial proposal called for constructing an additional cath lab within the existing hospital walls, in a separate location from the other two. The budget would be $4.5 million to transform and equip the space. While CEO Vicki Briggs was willing to consider the third cath lab, she wondered whether RMCA could get more for its money.

The Vision: Hybrid OR

Enter cardiovascular surgeon and RMCA's chief medical officer, Charles Wyatt, MD, with the idea of creating a hybrid OR. The hybrid OR combines "conventional operating room capability with state-of-the-art endovascular imaging. The need for these hybrid operating rooms has evolved as the endovascular revolution in vascular surgery has progressed."[2]

Cardiac surgery is becoming less invasive than it once was; conversely, cardiac catheterization, an imaging procedure, sometimes transforms into a situation requiring immediate surgical intervention. The blending of one procedure into another creates the need for a well equipped operating suite with advanced imaging capabilities.

Current Layout: Challenge and Opportunity

The hospital's third floor had become a sort of overflow area. If the ICU, CICU, Medical-Surgical or Telemetry departments on other floors exceeded their capacity, those patients flowed to the five-bed MICU on the third floor. The third floor also housed patients who came in for outpatient surgery and dialysis. (The dialysis locations had originally been configured as two C-section rooms, so they were the size and specifications of surgical suites, as shown in Figure 5.4.)

Dr. Wyatt envisioned consolidating all cardiology surgery services in one area—possibly the third floor. The areas currently used by cardiology on other floors would be freed up for other functions, making better sense of the layout all the way around. Dr. Wyatt envisioned working in a team to come up with ideas. That led to an intense, highly specialized 4-day 3P event at RMCA—before anyone ever called an architect.[3] The idea: let us determine how we want our space to work before we turn the job of design over to the architect.

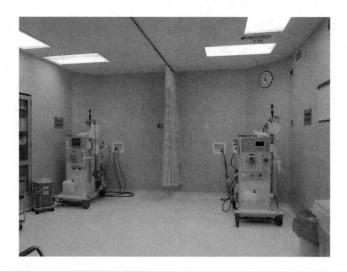

Figure 5.4 Current dialysis rooms, originally two C-section surgery suites, would become cardiac surgery suite and hybrid OR. (Courtesy RMCA.)

Said one hospital architect:

> It's always a good idea to include the architect on the beginning phases of the work. But sometimes, it's understandable when hospital staff members first want to get a handle on the size and scope of the project before going through the whole process of interviewing and hiring the architect."

Preplanning with Kaizen

Two weeks before the 3P, multidisciplinary teams, under the guidance of Lean practitioner Ken Lowe, conducted a kaizen (or rapid improvement) event in the catheterization lab. The plan called for the addition of a third cath lab. If enough capacity could be freed up through process improvement, perhaps it might not be needed right away.

The kaizen team focused on the pre-op holding area and discovered that patients stayed there 46 minutes longer than necessary. The team standardized processes and put into place a signal to call for the next patient to be transported (a "pull" rather than "push" system). The improvements reduced wait times by 20 minutes. The team believes that, over time, further improvements will reduce the wait even more.

By calculating takt time (the time available divided by the number of patients to see), the team members discovered that they could conduct 14 cases per day, on average, using just the improvements they had made in that one week, even in the current layout. Further Lean process improvements, like faster turnaround times and reconfiguring the rooms, opened up more capacity.

The team calculated a hypothetical takt time for a new hybrid OR that can handle both regular surgery and advanced endovascular surgery. The hybrid OR would accommodate 3.27 cases per day. The numbers are clearly theoretical at this point because at least one new surgery, for the Ercut heart valve, will be introduced to Louisiana at RMCA once the hybrid OR becomes available. Nevertheless, these calculations and process improvements provided a more complete understanding of the capacity at hand and the possibilities ahead.

Event Kickoff

The four-day 3P event at RMCA started with a Lean review with consulting Lean practitioners; however, much of the session was conducted by staff members like CMO Wyatt and others (Figure 5.5). The team consisted of 14 people from across the hospital, including a certified nursing assistant (CNA), administrative assistant, chief medical and nursing officers, clinical ICU supervisor, director of telemetry, and others. Together they agreed on

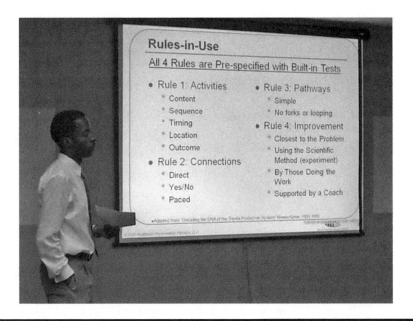

Figure 5.5   Leadership matters. Here, the chief operating officer reviews Rules in Use. (Photo by HPP, permission of RMCA.)

Figure 5.6   3P team observes cath lab recovery, second floor. (HPP photo, permission of RMCA.)

- *Scope:* to create a dedicated cardiovascular destination at RMCA
- *Objective:* to evaluate underutilized space in MICU, overflow, and cath lab in support of the dedicated cardiovascular unit

Together the group went to gemba, or the place where the work is done, to observe. They discovered the possibilities on the third floor, such as reusing the open hub area now sometimes used for storage, and on the second floor, in the area currently used for cath lab recovery (Figure 5.6).

Two Teams, Six Options

The group broke into two teams, each charged with brainstorming three separate options for creating a cardiovascular center and reassigning other functions that would have to move, such as dialysis and the gastrointestinal (GI) lab. Each group then took the best features of the schemes and consolidated them into one, which they presented to the group.

Once the teams had arrived at the scheme they favored, they still had important work to do:

- They had to test it by inviting frontline workers in the affected areas to consider their work. In the photo in Figure 5.7, a hospital leader asks a cardiovascular (CV) technician whether this plan could work for her. The resulting suggestions were incorporated. Inviting frontline feedback helps validate the work and generates buy-in from other staff.

Figure 5.7   Leader solicits ideas and validation from frontline technician. (HPP photo, permission of RMCA.)

Figure 5.8   3P exercise at Regional Health System of Acadiana, Louisiana. Colored yarn helps the team envision how each process in the cardiovascular lab could work and how each worker will move in the proposed new space. (HPP photo, permission RMCA.)

■ They had to take a detailed look at the "future state," or how the areas would really work. To do this, they conducted a yarn exercise, using colored yarns to indicate the pathway of work for specific staff members, like the circulator, respiratory therapist, patient, and so forth (Figures 5.8 and 5.9; also, note the cover illustration). The exercise showed the pathways for work and revealed problems like looping or forking, where workers retraced their steps. When the process becomes this visible, everyone learns.

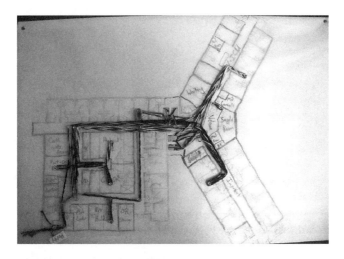

Figure 5.9 **Yarn denotes pathways of different workers. Pathways are direct, without loops or forks. (HPP photo, permission RMCA.)**

Figure 5.10 **CEO Vicki Briggs (right) lends a hand during report-out. (HPP photo, permission RMCA.)**

■ Along with safety for patient and worker, each team also had to consider capital, staffing, space, patient flow, implementation time, and capacity (current and future) as it developed its schemes.

On the third day of the 3P exercise, the teams presented their schemes to a cross section of hospital leaders and frontline workers. CEO Briggs remained at the report-out session to learn more (Figure 5.10). In the end, recommendations from both teams were incorporated, including:

- Consolidate all cardiac functions on the third floor.
- Convert the two dialysis suites to ORs, with one being the new hybrid OR. Move dialysis to the fourth floor, where other outpatient offerings, like physical therapy, reside.
- Continue plans to install a third cath lab adjacent to the other two to handle future growth.
- Move GI's endoscopy suites to the second floor, where the cath lab is now.

Was It Worth the Effort?

Assembling a team of 14 people for 4 days and inviting in an outside firm to facilitate a 3P—these costs add up. Still, CEO Briggs believes that the exercise was worth the investment on several levels.

"The 3P exercise was about more than physical layout," said Briggs. "It helped us see how the operations would flow best."

It may be unusual for a hospital to become this involved in looking at its processes before it ever calls the architect. Rather than relying on architects to make the initial recommendations, RMCA leaders saw the wisdom in assembling their knowledgeable frontline staff—including ancillary services, physicians, and nurses—and coming up with basic data and preliminary ideas based on actual processes.

Several important things happened:

- For 4 days, the concentrated focus allowed everyone to hear one another's perspectives. They discovered how certain problem areas had evolved and came to appreciate just how hard everyone was working. This broke down barriers. According to one participant, nurses respectfully challenged doctors' ideas and doctors were receptive. Everyone on the team quickly saw the advantages of looking at work flow and systems, not just space.
- Ordinarily, hospitals interview architects and ask them to make recommendations. Now, with data from their 3P, hospital leaders believe they can arm the architects with process data up front, which will help them make better recommendations. Entering a relationship with the architect from a position of self-knowledge should alter that relationship for the better.
- Data from the 3P can herald change in the architect's usual work cycle. Traditionally, architects will meet and speak with hospital people time and again, only to return and redraw, hoping to close in on meeting the client's needs. In Lean terms, this is the waste of rework. (One architect

refers to the cycle as "groundhog day," where each round of drawing seems only to beget another.) The 3P process creates a better informed client, which should reduce the architect's frustration and time line.

Briggs likes the outcomes of the work. With a dedicated cardiology hospital-within-a-hospital on the third floor, the second-floor OR can now better serve orthopedics, otolaryngology (ENT), and other specialties. She also expects Lean thinking and kaizen to expand efficiencies as they spread.

But perhaps most important, she says, "3P not only gave us valuable data, but it intensified our teamwork. This building project will proceed more smoothly all around."

Hospital workers are not designers, but they understand how a space needs to work. Developing that full understanding before turning it over to the architect changes the paradigm. Processes like 3P can help build a culture of safety and change.

Summary

The 2-year-old hospital in Lee's Summit, Missouri, seemed to be bursting at the seams. Plans were under way to add on, build up, and somehow gain more space. But leaders looked more closely and discovered that, not only was there adequate space, but that they also could increase throughput and use the entire facility more efficiently. The problem was the process.

Few hospitals can build new facilities or add on. At the Regional Medical Center of Acadiana, staff went through a comprehensive preplanning exercise before ever calling in the architect. They discovered space and an efficient layout for a new cardiovascular surgery unit within their walls.

Discussion

- What did Lee's Summit Medical Center do to gain space? Was it space they gained or needed?
- Why was Lee's Summit so overstocked with linens? Does anything like that happen in your facility?
- What would be the reason to go through a 3P before calling the architect? Do you think having the architect there for the 3P would have helped? Or would doing the 3P first help the hospital decide which architect to hire?

Notes

1. Spear, S., and Bowen, H. K. 1999. Decoding the DNA of the Toyota production system. *Harvard Business Review* 77 (5): 97–106. See Chapter 1 in this text for additional discussion on Rules in Use.
2. Belkin, M., MD, chief, Division of Vascular and Endovascular Surgery, Brigham and Women's Hospital, Boston, MA. The design and implementation of hybrid operating rooms. *Proceedings of Veith Symposium,* Cleveland Clinic Foundation, www.veithsymposium.org/pdf/vei/2761.pdf (accessed October 13, 2010).
3. 3P is defined in Chapters 2 and 3, and examples are in Chapter 7.

Chapter 6

Standardization Supports Flexibility

You can come surprisingly close to eliminating hospital-acquired infections with standardization as opposed to resources.

—Richard P. Shannon, MD
Frank Wister Thomas professor of medicine, University of Pennsylvania School of Medicine; chairman, Department of Medicine, University of Pennsylvania Health System

Case study: Monroe Clinic, Monroe, Wisconsin

Introduction

In 2004, Dr. Richard Shannon and his colleagues in two intensive care units at Allegheny General Hospital in Pittsburgh eradicated central line-associated bloodstream (CLAB) infections[1] within 90 days.[2,3] They did so without costly new equipment or supplies. They did it mainly by standardizing the way that they inserted and cared for these IV lines, by removing them as soon as they could, and by adhering scrupulously to basic hygienic requirements for staff and visitors. They discovered that, by doing work the same way every time, if an infection or bad outcome occurred, they had a scientific way to walk back through the process, see what had gone wrong, and fix it. The free exchange of this information in a feedback loop meant that they continuously refined and improved their processes.

In 2004, 32 patients acquired CLABs in Allegheny General's two target ICUs. As of January 2010, those ICUs had posted only one bloodstream infection over the prior 56 months, despite the admission of more and sicker patients. Significantly, overall ICU mortality was down by 23%.[4]

Standardization: Easy to Say, Hard to Do

Do it the same way every time is a simple concept, rooted in the scientific method; yet, standardization remains a hard sell in medicine, particularly when it comes to medical procedures. Although the correct use of check-lists, which help to promote adherence to standard procedure, has helped make aviation among the safest of human endeavors, their use in medicine remains largely misunderstood, and their deployment lags behind that of other industries.[5,6]

Says John Toussaint, MD, of Wisconsin's ThedaCare, "Dramatic variations in performance...[are] more the norm than the exception in American healthcare, where scientific methods have not been used in organizing work sequences."[7]

Captain Chesley B. "Sully" Sullenberger, a renowned aviation safety expert even before his famous 2009 emergency landing on the Hudson River, said, "Whenever possible, standardizing equipment and procedures not only simplifies things, it improves performance and outcomes...Aviation has many complex systems; medicine has many more. Relying on human memory to navigate them is untenable."[8]

The concept of "same every time" has also eluded hospital architects in the past, but that is changing. More architects have come to understand the theory behind human error—that human beings inevitably make mistakes and that their environments and processes need to be deliberately standardized to help them become "mistake proof."[9] Architects are realizing that by standardizing the environment, they can help design safety into the building.

Slowly but surely, hospital rooms—exam rooms, patient rooms, operating rooms, storage rooms—are being standardized. When supplies, equipment, and people are in the same place every time, then everyone—from doctors to the technicians who stock supplies to "floater" nurses to new employees—can find what he or she needs quickly and reliably. When moments count, the reliability that comes from standardization can make a life-or-death difference for patients.

Standardized environments make it easier to do things the same way every time. For example, a pilot entering a cockpit knows that the first officer sits on the right and the captain on the left. Each crew member's equipment is located in the same place every time. They have drilled and practiced their procedures time and again in this standardized environment, all in the interest of flight safety. If something goes wrong, they are at least in a stable and reliable environment with well known procedures at hand.

Flexibility: For Those Moments of Truth

Of course in medicine, as in aviation, the moments of truth come during emergencies. No two situations are the same. No two patients are the same. Brent James, MD, executive director for Intermountain Healthcare's Institute for Healthcare Delivery Research, has said that physicians must retain the ability to provide 100% customized care at the bedside, depending upon the need of the patient at that moment.[10,11] He cites an example where a patient's heart was actually located on the right side of the chest, necessitating adjustments to many procedures.

How can standardized rooms and processes help in a case like that? If everything is predictable—the room is laid out exactly the same and processes are reliable—then nobody on the team wastes a moment's thought or motion finding or fixing things during a critical moment. All thought can go into the procedure and the patient at hand. Self-inflicted complexity has been designed out of the environment. If a clinician needs the latitude to do something unique for this patient—the medical equivalent of landing on the Hudson—it can be done in a stable environment.

David Sharbaugh, senior director at UPMC's Center for Quality Improvement and Innovation, touches on the link between standardization and flexibility. "The hard things will always be hard," he says. "Let's make sure the easy things are always easy."

What Is a Standardized Room?

"When a trip to the medication room turns into a wasteful game of hide-and-seek for the nurse, it is not hard to see why it frustrates the nurse and degrades patient safety," says Lean practitioner Teresa Carpenter, RN.

When the idea that standardizing rooms could enhance patient safety took root in 2002 at St. Joseph Hospital in West Bend, Wisconsin,[12] there were still many definitions for "standardized rooms." The push for single-patient rooms as a patient-safety enhancement was not yet in full swing. At that time, "standardized rooms" might have meant any of the following three things:

■ *Same equipment in each room.* There might be one or two patients to a room. The patient might be to the right or left of the practitioner entering the room, and the supplies kept in different drawers from room to room, but as long as each room contained a bed or beds, sink, chair, cupboard, computer desk, bandage supplies, and so forth, it was deemed "standardized." (It is not.)

■ *Same-handed.* Same-handedness considers that the practitioner always approaches the patient from the same side, so rooms should be oriented in the same direction, not mirror images. Carpenter notes that physicians in training always approach patients from the right side, whether they are right- or left-handed. Thus, it may make sense to set up hospital rooms so that the door is closest to the patient's right side.

Same-handed rooms may be more expensive to build than mirror image rooms. With the mirror image room, the plumbing for bathrooms and other infrastructure share a common wall, saving some initial construction costs. But while creating rooms with identical orientation may be more expensive up front, many believe the benefits will accrue over time.

Still, same-handedness does not necessarily imply that the rooms are identical, that equipment is always in the same place, or that the supplies in the closets and drawers or the outlets on the headwalls are consistent from room to room. Nevertheless, until recently the same-handed room was also deemed "standardized." (It may or may not be.)

■ *The standardized room.* St. Joseph Hospital of West Bend, Wisconsin, was an early adopter of the truly standardized room.[12] In that hospital, every patient room was a single-patient room and same-handedness a given. Each was designed to be exactly the same size and configuration, with the practitioner approaching from the right, family members always to the left of the patient, and TV and information boards always on the foot wall. The location of common medical gases and other items in the headwall is consistent from room to room. Supplies and equipment are close to the point of service (no running down the hall for sheets) and 100% consistently located. Everything about the room was designed to foster safety and efficiency. Those familiar with Lean philosophy will understand the theory behind this kind of standardization, as it incorporates:

- Visual control, sometimes called "status at a glance." When visual control is used, for example, the presence or absence of a piece of equipment, along with its cleanliness and readiness, is apparent at a glance.
- Less waste in terms of motion, defects, excess processing, and waiting.
- One-by-one processing, continuous flow, with no batching. Waiting until things pile up before working on them is a wasteful practice fraught with potential error. When thoughtful design takes into account the way in which work is done—in U-shaped cells or with a discrete computer nook for every patient room, for example—the design of any room can make it easier to do the work as it comes in.

Acceptance of the single-patient, standardized room as a prerequisite to patient safety is not yet universal, but it is growing. Here is a profile of the Monroe Clinic in Monroe, Wisconsin, that used Lean-led design to decide to create standardized rooms, while simultaneously using Lean philosophy to transform their operations.

Monroe Clinic: Lean-Led Design Meets Lean Process Improvement

As described in Chapter 2, during the earliest stages of master planning, one hospital in the southern United States found a way to flex ambulatory surgery beds for use in the ED in off hours, creating major efficiency. This opportunity would quickly have been lost had the plan proceeded to more complex architectural drawings before it was discovered.

Monroe Clinic

Monroe Clinic is a not-for-profit health system featuring a multispecialty clinic and 100-bed hospital. Sponsored by the Congregation of Sisters of St. Agnes, Monroe Clinic offers comprehensive healthcare with more than 80 providers, a 24-hour emergency room, and home care and hospice services, as well as multiple clinic locations in southern Wisconsin and northern Illinois. (Architect: Kahler-Slater)

Fortunately, in 2007, the Monroe Clinic in Monroe, Wisconsin, was still at the sketching stage with the architects when Lean thinking began to take hold.

The timing was interesting. Monroe leaders had already decided to redesign their outmoded 290,000-square-foot main hospital, which had been built in the 1930s, then added onto in the 1950s and again in the 1970s. Said Steve Borowski, director of Facilities and Materials Management, "We did look at reusing our existing building, but code requirements made it uneconomical to retrofit. It was going to be less expensive and result in a better, more efficient hospital if we built new."

Monroe leaders had engaged their architect and had begun looking at preliminary sketches (Figure 6.1). Concurrently (and coincidentally), the hospital contracted with Lean practitioners to help staff learn about Lean process improvement, with an eye toward transforming the hospital culture.

As Lean thinking was introduced on the front line, workers began changing and improving the way in which they worked, and they discovered how some features of the existing building got in their way. Monroe's leaders were determined to avoid designing a new building around processes

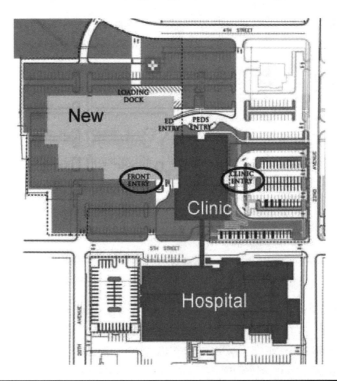

Figure 6.1 The new hospital is actually an addition to the newer clinic building, which is across the street from the existing hospital and connected by a sky bridge. (Courtesy Monroe Clinic.)

that weren't as efficient as they could be. They quickly saw the wisdom in expanding Lean thinking to their building design.

"Changing people's way of thinking wasn't easy," said Cindy Werkheiser, Monroe's director of service and process improvement. "People can hardly envision working any other way than the way they've been working. To introduce something as foreign as continuous process improvement was a real challenge. Understandably, the staff wanted evidence that change would make patients safer."

Fortunately, ample evidence shows that reducing waste—from hunting to handoffs—reduces risk to patients. Designing the structure to reduce steps, repetition, and uncertainty would help. But the building itself is not enough: It would take continuous improvements to the processes inside to continue making progress over time.

Carpenter and quality engineer Brad Schultz led kaizen events[13] in conjunction with the meetings with architects from Kahler-Slater. Monroe's staff members emerged from these events understanding that their processes contained waste—and absolutely committed not to import that waste into their new hospital.

"Although they were past the master planning phase, which is the ideal time, Monroe was fortunately still early enough," Carpenter said. "We were able to do Lean-led design work concurrently with the Lean process and operations improvement. It may be an overused term, but what we had was *synergy.*"

Initially, the architects may not have been aware of how much the process improvements would affect design. That would soon change.

Lean Synergy: Process First, Then Design

Architect Tom Wallen, who worked on the prototype hospital in West Bend, wants to know, "Why do we spend so little time designing the operational processes functioning within the hospital before designing the building?"[14] Monroe Clinic decided to start with operational redesign and let that inform building design.

The ambulatory surgery center (ASC) provides a good example of the synergy between the architect and Lean process improvement team. As the kaizen teams looked at more processes, more design opportunities surfaced. The preadmission testing area and ASC in particular provided rich opportunities for savings, consolidation, and improved performance. The following sections offer some examples.

Patient Registration

Brad Schultz said:

> There were little pockets of registration in different areas of the hospital. The kaizen team quickly saw the inefficiency, and they didn't want to repeat those little pockets in the new building. But had we not looked deeply into this at this early stage, the architects would have designed it with little pockets of registration. They could only have assumed that's what was desired.

As Werkheiser and Carpenter worked with the ASC frontline team to examine current operations more deeply, workers began to see the inefficiency in which they had been working. "In preadmission testing, at first people couldn't see anything to change or fix," Carpenter said. "But when we mapped out a spaghetti diagram of the patient's experience, we realized that patients had to stop in 16 different places, on four different floors, over 2 days, to get through their day surgery." (See Figure 6.2.)

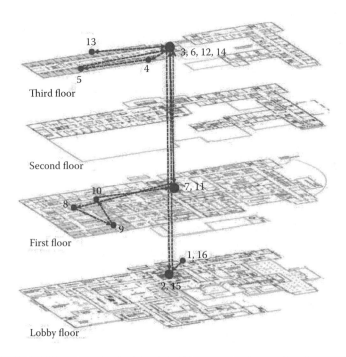

Figure 6.2   A depiction of the many paths a patient had to traverse in the original hospital to get through his or her day surgery. (Courtesy Monroe Clinic.)

The team, comprising people along the entire value stream—from the physicians' offices to the anesthesiologists—decided not to wait for a new building to try to fix the process. Together, they transformed a space in the existing clinic into a one-stop shop for preadmission testing. Now patients can register in the clinic lobby as soon as surgery is deemed necessary. Lab, EKG, and preadmission testing of all kinds are done then and there. Because redundant forms were consolidated, patients were asked certain questions only once. Sixteen steps (and 16 opportunities to wait) over 2 days became one quick stop. (See Figures 6.3 and 6.4.)

"We've worked hard to eliminate silos. We view everything as one continuous, horizontal path of the patient," said Werkheiser. Added Borowski, "Through the initial process work, we eliminated several classic wastes: time, motion, travel. Our new building will focus on process, deliberately defining service adjacencies for quick access."

Not only did this work produce a smoother process, it started transforming what had been proprietary and somewhat defensive silos into a collegial culture. The new process was so successful that it quickly fanned out all across the large physician practice.

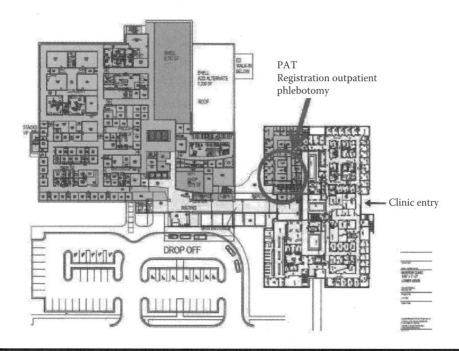

Figure 6.3   The team decided to consolidate all preadmission testing, admitting, and registration in the same area. This significantly affected the design of the new facility by removing scattered "pockets" of these functions. (Courtesy Monroe Clinic.)

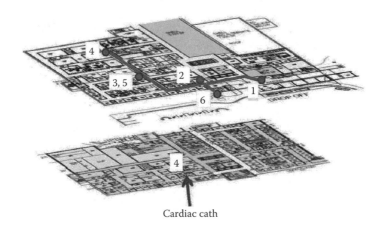

Cardiac cath

Figure 6.4   The much simplified process for outpatient surgery following the design of the future state. (Courtesy Monroe Clinic.)

The new way held definite design implications. The new building would colocate the lab, phlebotomy, outpatient testing, registration, and preadmission testing in one department (Figure 6.3). This design and the efficiency that it engenders would have remained unimagined without the Lean process work, which occurred early in building design.

Pre- and Postoperative Rooms

The team examined more design-influencing processes. Over 60% of surgical cases are under an hour in length. Was it really necessary to prep patients in one area, move them to a separate postoperative area, and then another recovery area? Rather than a "tour de hospital," what if they returned the patient to the same area after surgery was complete?

The disadvantage was that the space would be unoccupied while the patient was in surgery. The advantages included:

■ The cost of turning over the pre-op, post-op, and recovery areas is considerable. And extra steps introduce the possibility for error or hospital-acquired infection.
■ Providing two or three separate areas when one would do is a waste of space. Consolidating in to one pre-post area made sense.
■ The family can wait or browse in the cafe or gift shop.
■ The same staff members care for the patient pre- and postoperatively, providing better continuity of care. Reducing the number of staff members in contact with the patient reduces the possibility of infection.

How Many Rooms Are Needed?

As is usual practice, the architect used a formula including current hospital operations and projections to recommend how many rooms to build in the new ASC.

"Yes," said Carpenter, "taking into account the way things were currently done, the architect's calculations would have been correct. But if the front line could improve operating performance just a little, we suspected that they could do with fewer rooms."

Initially, day-surgery employees feared that they would not have enough rooms. On closer examination, surmountable problems surfaced.

"Mainly, we needed to create better access to information and scheduling," said Werkheiser. "Is there a room? Is it clean? There was no reliable way for nurses, housekeepers, and bed techs to know. Once we fixed the flow of information, we found that we could turn these rooms three or four times a day. We will have enough beds."

In the final analysis, the area will have one less room than originally planned. The savings can be applied to other areas and amenities in the new hospital.

The Stat Lab

Nervous employees also insisted on the need for a stat lab in the new hospital, to process lab samples quickly in an emergency. But on further examination, the team discovered that streamlining processes and fixing communication gaps allowed all lab samples to be processed more quickly. They created a better way for stat orders to be processed using existing facilities. The process improvements, coupled with a better pneumatic tubing system in the new hospital, will eliminate the need for a stat lab.

"They ended up not building a stat lab," Carpenter said. "They solved the process problem instead."

Creating better flow today is a good thing. Creating a streamlined building that makes it easy to do things right every time is even better (Figure 6.5).

Waiting Areas

Traditionally, each department has its own waiting room. In the new Monroe Clinic, there will be one waiting area per floor, with access to views of nature and natural light. Pagers and other forms of technology will notify

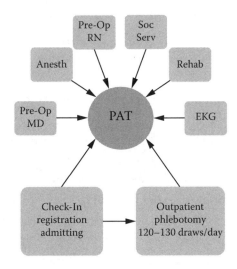

Figure 6.5   The new, simplified flow of registration, admission, phlebotomy, and other processes all feed off of the preadmission testing function. (Courtesy Monroe Clinic.)

family members when the physician is ready to brief them and when their loved one has reached a certain point in the procedure.

"If you have five departments on one floor, you would typically design 20 seats for each one, although you never use all 20," said Borowski. "A generous centralized waiting area means you meet the need with fewer seats. When you allow people to circulate to the coffee or gift shop, there will be fewer still. And fewer seats mean less heating, cooling, and cleaning as well."

Storage

Currently, major storage is overseen by Operations, Materials Management, and Sterile Processing. The Monroe team consolidated those departments and began taking a close look at efficient, high-density storage. They removed unneeded inventory. They looked at their processes to see whether they could move closer to just-in-time ordering and other supply-chain improvements.

"We were not trying to replicate what we have today, but we were trying to be visionary," said Borowski. "We were not asking, 'How does it work?' but 'How should it really work?'"

The result is 30%–40% less storage space planned for the new facility. The hospital is undergoing workplace organization and standardization before move-in to the new facility and is confident that storage will be ample.

The Journey to the Standardized Room

Cindy Werkheiser will not sugarcoat it: Making the decision to standardize every patient room was the most difficult and contentious decision that leadership had to make. The decision, of course, was made with ample input from frontline staff members. "We couldn't have done it without them," Werkheiser said.

Monroe Clinic contacted architect Tom Wallen, who had worked on the "safe by design" hospital in West Bend.[12] He described the necessity of standardized processes and standardized rooms, and he answered staff concerns. Would this be cookie-cutter medicine? Would having things always at the ready and always in the same spot erode their critical thinking skills? Wallen persuaded them, with evidence from the West Bend experience, that standardization releases the mind from the trivial to work on tasks that require critical thinking. Evidence clearly showed that patients were safer.

Using the FMEA Unconventionally

Of the tools at the disposal of Lean quality engineer Brad Schultz, one of the most sophisticated is the failure modes and effects analysis (FMEA). Traditionally, FMEA is used to highlight flaws within the design—either active or latent, show the flaws to the team before an actual failure occurs, and collectively decide what to do about them. The team will typically consider:

- What is the probability of failure?
- What is the severity of the effect if a failure does occur?
- Is a failure detectable or not detectable?

Because both the architects and hospital leaders had stalled over the issue of standardizing the rooms, Schultz and Carpenter decided to use FMEA in a slightly different way. In addition to showing the weak spots in a nonstandard environment, FMEA could be used as a decision-making tool to break the logjam.

The question was deceptively simple: *Would standardized rooms present more or less risk to patients?* FMEA helped the group to analyze the question and generate consensus on the answer. Together they analyzed risk (1) where the room was standardized and (2) where it was not.

The team accepted ICU care, with its low nurse–patient ratios and 100% patient visibility, as the "gold standard" for patient care.[15] Lack of patient visibility, then, was one risk analyzed. When the room is oriented so that the patient's head is at the left wall, a nurse entering from the left will see the patient, head to toe, upon entry. But a nurse entering from the right will not always have a clear view of the patient's head—and that is a risk factor.

In mirror-image rooms, risk factors multiply. Caregivers must move right to left in one room and left to right in another. And supplies and equipment are not in the same place each time, but now on the right, now on the left.

Regarding potential cost savings of mirror-image rooms, facilities manager Borowski added:

> It doesn't make sense to place patient care in the hands of the plumber. If we must, we will spend more in piping to get 100% standardization, but we will save money because standardized things can be constructed off-site, in a shop.[16] There are construction efficiencies, but the main reason for standardization is that the patient safety implications over time are huge.

Returning to the aircraft analogy, pilots flying one type of aircraft do not expect to find the fuel switch on the right today, but on the left tomorrow. In the cockpit, aircraft designers and human factors engineers have deliberately created an environment where every instrument and every piece of equipment is in the same place every time, and pilots have trained on routine procedures over and over. In a busy cockpit or in an emergency, this level of standardization means that the underlying routine is almost automatic, freeing the minds of the crew members to solve the more urgent problems at hand.

Schultz says that a nonstandard environment tends to perpetuate nonstandard practice because it opens the door to opinion and preference. "If I change one thing in one room, then I've just created two possible configurations," says Schultz. "If I change two things, I have four configurations, and so on. Each change doubles the deviation from standard. It doesn't take long for the risk to escalate significantly."

To standardize the hospital rooms or not: This became a decision point for hospital executives. "Stopping short of standardizing the rooms would have compromised our commitment to our newly adopted Lean methodology," said Werkheiser. "The FMEA helped us see that standardization was nonarguable."

The executive leadership decided to design the new Monroe Clinic with standardized rooms, which will support Lean work into the future. The architects agreed to design standardized rather than mirror-image rooms.

"Reaching for an FMEA to help build consensus may have seemed a little unorthodox," said Schultz, "but it turned out to be a good call. When we applied Lean principles to the pros and cons, we arrived at a clear consensus: Standardization was the best way to go."

Using Workplace Organization Now to Prepare for the Move

As part of preparing for moving to a new building, each department of the Monroe Clinic is undergoing a thorough 5S and visual workplace concepts exercise, known collectively as workplace organization.[17] All service lines and all departments are expected to have completed workplace organization well before the new hospital is occupied in 2012. The objective is to arrive in the new building with nothing superfluous.

"This meant establishing par levels and an inventory replenishment system. It meant an end to stock-outs and an end to hoarding," said Werkheiser.

In one example, an equipment room had become so overloaded that nobody could safely walk in and search. After everything came out of the room, pieces of equipment that had not been used in decades were discovered. They designed a better space, taped the floors, and installed visual cues and a process for keeping the equipment clean and in place (Figure 6.6).

In the new hospital, says Werkheiser, "We're designing space that's far more relevant to the work we do."

Although workplace organization began in earnest after the architectural design was under way, staff members were able to make a credible estimate of the storage space needed, and have made a commitment to work within that space.

"By doing 5S now, they can count space avoidance as a cost savings," said Carpenter. "They won't cram things in. There's a lot of big, bulky equipment they'll be able to leave behind."

To give everyone at Monroe Clinic a chance to learn the basics of 5S, the training team created a type of "5S in a box." It is a standardized plan,

Figure 6.6 Introducing workplace organization into the existing hospital allowed for a tremendous amount of unneeded supplies and equipment to be eliminated. That was stock that never had to be transported to the new hospital. (Courtesy Monroe Clinic.)

checklist, prepackaged materials, and everything needed to conduct 5S and begin a visual workplace. When a department sends a request, it receives the materials and a facilitator.

"This is one of the most creative things I've ever seen from a client," said Schultz. "It was so clear that people who had been through the training can do 5S themselves."

Culture Change Barometer

As they continue to look at current processes and how they want to work in their new building, the staff at Monroe Clinic seems well on the road toward culture change. Positive road signs include:

- Staff is managing operations more visually, posting performance metrics in each department. They post their performance numbers, whether favorable or not. They celebrate successes. If they fall short, they post the reason why and what measures they are taking to improve. These posts are kept current.

- Leadership spends a significant amount of time on the floor looking at the work and helping to solve problems, rather than in marginally productive meetings.

- Rather than being escalated to management, problem solving is moving closer and closer to where the problem occurs, in real time, in the course of work.

- From the earliest design through construction, over 200 of Monroe's 900 full-time employees have participated directly. During construction, even before the hospital was fully enclosed, groups of employees went through critiquing the subtle things, like outlet heights.

Said Facilities Director Borowski, "This design process was not management driven. Employees were on every team, challenging everything, and they were right up front in decision making. They are totally committed to working through any difficulties."

By the Numbers

Borowski also notes that the planners initially assumed that the new hospital would be a bigger hospital. New equals bigger: Bigger equals better. As it turns out, Lean-led design helped Monroe Clinic to moderate that assumption. Said Borowski: "Because of the way we have designed adjacencies, we have less corridor, storage, and waiting space. It's difficult to say exactly how much money we have saved, but it is in the millions."

By building a new hospital, rather than trying to rehabilitate a hospital disfigured by numerous add-ons, Monroe Clinic benefits in several ways. Borowski said:

We've achieved operational efficiency, sustainability, technology, standard patient rooms, evidence-based design, and environmental sensitivity. Everything about the building is welcoming and home-like. But perhaps most important, we believe we have designed a safer hospital.

Summary

Wisconsin's Monroe Clinic had already begun its Lean journey, learning to infuse Lean thinking and process improvement into their existing work environment. When the old hospital was deemed too expensive to retrofit, plans for a new hospital emerged.

Leaders saw the opportunity to create Lean efficiency in the hospital design. Along the way, they discovered that they could consolidate waiting rooms and pre- and post-op areas, achieve better functionality, and build a more efficient facility than they currently occupy. They overcame some initial difficulty agreeing to standardize patient rooms.

Using a failure modes effects analysis—a tool designed to detect latent design flaws—staff were able to see objectively why standardization was a good idea.

Discussion

- Rule 1 of the Rules in Use states: *Activities of work shall be highly specified as to content, sequence, timing, and expected outcome.* In other words, work should be done the same way each time, or standardized. How does standardizing the work space foster the standardization of procedures?
- What were the advantages of starting 5S well before move-in?
- What were the advantages of trying to reconfigure the old space for preadmission testing before the new hospital was complete?
- How does the design increase respect for patients?

Suggested Reading

Gawande, A. 2009. *The checklist manifesto: How to get things right.* New York: Henry Holt & Co.

Pronovost, P., and Vohr, E. 2010. *Safe patients, smart hospitals: How one doctor's checklist can help us change health care from the inside out.* New York: Penguin Group.

Reiling, J., ed. 2007. *Safe by design: Designing safety in health care facilities, processes, and culture.* Oakbrook Terrace, IL: Joint Commission on Accreditation of Healthcare Organizations.

Shannon, R., Frndak, D., Grunden, N., et al. 2006. Using real-time problem solving to eliminate central line infections. *Joint Commission Journal of Quality and Patient Safety* 32:479–487.

Shannon, R., Patel, B., Cummins, D., et al. 2006. Economics of central line-associated bloodstream infections. *American Journal of Medical Quality* 21:7S–16S.

Toussaint, J., Gerard, R., and Adams, E. 2010. *On the mend: Revolutionizing healthcare to save lives and transform the industry.* Cambridge, MA: Lean Enterprise Institute.

Notes

1. A central line-associated bloodstream infection refers to hospital-acquired infections that can result when intravenous catheters are introduced into a patient's main blood vessel to deliver life-saving medication, nutrition, or hydration. Unfortunately, these catheters, if inserted or handled improperly, provide an easy and direct way for bacteria to enter the bloodstream. As these central lines are usually reserved for the sickest patients, typically those in intensive care units, the effects of life-threatening bloodstream infections can be particularly devastating. The U.S. Centers for Disease Control and Prevention estimates that at least 100,000 people every year acquire CLAB infections in American hospitals.

2. Grunden, N. 2008. *The Pittsburgh way to efficient healthcare,* Chapter 2. New York: Productivity Press.

3. Shannon, R., Patel, B., Cummins, D., et al. 2006. Economics of central line-associated bloodstream infections. *American Journal of Medical Quality* 21:7S–16S.

4. Shannon, R. 2010. Approaching the theoretical limit in healthcare: Is it possible? Is it sustainable? Is it worth it? Presentation, Lean Power Day, Nashville, TN, May 20, 2010.

5. Bosk, C., Dixon-Woods, M., Goeschel, M., and Pronovost, P. 2009. Reality check for checklists. *Lancet* 374 (9688): 444–445. In medicine, checklists are too often treated as lengthy and optional step-by-step instructions, and they are not understood to be organizing, summarizing, and team-building, as well as standardizing.

6. Gawande, A. 2009. *The checklist manifesto: How to get things right.* New York: Henry Holt & Co. In Chapters 5 and 6, Gawande discusses the difficulty in creating checklists that are short, that summarize only the key points, and that can and must be used every time. He describes the science behind the checklist, which is not yet fully understood or deployed in medicine.

7. Toussaint, J., Gerard, R., and Adams, E. 2010. *On the mend: Revolutionizing healthcare to save lives and transform the industry.* Cambridge, MA: Lean Enterprise Institute.

8. Sullenberger, C. B. (with Grunden, N.). Keynote address. Health Information Management Systems Society, Atlanta, GA, March 4, 2010.

9. Reason, J. 1990. *Human error.* New York: Cambridge University Press.
10. James, B. 2010. Breakout session, Shingo Prize Conference, Salt Lake City, UT, March 2010.
11. The requirement for 100% customization aligns with the concept of Ideal, popularized by S. Spear and H. K. Bowen in the 1999 *Harvard Business Review* article, "The DNA of the Toyota Production System" (77: 97–106). Ideal is defined as care that is exactly what the patient needs, defect free; care delivered to one patient at a time, customized to each patient, on demand, and exactly as requested; with immediate response to problems or changes; without waste, in an environment that is physically, emotionally, and professionally safe. Dr. James's requirement for flexibility is a request for the Toyota version of Ideal care.
12. Reiling, J., ed. 2007. *Safe by design: Designing safety in health care facilities, processes, and culture.* Oakbrook Terrace, IL: Joint Commission on Accreditation of Healthcare Organizations.
13. Chapter 1 includes a definition and discussion of kaizen.
14. Wallen, T. K. 2007. Chapter 6 in *Safe by design: Designing safety in health care facilities, processes, and culture,* ed. J. Reiling. Oakbrook Terrace, IL: Joint Commission on Accreditation of Healthcare Organizations.
15. Donchin, Y., Gopher, D., Olin, M., et al. 2003. A look into the nature and causes of human errors in the intensive care unit. *Quality & Safety in Health Care* 12:143–147. This ICU human factors study cites an estimated number of 1.7 errors per patient per day and an average of 178 activities per patient per day.
16. See example from ThedaCare in Chapter 8.
17. In common usage, 5S usually refers to a rapid improvement event in which a department conducts the exercise (sort, set in order, shine, standardize, sustain) usually in a closet or work room. Workplace organization implies a large-scale 5S plus visual workplace, potentially reorganizing and standardizing the entire hospital.

BROADENING COLLABORATION

3

Chapter 7

When to Break the Rules

The architects were surprised to see me, a physician, show up at that early planning meeting. I told them we'd been doing Lean process improvements here for 4 years, and we'd made a lot of progress, and I wanted the design of the new bed tower to help and not hinder the effort.

—James Nesbitt, MD (MMM)
Project Manager, Operational Excellence
Providence Alaska Medical Centers

Case study: Boulder Community Hospital, Boulder, Colorado

Introduction

To Boulder, Colorado, the community-owned hospital is more than a health-care facility. For nearly a century, the hospital has been an indelible part of the community's identity. As such, any change to its services or physical space must be approached with great care and attention to community values, especially patient safety, environmental sensitivity, and resource conservation.

Boulder Community Hospital

Founded in 1922 as a community-owned and -operated, not-for-profit hospital, Boulder Community Hospital encompasses the following major facilities (Architects: Boulder Associates):

- Boulder Community Hospital, a 159-bed acute care hospital with 24-hour emergency department.
- Boulder Community Foothills Hospital, a 60-bed acute care hospital with emergency department plus maternity and pediatric services.
- Community Medical Center, housing urgent care, physician offices, and special medical services.
- Mapleton Center, housing centers for sports medicine, rehabilitation, and behavioral health.

The decision was made to phase out the old, original hospital building downtown in favor of centralizing services at the newer Foothills campus. Doing so would require a major renovation and expansion to the campus, which had been awarded a silver LEED designation[1] when it opened in 2003. Site constraints limited the footprint of the new hospital, so space was one resource to conserve.

"Hats off to everyone on this project," said Lean practitioner Ronnie Daughtry. "The architect was willing to step out of the box, and the staff members, who started out as strangers, put their heads together to optimize the whole patient experience, not just pieces of it."

Boulder Community Hospital: Complex Project Yields to Simplicity

The Boulder project was complex. Not only were two campuses to merge into one, but also, during the project, a portion of the new hospital would have to remain available as the community's ED. Building codes tightened after the 2002 completion of the Foothills campus: New construction on that site now must withstand a 500-year flood, a requirement that circumscribes the horizontal spread of the building and reduces the utility of parts of the basement. The project time line is also ambitious, with opening scheduled for 2014.

"We can't afford to build one square foot of something that adds no value," said one hospital staff member. "Making people walk more because it's a bigger room doesn't add value."

Boulder Community Hospital's laboratory had been engaged in Lean process work for a few years before the kickoff of the new hospital project; however, the Lean journey for the hospital had just begun. Early in the project, while still in concept design, the hospital started using Lean-led design to help determine the best function and form for the new building.

"Like so many other hospitals, we did not want to inadvertently build in the same process problems," said Paul Lewis, MD, chief medical officer. "The 3P process brought out the best thinking of our staff and the architects. The solutions we designed together exceeded what we thought possible."

Getting Started

Ordinarily, the first order of business would be to create a master 3P, the grand Lean plan that identifies the seven service families, creates goals, clarifies the business case, and identifies teams to conduct a design 3P for each service family (as described in Chapter 3). But the Boulder team was already in concept design; architectural drawings had already begun in a core area of the hospital that housed Invasive Services. Because it was a critical area at a critical time, designing that area took precedence.

From the patient's point of view, Invasive Services comprises the journey through any intervention involving prep and recovery. Patients usually undergo three phases of pre- and postsurgical care. Immediately after surgery, patients go to the stage 1 or post anesthetic care unit (PACU). Once awake and stable, they are transferred to a step-down or stage 2 recovery unit. From there, ambulatory surgery patients are usually discharged, while inpatients return to their care units.

Just as in most American hospitals, Boulder Community had separate departments to handle the various types of invasive services such as surgery, cardiac catheterization, interventional radiology, endoscopy, transesophageal echocardiogram, and non- and minimally invasive cardiac procedures. With two hospital campuses came two of each department. Staff members from the various departments rarely mingled. Merging the departments into one hospital would be one kind of challenge; doing so with space constraints in the new building seemed daunting.

The architect and Lean practitioners saw a potential opportunity to restructure the way in which work was done, streamlining processes and reducing the square footage required. Launching a 3P that covered all invasive services would show these fragmented departments how they could benefit by sharing capacity rather than competing for space.

A Bold Idea

The idea of consolidating services from several departments, times two hospitals, was a bold one. It would require a significant cultural shift to bring people together across departmental lines to look at the potential for sharing prep and recovery space for all invasive services.

Ultimately, team members selected from each hospital and department sat down together to look at the issue from the point of view of the patient— the one value on which everyone could agree. True, working together under the umbrella of one "invasive services platform" could reduce the number of patient handoffs and increase safety while saving space and improving communication and workflow. But this sweeping level of consolidation would require an unprecedented level of collaboration and leadership. And on a practical level, it quickly created a question they could not yet answer: *How many stage 1 and stage 2 recovery beds will be needed at the new hospital?*

The older downtown campus has several discrete prep and recovery areas for surgery, cardiac catheterization, interventional radiology, endoscopy, and other non- and minimally invasive cardiac procedures. The newer Foothills campus had its own set of prep/recovery areas as well. Forecasting space for the new, merged unit would be tricky.

Before the 3P began to look earnestly at merging services, the architect had begun to stage the number of prep/recovery areas required. At that time, each department was asking for as many prep/recovery beds as possible.

"They were asking based on fear of not having enough space to go around," said Lean facilitator Teresa Carpenter:

> As the architect tried to accommodate their perceived need for more and more prep/recovery spaces, it was eating into storage and other spaces. We realized that we could never have "enough" to allay the worry about shortage. We knew we had to base the ultimate decision on data, which these scientists respect.

Said designer Carrie Stahl:

> When we mentioned that we would like to combine some ser-
> vices that had not been combined before, we didn't yet have all
> the information we needed, like how the hours of operation varied
> for the different service lines. Staff at both campuses were siloed,
> and rarely crossed paths. We needed data to figure out how many
> recovery beds we'd truly need. 3P turned out to be the best and
> fastest way to look at consolidation, build support among the staff,
> and find out, scientifically, just how many recovery beds we would
> really need.

Other questions arose. What would be the impact on those in the waiting
room or on patient flow? Could this consolidation be accomplished within
the limited footprint of the Foothills site? The team turned to 3P to inform
the design, experiment with it, and determine how to operationalize the best
design for the future.

Building Trust and Building a Business Case

Staff members were not all well acquainted. Now they would need to collaborate to come up with a groundbreaking design that would work well
into the future. The first exercise involved building trust in collaboration
itself, using simple wooden blocks. The object was to remove any block
that could be removed and place it on top, building the tallest tower.
Round 1 was done competitively; teammates admonished but did not
help. In round 2, teams were told to work collaboratively, helping each
other and considering each move. The block towers were at least 30%
taller at the end of round 2, showing that collaboration really does produce the best results (Figure 7.1).

To examine the different services under the umbrella of Invasive Services,
the 3P staff broke into three multidisciplinary design teams to examine each
part: prep and recovery, operating room (OR), and imaging. Already something audacious was happening: Each group, with representatives from both
hospitals, would consider the issues not from a departmental or campus perspective, but rather from the patient's perspective alone.

The teams quickly had to determine what key design factors already
existed (for example, staircases and elevators that could not be moved) and

Figure 7.1 **In the block exercise, cross-functional teams decide which block to remove without causing a collapse. The idea is to encourage team thinking as design progresses. Pictured are Gary Gibson, Julie Jenkins, Maria Melouk, Kris Mickens, and Jennifer Ludlam. (HPP photos, permission of BCH.)**

what data they would need to describe the current state and design the future state. To move from a high-level look at the service value stream to a fine-tuned process value stream, they would need to start with the business case. Table 7.1 gives examples of the types of factors that each team considered.

Learning from Current- and Future-State Data

With the business case in hand, each team proceeded to collect data on the current state for their areas at both Broadway and Foothills campuses. The first step was for all three teams to conduct a "waste walk" in all of the Invasive Services areas at both hospitals, noting which processes worked well, which could be improved, and how design of new space could support

Table 7.1 Example of Teams' Considerations for the Business Case

Each team comprised multidisciplinary staff, physicians, architect, equipment planner, and Lean facilitator

	Prep and recovery team	OR/endoscopy/core support team	Catheterization/interventional radiology/procedure rooms team
Process parameters	Start: MD office End: postprocedure recovery/ disposition	Start: procedure scheduled End: patient goes to recovery	Start: procedure scheduled End: patient goes to recovery
Scope/ purpose	Number of beds, equipment; function; hours of op/ scheduling assumptions; overflow protocol; waiting seats for all services	Primary/secondary room function for procedures; one-stop sources for all room support; define connections between prep/recovery, cath/IR, SPD; equipment locations and work flow across all Invasive Services	Core supports all room needs; primary/secondary room function; define connections to/ from prep/recovery; equipment/ supply locations and flow; work flow for cath/IR; room utilization protocols
Key metrics	Room utilization; available beds (active prep or waiting time in room); turnover time; wait time; case start	Turnaround time; on-time starts; scheduling accuracy; number of times RN leaves the OR during case	Turnover time; on-time procedure start
Deliverables	Floor plan model (equipment location and pathways); big idea/concept and key assumptions; standard work instructions; number, spaces, location of wait chairs; number and allocation/types of beds; protocols for 24-hour use of prep/recovery; overflow protocols	Floor plan model (equipment location and pathways); big idea/concept and key assumptions; standard work instructions; staffing with special considerations/skill requirements; hours of operation and key assumptions; room designation	Floor plan model (equipment location and pathways); big idea/ concept and key assumptions; standard work instructions; staffing with special considerations/skill requirements; hours of operation and key assumptions; number of procedure rooms/utilization assumptions, secondary uses

best practices. They considered the "voice of the customer," looking at which activities add value for the patient. Said Stahl:

> Probably one of the best things to come out of the first part of the 3P was walking through each other's spaces. Each team had people from each department, so they could see their counterparts' processes. Before 3P, we would convene with individual departments, which never allowed user groups to see how other departments functioned. It allowed for some unintended insensitivity to the other departments' needs. Doing that walk with a cross-functional group really built mutual respect within and among the teams, which was great preparation for the hard work and big decisions ahead.

With this information, the teams created future-state visions, experimenting with possible changes.

"We use the current-state data to say, 'Now I see why this doesn't work well. If we changed this, this or this, would it be an improvement? Would it still work if we added a different patient type, on a different day, with a different shift?'" asked Daughtry. "The future-state map helps you visualize information flow and process flow. At that point in the 3P, we can start experimenting with options."

Key Assumptions Kick Off Seven Ways

At this stage of concept design, aligning with the "product" part of 3P, certain features of the new building, called "key assumptions," were already immutable. These are the things about the project that cannot be changed. It is important for the group to understand the key assumptions so that the seven ways exercises, simulations, and experiments will remain within the realm of the possible. The key assumptions were:

1. Quantity and size of procedure rooms are fixed.
2. Shafts, columns, stairs, and elevators are fixed.
3. Exterior walls cannot move. Square footage is fixed.
4. Locations of departments are fixed.
5. Three of eight ORs are dedicated: heart, DaVinci robot, and hybrid.

The three teams began the seven ways exercise, coming up with seven different ways to streamline the processes and design within the constraints of the key assumptions. As described in Chapter 3, this exercise encourages participants to look beyond the obvious or comfortable solutions to achieve breakthrough thinking.

Can We Break the Rule?

It was during the seven ways that the prep/recovery team came face to face with what seemed like an unrealistic and especially frustrating constraint—key assumption 4, which fixed the locations of departments.

"The assumption did not allow us to move surgery, IR, or the cath area," said Lean practitioner Maureen Sullivan, RN. "Some physicians had required that their areas be at a certain location, believing that it would shorten travel times for patients coming from ICU. But once we'd gathered the data and began experimenting, we found their good intentions created longer travel times for most staff members."

The existing layout called for locations of the cath labs, ICU, and ORs that increased the distance to Central Sterile (Figure 7.2). With the best intentions, early participants had enforced the opinion that moving patients should trump moving instruments—on its face, a perfectly laudable goal.

However, during the seven ways experiment, the prep/recovery team realized that the endovascular nurses and cardiologists would be walking great distances from the cath labs to the prep/recovery area, decreasing efficiency and wasting motion. If the layout were to break one key assumption—moving departments—other benefits would accrue. For example, moving Sterile Processing closer to the ORs would remove a significant amount of traffic from one corridor. The teams asked a bold question: *Can we break the 3P rule?*

The answer to that question for the prep/recovery team would affect the work of the OR and endovascular teams as well. The 3P stopped while everyone considered the option now nicknamed the "rule breaker."

With the full backing of hospital leadership, the 3P team recruited physicians from the affected areas to come and see the exercise under way, listen to the data on the number of steps, and decide whether to release the 3P team from the key assumption that troubled them.

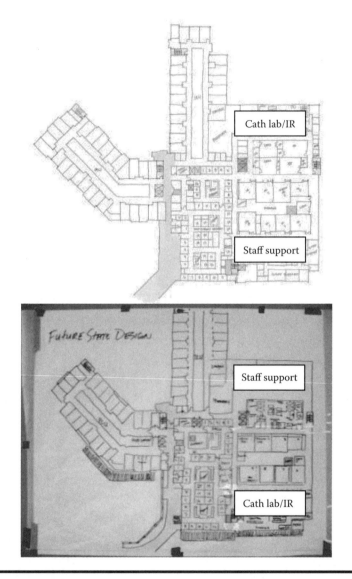

Figure 7.2 Before and after the "rule breaker." Top sketch shows original positions of staff support (bottom) and cath/IR areas (top), which had been considered sacrosanct. During 3P, one team showed a way to reduce staff travel while maintaining patient safety by flipping those locations (lower sketch). Once clinicians saw the data on staff travel, they agreed that this was one rule that could be broken. (Illustrations courtesy Boulder Associates.)

Having the architect on board as a team member at this time was crucial. The design was far enough along that changes this sweeping could wreak havoc with the structural grid. Certain structures, for example, made moving the ORs out of the question. On the other hand, the staff support area and the cath lab/IR cluster were not yet set in stone. Those areas could be interchanged or flipped without major structural consequences.

"Without the architect's in-depth knowledge to guide the team, it would have been impossible not to create more problems than we fixed," said Daughtry.

Even so, the changes created discomfort within the architectural team; after all, the physicians had signed off on the plan as it was. Changes at this stage risked upsetting physicians or being seen as failing to deliver on a promise. But the architects were bolstered by hospital leaders who gave the green light to further exploration of the question. If there was a better option that would make a better building, everyone would get behind it.

In preparation for the presentation to the physicians, Stahl drew up some examples, moving the cath lab 150 feet to the south (Figure 7.2), closer to prep/recovery, and then using AutoCad to examine travel paths and distances of patients, physicians, and cardiovascular nurses. Nurses simulated the walk, timing how long it took the patient to arrive from the ED. While the travel distance from the ED to the cath lab was a bit longer, a hairpin turn was eliminated and travel time was reduced. Their analysis showed that there was no decrease in quality or safety for patients by flipping the departments; in fact, it could decrease travel time.

Table 7.2 Number of Footsteps, Current versus Future State (If the Rule Is Broken)

Area or discipline	Current state	"Rule-breaker" future state	Notes
Patient	1110	1066	Steps reduced if rule broken
Visitor	608	608	Steps unchanged if rule broken
RN	2212	2055	Steps reduced if rule broken
MD	1876	1938	Steps increased slightly, but hairpin turn eliminated, transit time reduced. Physicians enter the building close to staff support area, which they appreciate.
From OR to sterile processing	481	360	Steps reduced about 25% if rule broken. This is a frequent route used by everyone.

Note: Physicians respond to data, so the team performed a simulation to gather it.

"This would have been the perfect moment for a formal failure mode effects analysis, or FMEA," said Carpenter:

> We didn't have time for a quantitative FMEA,[2] so we had a qualitative discussion to determine the frequency of occurrence, severity of a failure, and so on. Would moving the departments in any way degrade patient safety? We kept finding that it actually improved patient safety, and, on the whole, the facility would operate infinitely better, now and in the future.

One unanticipated benefit of breaking the rule was that IR and cath had much closer proximity to prep and recovery beds, which improved utilization of cardiologists' time. Cardiologists often do special, short procedures, such as transesophageal echocardiograms or elective cardioversions, between longer catheterization cases. The immediate proximity of prep/recovery beds makes it easier to serve patients requiring short procedures between those requiring longer ones, helping the physicians improve their productivity and getting patients out sooner.

"Architects don't like to break rules any more than clinicians do," said Sullivan. "Everyone had to step outside the box to come to the best solution here. It was an amazing bit of teamwork when you consider that, on Monday, these people had never met. By midweek, they were looking at each other, asking, 'How can we do great things together?'"

When the physicians, including CMO Lewis, and staff members, saw the data showing less motion, reduced turnaround time for patients, and potential productivity benefits, they agreed that it was time to break the rule (Figure 7.2).

Takt Time Reveals Savings

Core questions still remained as the team entered the "process" part of the 3P. As they combined several functions from two hospitals into an Invasive Services platform, how many PACU and prep/recovery areas would the new hospital need?

The architect's preliminary drawings reflected the staff's anxiety that there were not enough prep and recovery rooms. As the Invasive Services 3P began, prep/recovery consumed most of the available Invasive Services space and included 32 recovery spaces. Storage space had been cut nearly to zero. Still, staff and physicians worried that 32 recovery rooms would not be enough.

Based on the initial business plan, teams had already collected the data on patient volumes predicted beyond the 2014 opening date. To help predict room capacity, the teams measured takt time—that is, the time available (for example, a 12-hour shift) divided by the number of people going through the process. They knew patient volume around the clock and patterns of use by hour, department (cardiovascular, interventional radiology, and surgery) and patient type. They knew the maximum and minimum needs and the times when they occurred.

Based on 24-hour observations, the teams synthesized their data into a master histogram, showing how many PACU, pre-op, and recovery beds were actually in use at any hour. They were surprised to see that bed demand peaked at noon, with a 20-bed maximum. Said Stahl:

> If they improve a couple of processes, like throughput and scheduling, just a little bit, the work load could be leveled and that peak of 20 rooms could be even lower. Nevertheless, to accommodate future growth for prep and recovery bays, we designed for 24. Proposing that few would have strained credulity without the histograms, but the data showed conclusively that we did not need 32 bays. That freed up a lot of space for other support purposes—including consult rooms and storage.

When it comes specifically to PACU beds, Stahl noted that some states, like California, mandate a minimum number of 1.5 beds per OR. If such a formula had been imposed on this project, then eight ORs would have created the need for 12 to 14 PACU bays. However, since Colorado does not mandate minimums, the architects were allowed to base their decisions on the data. The new hospital will need nine PACU bays, plus a band of prep/recovery areas that can "flex" into PACU beds during times of high census.

"We figured out how to get three or four flex spaces situated between PACU and prep/recovery," said Stahl. "Those spaces can be used for either purpose without moving the patient from one place to another."

One unit may have a higher census in the morning, another in the afternoon. Cross utilizing beds during alternating slack times increases virtual capacity and creates what Lean calls "level loading." In other words, flexibility in a floor plan often has more to do with process than walls and floors. When it makes clinical sense, cross utilization can increase the number of patients served, reduce travel, and improve productivity.

The net result of the 3P reduced the prep/recovery area from 32 bays to 20. Sterile Processing was now closer to its major user, the ORs. And the teams validated that each area had enough support space to function properly.

"We found we only needed half the number of rooms than the 'fear factor' told us," said Carpenter. "This plan provides enough, and will provide enough for future growth. And we regained plenty of room for storage as well."

When space floods back into the floor plan—10% to 15% overall, according to Stahl—the tendency is for teams to stake claim to as much of it as possible for storage. It is a phenomenon that Carpenter ironically calls "post-traumatic space disorder."[3] But rather than grab all the storage possible, she challenged the teams to look thoughtfully at what type of space works best. What is needed, where? What is stored, why? Could a more reliable supply chain reduce the need for inventory? These questions will be part of the "preparation" or third P, and will continue to be worked on until staff is ready for move-in.

In the end, the teams at Boulder Community began to view and design storage areas differently. In Lean-led design, big, deep equipment rooms are not done, because they cause people to have to move things around inside and permit things to get lost or accumulate in back. Instead, the storage areas are shallow for easy access, and items have parking spots or alcoves. The essential layout of the OR was unchanged, but now the items will be easy to find every time.

The 3P provided a way to defragment several departments, leverage collaboration and standardization among them, and design according to the patient journey, not the silo. The result was more utility within the space, more collegiality among staff, and the potential for more and better service to patients.

The culture shift apparent with this 3P was sweeping, and yet more will be demanded. Optimal use of the flex space will challenge leaders to collaborate in new ways and staff members potentially to broaden skills to serve a wider patient mix. The standardization of the rooms and areas will ease any of these transitions and can make every area a learning lab. The staff at Boulder Community has already demonstrated its open-mindedness in collaboration and in its willingness always to be guided by the best interest of patients. The community's well known dedication to conservation and stewardship of resources seems to aid in the acceptance of Lean thinking.

Regarding the 3P process, Stahl says, "Everybody should be doing this, starting as early as possible—certainly before we put pen to paper."

Said CMO Lewis, "I fully support this process and believe it has affected much more than the floor plan. The use of data to drive decisions is what makes us a community of scientists."

Summary

Boulder Community Hospital, a proud, community-owned and -operated hospital, is undergoing a complex building project. The old downtown campus will be repurposed, and the newer Foothills campus will be enlarged to become the main hospital. Both hospitals have separate departments for the various invasive services—from cath lab to interventional cardiology to minor procedures. Space and sense determined that all departments falling under the Invasive Services umbrella, from both campuses, should merge into one department and design their space according to the patient journey, rather than departmental silos.

Discussion

- Why was this such a complex building project? Why was it complex from a staff point of view?
- Why did they start with Invasive Services?
- Why would it be important to start by gathering data for what they called the business case?
- Why did they have to break a rule of 3P? What did that involve? Why was it such a big deal?
- In the beginning, different departments feared that they would never have enough prep/recovery beds. In the end, they were satisfied with nearly 50% fewer. What happened?
- How does this work relate to the Rules in Use (activities, connections, pathways, improvements)?
- What management challenges are created by designing this way?

Suggested Reading

Cohn, K. H. 2006. *Collaborate for success! Breakthrough strategies for engaging physicians, nurses, and hospital executives.* Chicago: Health Administration Press.

Notes

1. The U.S. Green Building Council awards LEED (leadership in energy and environmental design) certifications as a way to promote sustainable building practices, based on measurable criteria. A silver award is the second highest. See http://www.usgbc.org for more information.
2. FMEA is discussed in Chapters 3 and 6.
3. See Carpenter's essay on this topic in Appendix D.

Chapter 8

At the Tipping Point

No wonder hospitals operate in silos. We build them that way!

**—Hospital architect, upon completion of
introductory Lean healthcare course**

*Case studies: Seattle Children's Hospital, Seattle, Washington; ThedaCare™,
Appleton, Wisconsin; Sutter Health, California*

Introduction

This chapter profiles three hospitals that have long experience with Lean
process improvements and the culture change it engenders within hospital
walls. They also have more than one successful, major Lean building project
under their belts.

Lean design means getting a broad, multidisciplinary group of frontline
staff and leaders together from the first day to figure out the best way to
work. It means including the architect in the process and, with an integrated facility design (IFD), it means also having the construction team in
the loop. IPD (integrated process delivery), as we learned in Chapter 2,
is a single construction contract that covers the construction trades and
architect, giving everyone a common goal and a stake in the outcome.
IFD holds a slight distinction, in that it refers to the entire process—from
value stream mapping through 5S on move-in—as one integrated continuum of work.

Both Seattle Children's Hospital and ThedaCare participants stressed the necessity of investing in a full-sized mock-up, which allows staff and family members, physicians and leaders, board members and others to walk through and "feel" how the space will work. Many, many glitches were caught at this stage, and unimagined improvements were made before the building began. In the case of ThedaCare, the mock-up stage was done as a way to test a care model, and it lasted 2 years.

Perhaps most significantly, these hospitals are beyond the "tipping point" with Lean. This is the way they run their hospitals. This is the way they build. Lean is their operating system.

Seattle Children's Hospital: Process Improvement Improves Building Design

The July 2010 opening of the new Bellevue Clinic and Surgery Center represented an important waypoint on the learning curve for Seattle Children's Hospital (SCH).[1] The Bellevue Center would increase access on Seattle's east side to pediatric subspecialties and outpatient care for otherwise healthy children. Plans called for the existing facility to grow from 12 exam rooms to 32. As noted in Chapter 1, the facility came in 25,000 square feet smaller than the estimated 110,000 square feet and $40 million below the original $100 million budget.

When first envisioned in 2007, SCH started to approach the building of the Bellevue Center in the traditional way—that is, to ask the architect to design the building. The economic downturn of 2008 forced leaders to look at design and construction in a new way, to maximize every resource. For years, the staff at SCH had infused Lean successfully into their organization, streamlining processes across the hospital; now, they would extend the philosophy and techniques to its building program.

"One thing we learned about continuous performance improvement, or CPI," said COO Pat Hagan, "is that everyone has to start out by shedding the way they thought about things in the first place. We tell people to check their opinions, assertions, and titles at the door. We are going to think together."

Founded in 1907, Seattle Children's is a 250-bed regional pediatric academic healthcare center serving Washington, Alaska, Montana, and Idaho—the largest service area of any children's hospital in the country. The hospital's physicians practice in nearly 60 pediatric subspecialties and the hospital handles over 14,000 admissions per year.

In addition to the hospital, Seattle Children's also comprises a research institute and hospital foundation, as well as several outlying clinics.

SCH has 4,492 employees and 1,118 medical staff members. Its guild association is the largest all-volunteer fundraising network of any hospital in the nation, with 7,000 members. In FY 2009, SCH provided more than $100,000 in under- and uncompensated medical care.

SCH uses continuous performance improvement (CPI) to evaluate healthcare from the patient and family point of view and to improve:

- Quality of care and service
- Cost effectiveness and financial strength
- Access to specialists
- Environmental safety
- Staff engagement

Integrated Facility Design

When it comes to designing a new facility, Hagan says, it cannot be a one-way street, with the architect presenting a design. It cannot even be a two-way street between the architect and hospital staff. It must be a multidisciplinary highway, giving voice to everyone involved in the continuum of design and construction—from CEO to construction manager, housekeeper to electrician.

Although their design process is infused with Toyota-based Lean philosophy, Hagan shies away from using Japanese and manufacturing terms like 3P.

"It's not what Toyota does, but how they do it," says Hagan. "When they talk about 3P—their 'production, preparation, and process'—what they really mean is that they're integrating manufacturing, engineering, and design with the builders of factories and the builders of assembly lines. That's the integrated, multidisciplinary approach we are after—from design through occupancy."

In the case of the Bellevue Center, SCH implemented an IFD, where a single contract covered the services of architect, builder, and construction subcontractors.[2] Sharing the contract meant sharing the risk and sharing the mental model that this would be the finest facility imaginable. This single contract encourages the entire team to operate according to Lean principles, saving time and money and building efficiency into their own processes.

It was a tall order.

As with hospitals, architectural and building firms are typically organized in a "siloed" fashion, with departmental barriers that can inhibit the flow of information and ideas. Also, as with hospitals, breaking down those silos and giving Lean systems thinking an environment in which to take hold across the continuum of work requires a shift in thinking and a great deal of leadership. And as with hospitals, different firms are at various points of maturity on their Lean journey, with some just starting to understand the concepts and others applying them in everyday work.

In *Leading the Lean Healthcare Journey,*[1] Wellman, Jeffries, and Hagan state:

> Selecting a core team with Lean experience was not enough. Process experience with the Lean concepts was an insufficient replacement for specific Lean design and concurrent engineering knowledge. Also, there was the belief that the non-SCH team members could learn as the project progressed, but the mismatch in levels of Lean understanding caused friction and delay. The architects and contractors were selected because of their Lean experience, but as the project unfolded, more education was needed than initially imagined.

Everyone had to shift and change, including SCH, which had about a decade of experience with Lean. Hagan notes that administrative leaders, in addition to their role as "owner," also had to collaborate with the architect and builder in a whole new way. Learning to collaborate genuinely was hard work, but rewarding.

"The risk melts away when everyone is at the table together from the start," said Hagan. "As it turned out, the Bellevue project was so successful that there were no big problems for me, as COO, to adjudicate."

Hagan notes that a project the size of the Bellevue Center would be expected to generate about 600 requests for information, or RFIs, which usually lead to expensive and sometimes contentious change orders. Instead, this project generated just 30 RFIs and no significant change orders. Due to this and other factors, the project was completed well below budget.

Designing for Communication

The facility is designed for collaboration, communication, and less complex handoffs. Separating the flow of patients ("onstage") from the flow of staff members ("offstage") reduces confusion and congestion (Figure 8.1). The traditional racetrack design (Appendix A) morphed into a very large team room surrounded by exam rooms. Different teams take care of different sets of patients, but all use the same team room. Rather than calling or texting a person across campus, clinicians and staff can usually confer face to face.

"We believe we have increased team communication by the way in which we designed the facility," said Hagan. "Reducing the footprint also reduced chances of miscommunication between one professional group and another."

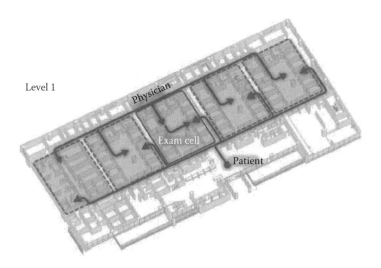

Figure 8.1   Cells of exam rooms feature collaborative areas. The design separates patient from staff travel areas in an "offstage–onstage" design. (Courtesy SCH.)

Bellevue Mock-ups

Even with everyone at the table sharing the enthusiasm, the learning, and the risk, the team for Bellevue Center quickly realized that the usual, months-long cycle of reviewing paper drawings from the architect would not work. It just took too long. Instead, the architects and contractors mocked up full-sized individual rooms, then entire floors, and then whole sequences of physical space at the hospital parking garage (Figure 8.2).

Staff members, administrators, and family members conducted walk-throughs and simulations. They mapped and remapped the flow of patients, staff members, and supplies. Engaging people in this way gave them a real investment in the outcome.

"We invited families in. We counted how many steps it took to complete a process. We ran codes. Until everyone sees the space mocked up, they cannot fully understand how it will be used, what sight lines will exist or how far the supply closet is," said Hagan (Figure 8.3).

This investment of time and space paid off, as dozens of glitches and potential design improvements were spotted within days and weeks, not months. Changes were made on the fly, immediately, and tested over and over. Finding inefficiencies and opportunities in the mock-ups saved time and money by preventing change orders later.

Figure 8.2   The mock-up gave team members a chance to see and amend the actual space before construction made it permanent. (Photo courtesy SCH.)

Figure 8.3   Code simulations in the mock-up helped staff see whether the design would work best for patients. (Photo courtesy SCH.)

Bellevue Results

At this writing, the Bellevue Center has been operating for 1 year. Is there evidence of success? Was it worth it? Hagan thinks so: "If we go by the quality, cost, delivery and safety that we are delivering, we are succeeding." Among other things:

- Access is improved and wait times are negligible.
- Staff engagement and client satisfaction, as measured on surveys, are way up.
- Safety metrics are not yet available for comparison, but Hagan says that with the visible lines of sight, reduced handoff complexity, and more staff communication, the indicators are lining up to the positive.

"You have to keep reminding yourself that this is a children's hospital," said Richard Shannon, MD. "It is unbelievably quiet and calm, and nobody is waiting around."

Hagan believes that time will show the new operation to be very cost effective. Meanwhile, on the capital side, saving $40 million on an 85,000-square-foot building has been an enormous success that sets the stage for future building projects.

Figure 8.4 Mock-ups are also used for team training. Here the space is put to the test in a disagreement and crisis management simulation. (Photo courtesy SCH.)

Lean Experiences Guide the New "Building Hope"

Several important lessons that emerged during the construction of the Bellevue Center are guiding the construction of the new 330,000 square foot, $176.5 million critical care/cancer care, Building Hope, at the main campus east of the University of Washington. The new eight-floor structure will house a 48-bed cancer wing on the top two floors. The sixth floor, housing 32 critical care beds, will connect to the main hospital by a sky bridge. The ED will move to its ground floor. The other floors will be shelled for future use, in keeping with SCH's plan to grow from 254 to 600 beds by 2030 in response to the rapid growth in its large service area.

Informing this construction program will be the lessons learned at Bellevue, including:

- Understanding the importance of running simulations in actual-size mock-ups, using a cycle of observation, value stream mapping, and on-the-spot problem solving (Figure 8.4).
- Bringing in ongoing process improvement work from the main campus, such as their superior demand-flow supply chain, to improve design and save space.

The Importance of the Mock-up

The lessons of the Bellevue Center mock-up were so compelling that when it came time for Building Hope, Seattle Children's rented 60,000 square feet of warehouse space to mock it up. They mocked up entire patient floors and invested the time of staff members, families, and others to run simulations for weeks at a time, in the presence of architects and construction managers.

"The idea is to test, test, test," said Hagan. "What will it be like to make rounds in this space? How will we function as a team?"

Already the investment in the mock-up has paid off. Building Hope was originally sited far from the main hospital, near the street, where it would be most visible. But when the mock-up revealed just how very long the travel distance from the new building to the existing one would have to be, the architects moved the building site much closer to the main hospital. Doing so allowed them to optimize the use of resources in the existing facility and ultimately shrink the new building to 50% of its originally intended size.

"We already saved a lot of staff time, inconvenience, and money in this building by doing one simple thing: siting it correctly," said Hagan. "When you mock it up, you can't miss that kind of thing. The closer site will save countless linear feet and steps far into the future."

Demand-Flow System: Design Benefits from Continuous Process Improvement

One example from SCH illustrates just how important ongoing process improvement work can be in the design of a new building. The continuous process improvement (CPI) staff at the hospital had long experience with the organizing principles of 5S and had gone through many supply areas reducing inventory. As a result of their work in the main hospital, the Bellevue facility was built with much less storage than originally envisioned.

But these supply chain experts knew there was room for more improvement when they discovered that a full-time registered nurse was spending 100% of her time ordering supplies. Could it really be that complicated?

As they drilled down into the process of ordering and receiving supplies, the CPI staff discovered that it took 57,000 labor hours a year. On average, it took 3.5 days to fill an order, which went through a "node" to central purchasing to the manufacturer and then back again.

Often, staff picked supplies only once a week, and often took extra to sustain them the entire time. Still, stock outs were as regular as they were distressing. In a valiant attempt to do their jobs, staff members would hoard supplies, exacerbating the shortages and sometimes causing

 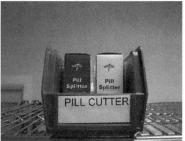

Figure 8.5   Blue plastic bins are low-tech, but the system behind their use is high-tech. (Photos courtesy SCH.)

over-ordering in response. Inventory doubled or tripled, in an attempt to keep up.

"We created standards for when to pick supplies," said Supply Chain Director, Greg Beach. "If you only pick them every seven days, you drain supplies and create stock outs. It's better to pull a few every day."

Thus began a facility-wide demand-flow system. Blue bins of predetermined sizes hold supplies and, when they are empty, act as visual cues to be refilled. Supply staff collect the bins at frequent, predetermined times. The bins are low-tech indeed, but the system behind them is very sophisticated (Figure 8.5).

Central Supply staff fan out to collect bins three times a day at specified intervals, 7 days a week. Even their routes through the hospital are analyzed so that they make more deliveries with fewer trips. They collect and scan the yellow, bar-coded inventory (kanban) tags on empty bins by 8 a.m. and receive the order by 8 p.m. the same day. Daily restocking takes place on the night shift, when the facility is less crowded and the elevators work faster. No more than 3 days' supply is kept on hand in the nursing units. Central Supply warehouse keeps a store for disaster preparedness and for replenishment of critical items.

The system is supported by a software dashboard developed by SCH staff (Figure 8.6). SCH negotiated with its supplier to deliver in frequent, smaller quantities exactly as needed, and to charge for the supplies only as they are used, at no increase in the price. In this way, the supplier is drawn in and becomes part of the Lean process continuum.

A value analysis group looks at each supply for value, function, and preference, and as a way to standardize materials.

"If you don't have a group analyzing what to order, you may end up with five different brands of the same item, and that is waste," said Beach.

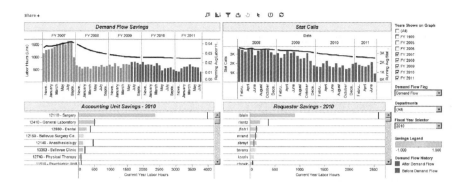

Figure 8.6 Demand-flow savings dashboard. The charts indicate requestor savings and "stat" calls to Central Service. Monitoring this information indicates where adjustments in supplies need to be made. (Courtesy SCH.)

Improvements from the demand-flow system include:

■ 48,000 fewer hours across the system in ordering and restocking per year. It takes 0.8 days to fill an order, down from 3.5 days.
■ Inventory was halved, from $1.1 million to $525,000.
■ No clinical staff order or stock. Their time is returned to patient care.
■ Central Supply staff no longer count out supplies, because the supplier provides them ready to use. The staff maintain and monitor the system, continuously improving it.
■ Excess and obsolete items are no longer a problem. If such an item should crop up, the team troubleshoots it to root cause immediately.

Beach emphasizes that, without senior leadership front and center at every turn, the CPI staff could never have made these sweeping improvements:

> You can put blue bins around, and you will see some improvement. But it takes capital and determination to create the monitoring and auditing system, to buy the racks and software, do the facility improvements, negotiate the contracts, and stand behind an aggressive rollout. When you're thinking this big, you must have senior leadership right beside you.

In addition to improving performance, the demand-flow system has freed up 70% of the space in the main hospital that was formerly used to store inventory. It has altered what everyone believed about how much storage space is really needed. And that has enormous design implications for the new Building Hope.

"By saving space in facilities here in the main building, we can see how to save a lot of space and money in the new cancer center," said Beach. "It's a perfect example of how improving processes can help improve design."

ThedaCare: Creativity before Capital

In 2007, ThedaCare's Appleton Medical Center was one of 12 hospitals selected to participate in a national initiative, called "Transforming Care at the Bedside," sponsored by the Institute for Healthcare Improvement. By the time of its selection, ThedaCare, a major employer and healthcare provider in Wisconsin, had already begun adopting Lean concepts with its ThedaCare improvement system (TIS), and it now sought, through this pilot program, to create an ideal patient care model and an ideal hospital room. The result was the collaborative care model, a creative, multidisciplinary way to meet patients' needs.

Concurrent with early development of the collaborative care model, leaders also realized that their buildings needed to be refreshed. They began to work on a master plan to phase in improvements over time.

With more than 5,400 employees at 43 sites, ThedaCare is the largest healthcare provider and employer in northeast Wisconsin and serves more than 250,000 patients in a 14-county area. The system has five hospitals: Appleton Medical Center (150 beds), Theda Clark Medical Center in Neenah, Wisconsin (173 beds), and New London Family Medical Center, Riverside Medical Center, and Shawano Medical Center (25 beds each).

In 2003, ThedaCare began to apply the principles and tools of Lean manufacturing and the Toyota Production System (TPS) to healthcare. The result was the ThedaCare improvement system (TIS)—an organization-wide quality improvement initiative.

ThedaCare gained firsthand experience through engagement with like-minded industries, including healthcare organizations that had already successfully applied Lean concepts.

Through TIS, ThedaCare improved processes and patient outcomes, eliminated waste, and developed revolutionary new models of clinical care based on these principles.

ThedaCare removed more than $23 million in costs without layoffs by continuously focusing on the value provided to customers (better outcomes with rational costs) (adapted from text at www.createhealthvalue.com/about/thedacare).

"We'd started work on our collaborative care model, and realized that if we just spent money on a new building, that would be okay, but it wouldn't necessarily support the model," said Kathryn Correia, who then served as president of the Appleton Medical Center and Theda Clark Medical Center, and senior vice president of ThedaCare. "We decided to find a way to create a building that could accelerate progress on our care model."

The Collaborative Care Model and the "Ultimate Mock-up"

In the collaborative care model, a nurse, physician, and pharmacist meet each new patient and his or her caregivers within the first 90 minutes of arrival in the unit and they develop a single, unambiguous care plan. From that point on, everything about collaborative care is interwoven with the design of the space.

In a bold move, leadership agreed to build the "ultimate mock-up," according to architect Albert Park, ThedaCare's director of facilities planning. They gutted an existing unit and created a 14-bed unit in the Appleton Medical Center to test and verify the impact of the collaborative care model.

"Before we committed to building a whole new replacement bed tower in Appleton, we built a completely functional trial unit just to test and perfect the collaborative care model, and we ran it for 2 years," Park explained.

As always, input from frontline workers was the key to developing the most useful design. A core cadre of healthcare staff, physicians, patients, and designers came together in a series of 2Ps (preparation and process—with the assumption of "patient" as the first P) that were focused on various aspects of the new facility. The team first created the design that they found most essential.

"The seven ways exercise[3] was especially helpful in getting us away from old ideas," said Park (Figure 8.7). "By the end of the fourth day of each 2P event, we had a conceptual plan laid out from the hands of everyone. The architect then used this as the basis for all subsequent design work in detail design meetings with project teams."

As a result, the traditional large, central nursing station was replaced with smaller work stations near the patient rooms. The team established a new standard: the private room with enough space for the care team and patient family.

Figure 8.7 ThedaCare employees abandon preconceived notions during their 2P and seven ways exercises. The result is an environment that best fits patient needs and thus makes work easier for staff. (Photo courtesy ThedaCare.)

The two design considerations that increased nursing "touch time"[4] (time with the patient) by 50% were:

- A patient server in each patient room ensures that individualized medications and supplies are always stored at the bedside. Because nurses have what they need every time, nurse travel has plummeted.
- A thoughtfully designed, easy-to-use electronic recordkeeping system gives nurses instant access to medication records, which makes it easier to achieve 100% medication reconciliation. The rational use of IT at the bedside has cut documentation time in half.

At the end of the 2-year trial, the metrics were undeniable. The collaborative care pilot unit achieved zero medication reconciliation errors for over 18 months. Costs declined by 25%, length of stay and readmissions declined, and patient satisfaction soared to 100% and stayed there. Staff satisfaction rose as well.[5] Said Correia:

In the beginning, we didn't know what we didn't know. By developing this pilot unit, we were able to design constantly as we went forward. Doing it this way engaged everybody, used everyone's minds and talents, and generated a lot of enthusiasm. And it was much cheaper than building all at once and finding the flaws later.

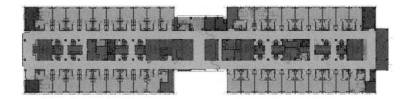

Figure 8.8 **The design features a collaboration area in the center rather than a traditional "racetrack." This is a typical floor from the Theda Clark Medical Center renovation project. (Courtesy ThedaCare.)**

Aligning the Space with the Model

According to Correia, once they discovered the power of the collaborative care model, they realized that the physical space inside the hospitals would have to change. The new standard would include larger, private rooms to promote the vigorous collaboration among care team and family that the model requires. Each room must have its own nurse server and computer interface and be large enough to accommodate diagnostic equipment as needed. (The idea is to bring the equipment to the patient as much as possible, rather than moving the patient from place to place.) The size and location of nursing stations would also need to change.

At Theda Clark in Neenah, the hospital was gutted and remodeled. Park noted that the hospital was originally sized for more patients, but whole units were being used for office space, rehabilitation, and other purposes. Two-patient rooms predominated. By vacating the spaces not used for patients and creating all standardized, private rooms, they achieved the environment that promoted the collaborative care model within the existing walls. (See Figure 8.8.)

At the Appleton facility, a new eight-story bed tower accommodates the collaborative care model. ThedaCare is offering it up as a design for the future. Salient features include:

- Admission trio (a system where three people work to reduce admission times).
- Daily bedside care conferences by team.
- Electronic medical record (EMR) supporting one plan of care and links to the evidence-based Milliman guidelines.[6]
- Visual production control management for care progression.

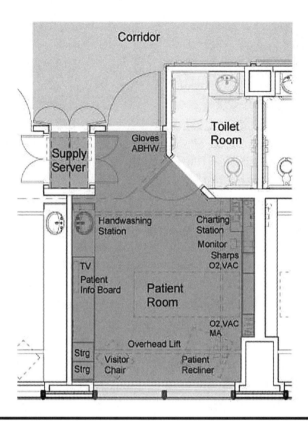

Figure 8.9 **A typical patient room is 13 feet, 10 inches by 18 feet, 7 inches (218 square feet). Toilet room is 8 feet, 8 inches by 6 feet, 6 inches (50 square feet). Note the pass-through for the supply server. (Courtesy ThedaCare.)**

- Clarification of all roles so that staff members can function at their highest scope of practice.
- A physical environment that promotes safety for patient and staff, and key processes that increase care team effectiveness and increase the quality of bedside care.

"There's nothing proprietary about our design," says Correia. "We feel we have been successful, and that creates the obligation for us to share with others." (Figures 8.8 through 8.11 show the design.) Note that the supply closet can be resupplied from the hallway in a "pass-through" arrangement, which reduces restocking time and may also address some infection-control concerns.

Lean Construction and IPD

Building a test unit, remodeling one hospital, and building a new bed tower at another tested the Lean thinking of construction personnel. In vetting

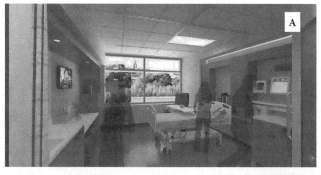

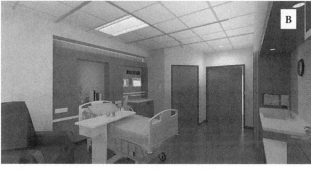

Figure 8.10 Interior of typical patient room at ThedaCare: (a) room interior with zones for bedside care, hand hygiene, and documentation; (b) interior of the room looking toward hallway and bathroom. (Photos courtesy of ThedaCare.)

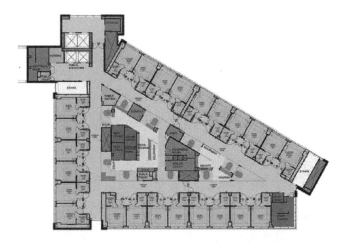

Figure 8.11 Typical unit floor plan in Appleton Medical Center new inpatient facility. This illustration shows 24 patient rooms and 19,750 square feet. (Courtesy ThedaCare.)

construction firms, Park and others decided to work with a firm that had been involved in Lean for many years and had built hospitals using the concepts.

ThedaCare also noted the advantages cited by SCH—namely, that the shared vision and shared risk created by a single, comprehensive IPD contract puts everyone on the same page. The advantages of Lean construction and an IPD included a faster time line, with less time at each stage and less lag time between steps (see Figure 2.1). All involved were joined in the determination to build a unit that simply worked better.

"Simple questions like 'How can we fabricate and install the headwalls in patient rooms more efficiently?' are ripe for Lean concepts, and the construction manager was experienced at dealing with them," said Park.

Several components were created quickly and efficiently off-site, inside climate-controlled buildings, and then brought to the site for installation (Figure 8.12). This way, work sequences could be scheduled closely, saving time, and weather was removed as a factor.

"The old way would have been to call the plumber to the site with numerous individual pieces. The new way is having a whole wall of plumbing preassembled and brought in, or having whole walls built off-site with plumbing already assembled, tested, and installed," said Park.

Both projects were completed ahead of schedule and under budget.

Process and Design: Chicken and Egg

Each room is equipped with a ceiling-mounted patient lift. Literature on evidence-based design[7] holds that installing ceiling lifts in patient rooms reduces worker handling injuries by 50% and patient falls by one-third.[8] Lost in that statistic is what it takes to ensure that nurses use patient lifts properly, every time.

"Lifts are a product," said Correia. "Using the lifts is a process." Correia said that nurses had not been trained on the use of lifts. Thus, in addition to installing them, they trained the nurses on how to use them. "Nurses started lifting each other," she said. "They could see the advantages right away. Usage of the lifts went way up."

This example shows that process and design are opposite sides of the same coin. And Correia notes that quality improvement and cost savings are not in the building, but in the engagement of the staff. "You have to apply the principles," said Correia. "Lean is not a building."

Figure 8.12 From the Theda Clark facility: (a) shower valve prefabrication; (b) sink prefabrication. Off-site manufacture can save time and money and promote standardization. (Courtesy ThedaCare.)

The Cost and Benefit

At a time when other hospitals are delaying or even halting building projects, ThedaCare remains confident that these major building and remodeling projects are the right thing at the right time. "Adding an eight-story bed tower will add more fixed cost," notes Park. "We are planning for the long term,[9] though, and we believe that, in the long term, it will prove wise."

"Once the collaborative care model is in full swing," said Correia, "we firmly believe we will show better outcomes for patients. And the cost savings from the improved quality will pay for the project."

Sutter Health: Rethinking Everything

The 1989 Loma Prieta earthquake in northern California collapsed part of the Bay Bridge and approaching freeway structure, killed 62, injured thousands, and resulted in about $7 billion dollars in damage. Afterward, state legislators began to heed the warnings of geologists. Dozens of hospitals remained in harm's way: Eight of them are located within a mile of the Hayward Fault, predicted to be the next to rupture in that part of the state.

Sutter Health

Sutter Health serves patients and their families in more than 100 northern California cities and towns. Its doctors, not-for-profit hospitals, and other healthcare service providers share resources and expertise to advance healthcare quality and access.

Then, in early 1994, the Northridge earthquake in Southern California killed 57, injured 9,000, and caused about $20 billion in damage. The temblor caused $3 billion in damage to hospitals, rendering 12 hospital buildings unsafe for occupancy. In 1995 California legislators passed Senate Bill 1953, which called for retrofitting the state's seismically vulnerable hospitals—including 2,500 buildings on 475 hospital campuses.

Sutter Health faced a major challenge. Of its 28 hospitals, about half would need to be replaced or rebuilt. According to architect David F. Chambers, who was then Sutter's director of planning, architecture, and design, the challenge was not merely to build a seismically safe hospital but also to rethink what a hospital could be.

Fragmentation

Chambers contends that the same fragmentation of production and performance plagues healthcare delivery as well as the architecture, engineering, and construction (AEC) professions. The healthcare industry segments care by department. Architecture, engineering, and construction participants, typically separate business entities, are selected to deliver their respective parts of facilities. Both industries, encumbered by the eight wastes,[10] are

Table 8.1   Examples of the Eight Wastes that Plague Both the Construction and Healthcare Industries

Type of waste (DOWNTIME)	Construction example	Healthcare example
Defects	Worker injuries, poor work quality, rework.	Patient/staff injuries, medication errors, infections, readmissions.
Overproduction	Duplication of overhead support components for above ceiling assemblies.	Multiple registration points, completion of redundant discrete records.
Waiting	Queues are created by discreet subcontractor coordination.	Queues are created by departmental handoffs/ fragmented care delivery.
Not using staff	Productivity affected by fragmented processes.	Productivity affected by fragmented processes.
Transportation	Multiple material touches created by complex staging of raw materials.	Multiple inpatient transports to discrete departments mean many stops for one service.
Inventory	Stock on hand requires staging space/hides defects, costs to store.	Clinical teams store extra supplies which become dated and must be discarded.
Movement	Handoffs between trades often require returns due to poor definition of "complete".	Patient movement between discrete points of service due to departmentalization.
Excess processing	Coordination of multiple systems creates multiple system conflicts.	Multiple system interfaces in complex patient care environments.

Source: Courtesy of David F. Chambers.

hampered in their ability to deliver value to the client consistently. They answer to performance measures that are complex, ambiguous, and disassociated from each other. That complexity creates the perception that more regulation is needed.

"Fragmentation of work, whether in healthcare delivery or facility design and construction, leads to optimization of the piece, not the whole," says Chambers.

> Division between participants erodes trust. Contracts or departmental work is based on transactions, not relationships. No wonder, then, that the focus in a traditional design–bid–build scenario is on "risk shedding." Consider also the disclaimers a patient must sign

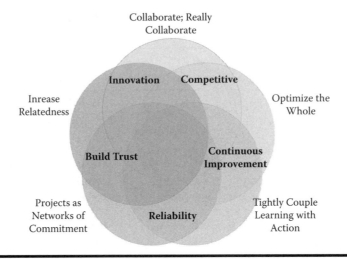

Figure 8.13 Sutter Health's five big ideas. (Courtesy David F. Chambers.)

before he or she actually receives care. Providers, just like AEC participants, think discretely about their specific risk before they think about ultimate success because they are not evaluated as a team that is accountable for a definable outcome.

Chambers and his colleagues at Sutter Health determined that eliminating waste and creating high-performance teams was the best way to "pull value to the customer." Achieving that ideal requires that all of the participants strive for the ideal, encompassed in Sutter's five big ideas (Figure 8.13)[11]:

■ *Collaborate, really collaborate.* Design is an iterative process, requiring input from everyone involved—from frontline caregivers to every subcontractor. The result is a building that is designed for efficient work, affordable construction, and easier maintenance.

■ *Increase the relatedness of the participants.* Develop relationships intentionally, increase respect for each member's unique skills and the value of his or her contribution, and introduce ways to problem-solve and share mistakes as learning opportunities.

■ *Develop a network of commitments.* From a vision created through process design and value stream mapping, from design through all phases of project execution, the work of building relies on networks of relationships and commitments. Leaders must keep the project moving toward the goal while managing these commitments.

■ *Optimize the whole, not the pieces.* Setting the directional arrow toward "ideal" and concentrating on smoothing the pathways (see Rules in Use,

Chapter 1), means less fragmentation and more assurance that one task relates directly to the next.

■ *Tightly couple learning with action.* Establish a learning loop by using real-time feedback on what works and what does not, and by doing work one by one (no batching).[12]

Co-opetition

In 2006, Chambers and colleagues set about to create a prototype hospital initiative. They intended to quickly generate the best and most progressive ideas for building safe, efficient, flexible hospitals. They called it a "co-opetition."[13]

Sutter Health's Co-Opetition

This cooperative competition, where information was shared regularly among three sets of architects and builders, led to rapid insight and learning that would not otherwise have been possible. The co-opetition had four goals:

■ Improve safety.
■ Enhance clinical efficiency.
■ Maximize flexibility for future changes.
■ Reduce the facility's cost, up front and long term.

Sutter invited three self-assembled teams, which included the architects as well as engineers, general contractors, and clinical process experts, to combine their expertise to find ways to eliminate waste in (1) healthcare delivery processes and (2) facility design and construction. Each team was provided $500,000 to participate in the co-opetition; teams would learn together by presenting their progress at key milestones to Sutter Health and to each other in open critiques. Teams were assured that their collaboration would be rewarded with continued project work as long as each team fully and openly shared its thinking at each critique (Figure 8.14).

Deliverables would include a strategic plan and an early schematic package with plans, elevations, and cost models. In addition to these fairly typical deliverables, participants were asked to include a staffing model based on a strategic plan indicating volumes and case mix index provided by Sutter Health. The teams also developed consensus-based project scheduling, to

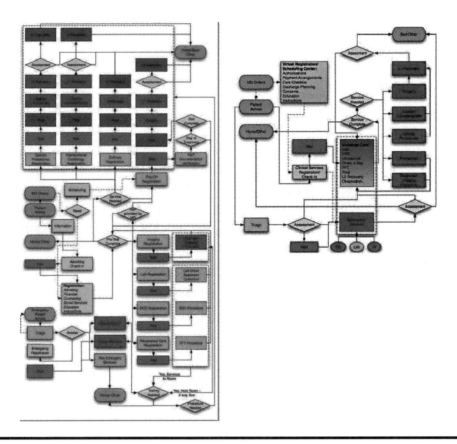

Figure 8.14   Starting with simple, high-level process maps, co-opetition participants looked at ways to streamline processes by removing steps, handoffs, departmental barriers, and queues. The diagram on the left represents a comprehensive range of services from Surgery and Diagnostics to Emergency and Observation as they are often configured in the current state. The diagram on the right provides a vision of these same services optimized for patient flow while also envisioning the way in which care teams (rather than departments) might begin working to optimize outcomes. (Diagrams courtesy David F. Chambers.)

see how quickly they could meet their deliverables. The entire co-opetition was completed in approximately 4 months.

"We needed our affiliates and aligned stakeholders—both in healthcare and in AEC—to recognize that their processes were broken," said Chambers. "We needed a deeper understanding of those problems and a path to their solution before we spent billions of dollars building hospitals."

To that end, Sutter Health also formed a project steering committee comprising leader-level physicians, nurses, healthcare executives, and project representatives. As teams were asked to think differently, so too were Sutter Health's leaders. The co-opetition had four goals:

- Improve safety.
- Enhance clinical efficiency.
- Maximize flexibility for future changes.
- Reduce the facility's cost, up front and long term.

"These goals set teams to thinking about how to provide more capacity for staff to give care, with expectations for greater quality outcomes," said Chambers. "They could do it if they configured the space to work with the least number of handoffs and patient movements."

Early on, Sutter Health expressed concern that if all participants saw each other's ideas, their outputs would all be the same, but that did not happen. "They shared ideas, but still came up with different ideas and designs," noted Chambers. "It's like a football game. The players know the rules, but they will play differently. When you assign three teams to a project and give them all the same parameters, you are likely to get half a dozen results." (Maybe even seven ways.)

In the end, Sutter Health's steering committee vetted the deliverables from each team. The results, if fully implemented, could change the fundamental relationship of value to cost for the delivery of healthcare, as well as the projects that house healthcare.

Cellular Care

Chambers was intent on eliminating steps that add no value, such as patient movement and queues. Rather than giving care in silos, the idea was to adapt cellular manufacturing ideas to healthcare and deliver more related patient services at a single point. Cellular care is delivered in a universal care unit that can include, for example, centrally locating preadmission testing, preparation, observation, and recovery beds, which are shared between the ED, medical imaging, and surgery.

"Early planning on one hospital showed that if we went to a cellular care model, using a robust universal care unit, we could create the capacity of a 180-bed hospital with just 130 beds," said Chambers. "With our prototype hospital initiative, we created more capacity for staff to give care by configuring work without handoffs and patient movements. And by providing the right care in the right place at the right time, bed utilization is more effective."

According to *Health Facilities Management*,[12] strategies such as cellular care; separating patient, visitor, staff, and service pathways; and delivering vendor supplies directly to the point of use were expected to result in "a 42%

improvement in workflow, a 35% reduction in space, a 32% reduction in the use of natural resources, and a maximum 53% reduction in time to design and build. Workflow improvements are expected to enhance safety as well."

The prototypes developed during the co-opetition confirmed the notion that, as Chambers said, "fixing processes has remarkable impact on the ability of care professionals to serve patients. We need to find a way to provide care to more people, and this is a way to leverage our expertise."

Lessons Learned

"Collaborative models—whether in healthcare or project delivery—can drive out waste," says Chambers. "We are plagued with too many handoffs and restarts and too much waiting, movement, underuse of staff, and defects."

Mind-sets will have to change, but the status quo will not work in the future. Collaborative models force the optimization of the whole, rather than the pieces. An unimaginably better product can emerge.

Summary

In addition to using Lean design, Seattle Children's Hospital, ThedaCare, and Sutter Health have discovered huge benefits from having the entire project—including all aspects of construction—included as a seamless whole. The resulting IPD (integrated project delivery) or IFD (integrated facility design) means that communication among all stakeholders must be as close as possible at all times.

Sutter promoted the exchange of ideas through an innovative "co-opetition." The other hospitals found special use for full-sized mock-ups; ThedaCare used its mock-up for 2 years as it perfected its care delivery model. All three hospitals demonstrated that design and construction are inseparable and that, when Lean leads the thinking, paradigm-shifting results can ensue.

Discussion

- Why is the integrated approach so revolutionary? What is the usual role of the owner, the architect, and the construction firm? Is it as productive as it could be?

- What about the life-sized mock-up was so important?
- How does Correia's last quote about investing for the long haul reflect Liker's first rule of management (Chapter 1)?
- How has leadership evolved in these two hospitals that have been on their "Lean journeys" for a decade or more? How does this leadership style contrast with the "command and control" and "management by objectives" styles of so many American business leaders?
- Lean promotes respect and dignity for everyone. How does that play out in a collaborative IPD for the owner? Architect? Construction managers and subcontractors? How does it play out for hospital staff members? How about the patient?
- At Sutter, the "five big ideas" help "pull value to the patient." How?
- What were the benefits of "co-opetition?"

Suggested Reading

Gladwell, M. 2002. *The tipping point: How little things can make a big difference.* New York: Little Brown.

Heath, C., and Heath, D. 2010. *Switch: How to change things when change is hard.* New York: Crown Publishing Group, Random House.

Notes

1. Wellman, J., Jeffries, H., and Hagan, P. 2011. *Leading the lean healthcare journey: Driving culture change to increase value.* Boca Raton, FL: CRC Press.
2. Typically, this arrangement is referred to as an integrated project delivery, or IPD. At Seattle Children's, they refer to it as integrated facility design, or IFD, to ensure that the term encompasses every aspect of design and construction and is not seen as being limited to a production process. SCH uses the term inclusively; that is, it refers not just to the construction trades, but also to the design work that precedes it and the move-in that comes at the end.
3. See Chapter 4.
4. In Lean parlance, "touch time" refers to the time when the product is actually being worked on, when value is being added. In medicine, the term is doubly meaningful because it refers to caring for patients.
5. On a scale of 1 to 5, nurse satisfaction was 3.72 in 2007; in 2008, after the implementation of the pilot unit, the score rose to 4.37. Source: http//www. createhealthcarevalue.com/resources/case-studies/collaborative_care/
6. http://www.milliman.com/expertise/healthcare/products-tools/ milliman-care-guidelines/

7. http://www.milliman.com/expertise/healthcare/products-tools/milliman-care-guidelines/

8. Sadler, B., Berry, L., Guenther, R., et al. 2011. Fable hospital 2.0: The business case for building better health care. *The Hastings Center Report* January/February 2011. http://www.thehastingscenter.org/Publications/HCR/Detail.aspx?id=5066&page=7 (accessed May 21, 2011).

9. See Chapter 1, Liker's 14 principles. Note how Park's comment aligns with the first principle.

10. These are defects, overproduction, waiting, not using talent, transporting, inventory, motion, and excess processing. See Chapter 1 for a fuller discussion.

11. Developed for Sutter Health by the Lean Construction Institute: http://www.leanconstruction.org

12. Lichtig, W. 2005. Sutter Health: Developing a contracting model to support lean project delivery. *Lean Construction Journal* 2:105–112.

13. Wagner, S. 2008. Sutter Health's "co-opetition" created hospital prototypes. *Health Facilities Management* (online) January 2008.

EXTENDED APPLICATIONS

4

Chapter 9

Cultural Context for Lean-Led Design

Would this [immigrant health screening center] be a place of bureaucracy and fear of illness, where a chance of deportation hung in the air? Or could it be a totally different kind of place? We decided on a simpler message: Welcome to Abu Dhabi.

—Lou Astornio
Architect

Case studies: Nanaimo Regional and Fort St. John Hospitals, British Columbia, Canada; the Abu Dhabi Health Service (SEHA) foreign worker Disease Prevention and Screening Center (DPSC)

Introduction

The design of a health facility must take into account the fabric of the community that it will serve. This sounds obvious, but it may not be. Who are the people of this community? What are their predominant health needs? Are there strong religious and cultural preferences? Can the design of the building respect local beliefs and customs and still provide the best of modern healthcare?

Nanaimo Regional and Fort St. John Hospital: Cultural Sensitivity Improves Quality

The hospitals of British Columbia (BC) serve a large population of indigenous people, including First Nations and local aboriginal people. Some of the beliefs that permeate those cultures have influenced hospital design in the region:

■ When a tribal member dies, custom requires the immediate return of that person's soul to nature, preferably through an open window. But in frigid temperatures, within the limitations of modern HVAC design, opening a window presented a problem. At Nanaimo Regional General Hospital, BC, this need was accommodated by integrating a "venturi" window (a small window within a window) into designated spiritual rooms (Figure 9.1).

■ Smudging is a common spiritual ritual practiced by Pacific Coast indigenous people. The ceremony, which involves wafting the smoke of burning sage, cedar, or sweet grass, is meant to cleanse the ill person of negative thoughts and feelings and set the stage for healing. Aboriginal housing standards in BC encourage design that allows people to practice smudging.[1] The new Fort St. John Hospital and Residential Care Facility in northern BC created two spiritual rooms where smudging can be done.[2] Designers had to ensure that the ventilation systems for these rooms could accommodate the practice, while preventing smoke from penetrating other areas.

Nanaimo Regional Hospital and Fort St. John Hospital

■ Nanaimo Regional General Hospital is part of the Vancouver Island Health Authority (VIHA), which provides healthcare to over 750,000 people on Vancouver Island, the islands of the Georgia Strait, and in the mainland communities north of Powell River and south of Rivers Inlet.

■ Fort St. John Hospital and Residential Care Facility is part of Northern Health, which delivers healthcare to the approximately 300,000 inhabitants across northern British Columbia, including acute care, mental health, public health, addictions, and home and community care services.

Figure 9.1   The "spirit window" designed into 15 labor/delivery/recovery/postpartum rooms at the Nanaimo Regional General Hospital, British Columbia. In addition to being culturally sensitive, the windows also introduce fresh air into the patient care space. (Photo: Viva Swanson, with permission from BC Health Authority.)

Designing out of respect for one "special-interest group" can end up creating a better facility for everyone. For example, hospital architects at a small community hospital thought that they had achieved a breakthrough when they penciled in a large waiting room adjacent to the ambulatory surgery center, where patients could wait, dressed only in their hospital gowns, for a bed to become available. It was seen as a decorous alternative to the current system, where gowned men and women sat in open hallways to wait.

The breakthrough came when one of the nurses brought up an important fact: The hospital served a large Mennonite constituency. Mennonites, especially women, are expected to be covered modestly at all times.

"Their husbands don't even see their bare legs," said the nurse. "It must be humiliating for them to be in a hospital gown with a bunch of other women—and men!"

Eventually, the group began to question why patients had to wait in gowns—or wait at all. They discovered that, if they prepared patients one by one, "pulling" patients in only when a bed became available, they did not need to warehouse them in a hallway or a waiting room. Anxious patients could stay with their families and then don the gown, get into bed, and reunite with their families.

The team did not wait for the new hospital to fix the process. They went to one-piece flow immediately, and the queue in the hall vanished. In the floor plan for the new hospital, that waiting room was repurposed.

The Abu Dhabi Health Service (SEHA) Foreign Worker Disease Prevention and Screening Center (DPSC): Cultures within Cultures

Even in familiar North American settings, cultural competence matters. Thus, when a Pittsburgh-based architectural firm was called upon to design a 250,000-square-foot foreign worker screening center in Abu Dhabi, United Arab Emirates (UAE), it realized that cultural context would play a huge role in that design. The cultural challenge was considerable. The company would be designing a facility for a Middle Eastern country that was foreign to *it,* and the clients for that facility would be arriving from several other foreign countries.

The program had even larger implications. One important goal of the new center would be to create a model for ambulatory care throughout the UAE.

To make sure that the processes and issues were examined from all sides, the company called upon the services of Lean practitioners, as well as its own in-house group of design researchers and cultural anthropologists.

Cultures within Cultures

"We all came as learners. None of us had ever been to the Middle East," said architect Paul Fisher. "The first thing we encountered when we went to visit the center was a crowded parking lot. And with that, the American architects began their journey."

The emirate of Abu Dhabi is just 50 years old; its capital city, Abu Dhabi, exudes an open-minded, eclectic metropolitan atmosphere. Everywhere, construction is taking place on an unimaginable scale. Maintaining the pace of construction in a country without the requisite manpower means importing laborers from other countries, also at an unimaginable scale—about 3,000 people per day. It is not uncommon to see 100 buses at each of a dozen work sites in the capital city taking migrant workers to and from their quarters at shift change.

Laborers arrive from dozens of countries and cultures, although 83% of them are from India, Pakistan, and Bangladesh. Among the immigrants, about 200 languages are spoken. The unifier seems to be a common faith: Most of the immigrants embrace Islam.

Abu Dhabi Health Services Company, or SEHA, is an independent public joint stock company founded to manage the curative activities of the public hospitals and clinics of the Emirate of Abu Dhabi. The establishment of SEHA is part of the government of Abu Dhabi's healthcare sector reform initiatives and represents another step in the realization of His Highness Sheikh Khalifa Bin Zayed Al Nahyan, president, of the UAE's vision to provide the people of Abu Dhabi with healthcare services that compare favorably with the best in the world. SEHA's mission is to transform the healthcare landscape of Abu Dhabi and realize that vision. We are committed to doing this in a socially responsible and cost-effective way. We will measure our achievement by benchmarking ourselves against international standards and by measuring our effectiveness in improving the accessibility, affordability, choice, and satisfaction of our patients.

—Welcome message, SEHA website, http://www.seha.ae
(Architect: Astorino)

Any worker who wants to stay in the country for more than 30 days must undergo an immigration clearance that includes a screening at a Disease Prevention and Screening Center (DPSC) run by the Abu Dhabi Health Services (SEHA), a quasigovernmental healthcare agency (Figure 9.2).

Figure 9.2   The Abu Dhabi Health Service (SEHA) foreign worker Disease Prevention and Screening Center (DPSC) processes up to 3,000 workers per day. (Photo courtesy Astorino.)

About 60% of the immigrants who move through the urban DPSC in downtown Abu Dhabi are male laborers; the women often come in search of work as nannies, housekeepers, or cooks. The site would require a design that could handle and segregate genders. (At an outlying rural facility in Musaffah, where about 2,000 mostly male laborers are processed each day, a mostly single-gender facility would be easier to design.)

The American team of architects, Lean practitioners, and design researchers quickly discovered the key to Middle Eastern culture: hospitality. "As an American viewing the Arab world, it is easy to misunderstand who they are and what they stand for," said principal architect Tim Powers:

> If we just rely on our media to get our information about the Arab world, we will get it wrong. Their priorities are really quite similar to ours—dedication to family, personal relationships, integrity, a thirst for education, and an appreciation for fine things. When they do something, they do it to the highest degree, but not out of ostentation. They believe it is their responsibility to provide the very best for their fellow citizens.

Current Condition

The health screening at the DPSC is just one part of a three-part process required to gain entry to the country. In addition, clients also go through processes set up by the Department of Labor and Department of Immigrations, currently at other locations in the city.

Immigrants coming to the DPSC for health screening undergo a five-part process consisting of (1) registration and a retinal scan (to identify people who may have been denied entry before), (2) physical exam, (3) blood work, (4) vaccination, and (5) chest x-ray (Figure 9.3). Only people with infectious

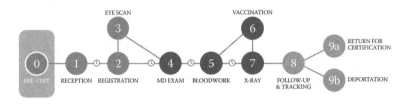

Figure 9.3 Simplified value stream map shows two occasions for disrobing, interrupted by a blood draw. Changing the order and increasing the numbers of dressing rooms improved the flow. (Courtesy Astorino.)

diseases are sent back to their home countries; about 99% of those screened are permitted to stay.

Yet, leaders at SEHA wanted to improve the experience and the efficiency of the existing screening center vastly, to align it more closely with renowned Arab hospitality.

"There was a waiting room to get into the waiting room," said Fisher. "Although it was as organized as it could be, it still felt confusing and chaotic. People spilled into the parking lot. They were told to come back tomorrow. They jammed the hallways because they couldn't find where to go next."

Poor ventilation and crowded waiting areas made clients feel closed in. Seeing practitioners in masks only intensified their fear of contagious diseases.

People had to undress and redress two times during the process: first for the physical exam and later for the x-ray. Each time, people left their clothes in dressing rooms, which rendered those rooms unusable until they returned. The physical exam and x-ray areas—primarily the changing rooms at x-ray—became bottlenecks in the process.

The travel pattern between rooms meant that gowned women had to cross a hallway to get to an exam room. When their x-ray was done, they doubled back to the dressing room, creating a loop in the process. Unable to understand the language, the newcomers were often lost or confused. Occasionally, a confused patient would open the door to the x-ray room only to find another person's x-ray in progress, accidentally exposing others to radiation. (*Where are my clothes? Where was that dressing room?*). To clear up the confusion, staff valiantly tried to provide continuous explanation.

The staff were very caring, but often frustrated. They wanted to provide better care, but were trapped in an uncooperative system.

The value stream map in Figure 9.3 shows the basic steps in the health screening. The process steps are shown in Table 9.1, along with the problems and consequences.

The most concrete requirement was the total segregation of men and women according to Islamic law. Screening for men and women was done in parallel, out of view of one another. Only women practitioners and staff members dealt with women and only men with men.

By law and tradition, women are accompanied to the center by a male companion or chaperone. These men often became concerned and required an explanation when the women were separated from them to go through the screening alone. To some, not being allowed to follow the woman at

Table 9.1   Current Condition, SEHA Immigration Center

Current process	Problem	Consequence
Arrive at reception Report for retinal scan for identification purposes	Two large waiting rooms No reliable way to schedule appointments Clients get lost on the way to the retinal scan	Clients wait twice Most have no appointments, so just arrive, creating unreliable work flow Staff must repeat directions
Proceed to physical exam area; undress; undergo exam; dress	Clients do not know where to go Clothing left in dressing room Client must find dressing room when finished	Staff must repeat directions; staff and clients frustrated Dressing room cannot be used while exam is taking place because clothing is stored there Time wasted finding dressing room after exam
Locate the lab; have blood drawn	Clients get lost	Staff must repeat directions; staff and clients frustrated
Proceed to vaccination station	Clients get lost	Staff must repeat directions; staff and clients frustrated
Proceed to x-ray; undress; have x-ray; dress	Changing rooms are small and few Machine idle while clients dress, undress for a second time	Work flow delayed by second round of undressing, redressing Idle machine creates delay
Exit the center; find escort	Clients exit at far end of the building, half a city block from where they entered	Clients have trouble finding where they came in Women looking for their chaperones feel intimidated
Receive test results Return to health center for certificate (if healthy) or for treatment or deportation (if not healthy)	Variable time to results: 5 hours to 2 days Returnees to health center clog the facility	Those who are ill may have exposed others Those seeking certificates must wait in long lines

a respectable distance through the entire process seemed an abrogation of responsibility. For some chaperones, the instruction to wait in the waiting room for the woman's return was upsetting.

When clients leave, they must be tracked and called back, either to receive their certification or to look into a health problem. Tracking thousands of people was difficult. Having them return to the clinic to receive their certificates bogged things down.

Emotional Profile

Working together with client representatives, the architects, Lean practitioners, and design researchers began to develop an emotional profile of the place. Preliminary observations highlighted the points of frustration, anxiety, and confusion in the process; these were viewed as points of opportunity. A unifying concept for the center was sought.

"This was perhaps the most transformational moment we had together as a team," said architect Lou Astorino. "Would this be a place of bureaucracy and fear of illness, where a chance of deportation hung in the air? Or could it be a totally different kind of place? We decided on a simpler message: *Welcome to Abu Dhabi.*"

With that key insight, the facility was transformed from an immigrant screening facility to a welcome center—from a harsh processing center to a refreshing oasis. The message of *welcome* resonated with the facility's leaders; they found it much more in keeping with the Arab qualities of collegiality and hospitality.

From this important pivot point emerged the eight guiding principles for the design of the center:

- Provide a welcoming experience.
- Create a holistic and healthy environment.
- Reduce fear of infectious diseases.
- Increase efficiency.
- Address cost implications for a revised process.
- Educate the customer and enhance understanding.
- Design with respect for local ecology and sustainability.
- Design a facility that embraces innovation and progress.

Moving from the current condition to this improved client experience would take thoughtful deliberation and attention to every detail in the process. Now that they knew their ideal state, their real work began.

Observations, Takt and Cycle Times, and Value Stream Mapping

Lean practitioners Mimi Falbo, DNP, RN and David Priselac began their observations of the hour-long health screening. The team included architects from Pittsburgh and Abu Dhabi, as well as the design researchers Christine Astorino and Erin Holland of the Fathom Group. The team gathered data about minimum, maximum, mean, and median times for each step at each station. Fathom also interviewed dozens of clients and staff members, yielding more information about what clients saw as the ideal experience.

The staff at the center already had an excellent system for observation as part of their emphasis on patient satisfaction. In a technique similar to the US Joint Commission's "tracer patient" methodology,[3] staff members routinely followed individual clients all the way through the process to find the bottlenecks. Falbo said:

> They already had quite a bit of good data. But we needed more detail on the timing, down to how long it took men and women to change clothes, how long each exam took, and how long the x-ray machine was idle between clients. We needed cycle times for each and every thing that happened. Our understanding of the cycle and subcycle times in each step of the process was critical to work design and subsequent facility design.

As described in prior chapters, takt time is the time available (for example, a 12-hour shift) divided by the number of people going through the process (in this case, about 3,000). Takt time helps determine the resources that will be necessary to move everyone through without delay. By streamlining the work and reducing the time that staff members spend looking for items and information, process improvements generally improve takt time.

In healthcare, there is a common misconception about what takt time is—and what it is not. Takt time is not a means to speed up the line, to rush clients through, or to cram as many cases as possible in on overworked practitioners. It is not prescriptive (dictating how fast practitioners must go), but rather descriptive (truly understanding how much time each step takes—learning the overall "cycle" time for each process step and then deploying adequate resources to meet customer demand). Knowing takt time and cycle time provides a way to measure how long clients and practitioners will realistically need to do a good job, account for the variations that occur, and promote a smooth process.

"The new design would need to support the clients at every step," said design researcher Erin Holland. "Without effort, they should be aware of what is going on and feel no fear or uncertainty."

Design Alternative: Queuing Model with "Lanes"

The staff at both centers concurred that the most significant design problem would be way-finding. It would involve more than a search for the perfect international symbols that could be understood by anyone (although that would happen, too).

Staff members at Musaffah and the city center had independently come up with the same idea: They wanted to explore the possibility of assigning a "lane"—that is, a single set of exam rooms tied together—to each client at registration. (See Figure 9.4.) Each lane would be self-guided; with assigned pathways plus explicit signage, getting lost would no longer be an option. Clinic personnel would always know where each person was. Their work-load would be reduced because they would no longer be directing traffic, answering repeated queries, dealing with a language barrier, and being frequently distracted.

Interviews with clients confirmed that they would prefer an assigned lane. But would such an arrangement make people feel closed in? Said Falbo:

> People were telling us that the current process made them feel like cattle and they did not like it. The option of having predefined corridors, especially when designed well—with natural light, great ventilation, and beautiful features—scored high with clients. They controlled their own journey, and it returned some autonomy to them.

Future State

In terms of process, the team quickly recognized the waste and discomfort in having people disrobe twice—once for the physical and again for the x-ray. They proposed reordering the screening in this way: register, undress for physical exam, go immediately to x-ray, dress, and then proceed for blood work and vaccination (see the future-state map, Figure 9.5).

Registration wait times accounted for 30%–50% of process times. By creating a reliable way to preregister by computer or phone, process times would plummet. Rather than operating on a purely walk-in basis, the center

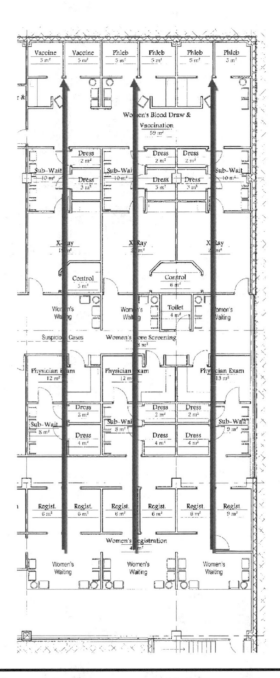

Figure 9.4 "Lanes" are stacked exam rooms with hallways between. Assigning lanes to each client makes it difficult for the client to get lost. In an environment where over 200 languages are spoken, this will be a major improvement. (Note: this is the women's side of the facility. The men's side is adjacent, but completely separate.) (Courtesy Astorino.)

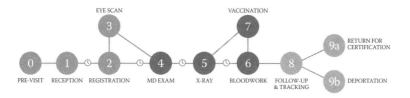

Figure 9.5 Simplified value stream map shows improved flow by doing the physical exam and x-ray in sequence. (Courtesy Astorino.)

would use a combination of open-access scheduling and limited walk-in hours. Staffing the reception area at all times, using standardized processes, and having a reliable set of backup personnel all helped to reduce registration times. The staff experimented with the new process and, rather than waiting for a new facility, they implemented it right away. The prewaiting area has already vanished.

The new design incorporates abundant natural light and ventilation, eliminating the "closed-in" feeling that heightened worry about contagion. Ceiling height variations and architectural details—along with shorter wait times everywhere—will enhance the feeling of spaciousness.

The new design increases the number of dressing rooms and places them adjacent to the exam areas that they serve. In addition to reducing the queue, the adjacency means that people will no longer have to cross a hall wearing a gown. They will carry their clothes with them and proceed to the next room, creating a smoother flow.

Distinctive corridors, or lanes, will make pathways clear, with no forks or loops and exits clearly marked.

Because the new center will be operated jointly by the departments of health, labor, and immigration, laborers will be able to complete all of their entry requirements in a single place. In addition to the health screening, workers' lanes will take them to other floors of the center for immigration paperwork and for the processing of ID and insurance cards. At the end of processing, clients will exit very near to where they entered, reducing confusion as they are reunited with their escorts and find their transportation (Figure 9.6).

The new design calls for a way for physicians to check x-rays in real time so that people with questionable results can be evaluated immediately, without being released for a few days and posing a health risk to themselves and the community. Patient education, in brochure or video form in dozens of languages, will be distributed as patients exit.

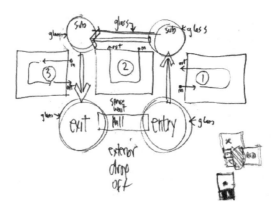

Figure 9.6 Early sketch shows U-shaped cell emerging. Although the final version had the end of the "U" upstairs, the concept was the same: Allow patients to exit near where they entered. (Courtesy Astorino.)

Customers with negative blood, x-ray, and physical exam results will receive their certificates on the same day and will be able to print the certificates themselves at kiosks. The goal will be to provide the health certificate for those with negative results within 30 minutes of their blood draw.

There was one more consideration: Some people wanted to be able to pay for a fast-track process where they could be assured that they would not wait for their screening. (Paying for a superior service is an accepted practice in the Middle East.) A second track would be developed to accommodate this perceived client need.

Queue Theory and Simulation: Drill-Down Reduces Waiting

Once the process was redesigned to eliminate two changes of clothes and the bottleneck in the changing rooms, the challenge would be to determine how many of each type of workstation or room and how many changing rooms would be needed in each lane.

The Lean consultants created a spreadsheet that utilized median cycle times for each process and the takt time for each volume projection to calculate the number of workstations or rooms needed. Could they design a process that was paced properly for clients and staff members, yet not leave machinery or people idle?

The answer to those questions would help the architects determine how much space would be needed for each station and for waiting areas, as well as how many lanes would be required to process 3,000 people per day.

The design team called upon queue theorists from the University of Pittsburgh to help create a simulation of the current and alternative clinic designs and work processes.[4] The goal was to discover how layout and resource allocation would affect the flow of clients through the clinic.

Expanding on the takt time data and other observational data from the Lean team, the simulation team calculated average wait time, queue length, and cycle time at each station. This helped them to determine the parameters for the queue at each station. They used various simulation models to evaluate various configurations.

The two high-value assets were the physician and the x-ray machine. Delay at this step was easy to anticipate. The model evaluated staffing "on the principle that every station should have enough capacity to ensure that the physician and x-ray always have customers (are not idle)."[4]

To make sure that these two stations were used efficiently, they were placed centrally, flanked on either side by a lane. Dressing rooms from both lanes opened directly into the physical and x-ray area. The simulation included enough dressing rooms at the physicians and x-ray machines that, while a client from one side was undressing, a client from the other side was undergoing the exam. From the client perspective, he or she would undress and go right in; from the physician perspective, he or she could see patients in an orderly way, without ebbs and flows in the work.

Although the observational team did not document an inordinate fluctuation in demand, the simulation team suggested a way to handle that possibility. Cross training the sometimes idle vaccination nurses to help in x-ray increased the pool of available helpers for busy times. The team also created a way for patients to change lanes, if necessary, to continue to the next step without delay, should the patient in front of them require more time. In other words, the new design promoted work flow leveling in the busiest times, which minimizes waiting and idle time.

The simulation, using a software solution called Arena Version 12,[4] worked as predicted, validating the observations of the team and demonstrating how the lanes would work. It also looked at the distribution of queues in the clinic, which influenced the size and location of waiting areas. The result was a design that minimizes downtime for the x-ray machine and physician, virtually eliminates patient waiting, and optimizes the sizes and numbers of waiting areas.

Information Technology

The health screening is only one of the three phases of immigrant processing; the departments of labor and immigration are also involved. Computer
programs currently require SEHA staff members to log in three or four times
to gather relevant visa and passport information about each client. A new
system will link SEHA to pertinent databases, making relevant information
immediately available.

When it came to registration, the challenge was to find a user-friendly
way to encourage people to preregister for an appointment. There will
be website access with the center where clients can retrieve data, make
appointments, and pay.

The registration function will be expanded in the new facility and will
become a gatekeeper to the system, regulating the flow of patients. Rather
than "push" patients in as quickly as possible, the registrar will admit clients
to a specific lane only when there is an available opening in the physician
dressing and waiting area before the physical exam. In the parlance of Lean,
this is a "pull" system, where the system itself notifies when it is time to
send in the next person.

Lean and Design Research

One unusual aspect of this program involved a detailed examination of the
emotional experiences of clients and staff with the process, as a way to understand how to create a more soothing and healing environment. The overarch-
ing vision was to transform immigrant processing into a welcoming experience.

To examine this aspect of care more fully, the architects called upon
Fathom, a design research team. "In Abu Dhabi, people place value on
emotion. They are very expressive people, very generous," said Alyssa Ilov.
"They are exuberant about their culture and they want to share and give joy-
ously to others. They care about how others feel."

Fathom interviewed dozens of people in seven user groups: SEHA, women,
men, VIPs, fast-trackers, male companions, and physicians and staff. Among
the questions were "How can the clinic provide comfort to its customers?" and
"What taste, scent, feelings, and textures can be conveyed through design?"

Using each step in the current-state value stream map (Figure 9.2), the
Fathom team inquired about the customer and employee experience in
terms of their feelings and emotions at each step. Likewise, they mapped
the ideal user experience and began to sketch out design elements such as

lighting, movement, pattern and texture, nature, form, and art that would enhance the experience. They focused on the colors (light), sounds (Qu'ran and traditional songs), and smells (coffee, herbs) that the clients found most soothing. Said Falbo:

> Design research is absolutely congruent with Lean. We have the same goal: to make the work environment less frustrating and to make clients and staff feel supported and enjoy the experience. Our work centers around the function of space as it relates to tasks. What are those tasks? Are they the right ones? The design researchers advance the goal through colors, music, art, and furniture that meet the emotional and cultural needs of the people.

Summary

The emirate of Abu Dhabi requires thousands of immigrant laborers for its building projects. The country wants to redesign the way in which it handles its guest workers, creating a one-stop shop for health, immigration, and labor clearance for the 3,000 people per day it handles in the urban center, as well as the 2,000 people processed at a suburban center.

Cultural considerations include language and customs; most of the immigrants are from Bangladesh, India, and Pakistan. Most are Moslems. Handling the health needs of these people with dignity and respect is the focus of this project.

Discussion

- In the introduction, the example is given of how considering the needs of Mennonite women improved the presurgical experience for everyone. How did that happen?
- The immigration center in Abu Dhabi was designed by architects from Pittsburgh. How did they deal with the culture in Abu Dhabi? How did the Emirates deal with the incoming cultures from central Asia?
- What was the pivot point for the design of this facility?
- One might worry that "lanes" or corridors would make people feel herded. How did designers plan to handle this? How did they know the design would be accepted by clients?
- What roles did takt time and cycle time play in this project?
- Is there a role for the queue theorist in healthcare?

Suggested Reading

Farmer, P. 2011. *Haiti after the earthquake*. New York: Public Affairs, Perseus Group.
Kidder, T. 2003. *Mountains beyond mountains: The quest of Dr. Paul Farmer, a man who would cure the world*. New York: Random House.

Notes

1. Aboriginal Housing in British Columbia: Community Engagement Sessions. Summary report. Prepared for the BC Office of Housing and Construction Standards, March 31, 2008. http://www.housing.gov.bc.ca/housing/docs/AbHousingEngagementSumReport2008.pdf (accessed May 16, 2011).
2. E-mail correspondence: Viva Swanson, RN BSN PNC(C), clinical lead. Acute Care Planning & Transition, Fort St. John Hospital and Residential Care Project, May 13, 2011.
3. Joint Commission fact sheet on tracer methodology. http://www.jointcommission.org/assets/1/18/Tracer_Methodology_2010.pdf (accessed May 20, 2011).
4. Luangkesorn, L., Norman, B., Zhuang, Y., Falbo, M., and Sysko, J. 2011. Designing disease prevention and screening centers in Abu Dhabi. Interfaces. *INFORMS* ISSN 0092-2102.

Chapter 10

Lean Technology

It takes a lot of hard work to make something simple, to truly understand the underlying challenges and come up with elegant solutions... Simplicity is the ultimate sophistication.

—**Steve Jobs**[1]

Case studies: Seattle Children's Hospital, Seattle, WA; Swedish Hospital, Issaquah, WA; University of Pittsburgh Medical Center (UPMC), Pittsburgh, PA

Introduction

Chapter 6 depicted the ways in which standardizing work spaces can save time and build a degree of safety and reliability into a new building. With most things in the same place from room to room, travel and search time decline. Standard work spaces can encourage the development of standard practices as well.

Toyota favors the low-cost, low-tech approach to standardizing processes—with reason: Quite often, it is enough. Thoughtless layering-on of electronics only creates complexity and waste. Nevertheless, Toyota is quick to adopt technology that makes sense—that is, when it makes work easier and improves quality.

The phenomenon of unnecessary complexity creeps into the most thoughtfully designed IT processes, says author Mike Orzen. He maintains that there is a correct order to designing IT solutions: "people, process, technology." It is the only way, he says, to ensure that technology supports effective operations.

In his book, *Lean IT,*[2] Orzen and coauthor Steve Bell describe the problem this way:

> Beyond the challenge of necessary complexity, there is an enormous amount of *unnecessary complexity*—self-inflicted pain—arising from the inappropriate design of business processes and supporting information systems. Lean practitioners call this the waste of *overprocessing:* excessive work where cost and complexity exceed the benefits…if stakeholders do not deliberately and continuously simplify and improve them, they naturally degenerate over time, becoming more and more complex, costly to maintain, and difficult to use. (pp. 7, 325–326)

One hematologic-oncologist observed, "I've seen this time and again. A doctor walks into a patient's room and immediately makes eye contact with… a computer. We have to remember that we serve patients, not machines."

IT deserves careful consideration as part of any facility design. The facility and adaptability of such a system have design implications. In the flexible space of the hospital of the future, will hard-wiring be a thing of the past? Furthermore, as this chapter shows, the design of the IT "solutions" bears careful scrutiny and can benefit from Lean methodology.

Seattle Children's Hospital: Cans and Strings

Seattle Children's Hospital (SCH) COO Pat Hagan says that he prefers a "cans-and-strings" approach over automation whenever possible. For example, the open office used in the Bellevue Outpatient Center creates easy face-to-face communication among members of the care team, reducing the complexity of handoffs.

"Certain things you just can't do as well by e-mail," said Hagan. "When we talk about the complexity of care, it's a systems problem. We can't assume that electrons are going to save the day. In fact, unless you have improved your processes in the first place, electrons compound the problem."

Virginia Mason's Gary Kaplan captures the sentiment this way: "Unless you address your processes, you will simply be moving [junk] at the speed of light."

Hagan notes the tension between cans and strings and electronics:

We have to improve processes before we can automate them and build a facility around them. We have to improve sequences before we build them in. I'm *almost* a Luddite, in the sense that I think we are far too beholden to IT. Look at our budget. I'd love to recapture some of the time we spend just trying to install software.

The Case for Low-Tech; the Place for High-Tech

SCH owned 70 secure cabinets, equipped with software that tracked when each piece of inventory was used and who used it. The high-tech cabinets were used to ensure security, but also to ensure that items in the inventory were properly billed, improving "capture" of reimbursements.

According to Supply Chain Director Greg Beach, once the supply chain was better understood, the use of these expensive cabinets came into question:

> Eventually, by the time we had installed 70 of these cabinets, we discovered that many of the items we kept in them weren't reimbursed by Medicare or Medicaid anyway, but were folded into room rates or procedure rates. We were asking the cabinets to hold everything, and they couldn't. As a result, we had about 1,800 stock-outs a month.

Using the cabinets was onerous for nurses. Every time a nurse wanted something, he or she had to swipe a card, enter a password, wait for the cupboard to unlock, pull the item, and then press a button to note that something had been removed. Repeat that dozens of times during a shift and you see that the "efficient," software-driven cabinets were eating a lot of time.

Since implementing a Toyota-based, low-tech, demand-flow system for supplies (see Chapter 8), SCH has removed all but three of the cabinets, which now hold only high-value items like replacement joints. This was the purpose, Beach notes, for which the cabinets were created. The low-tech solution—keeping low-cost items in blue plastic bins in the new demand-flow system—saves hundreds of nursing hours each month and about $100,000 in service agreements for those cabinets.

As a result of these findings in the main hospital, the new Building Hope, will have about 80% fewer of these electronic cabinets than would originally have been planned, saving another $100,000 in costs and reducing square footage.

One sophisticated IT solution—electronic cabinets with tracking software—may not have been the best answer for storing everyday items. However, another sophisticated IT solution—an inventory-tracking dashboard (see Figure 8.6)—proved absolutely vital to keeping the demand-flow system simple and efficient. With the behind-the-scenes dashboard created at SCH, the supply chain can be monitored closely. If a resupply is expected every 3 days, but begins to be requested every day, the system flags it for response. Likewise, items used less frequently than anticipated are flagged for a root-cause analysis and likely reduction or removal.

Lean enables simplicity. Simplicity can indeed be in the forms of cans and strings. But simplicity as applied to the design of IT has some fascinating possibilities as well.

Swedish Hospital, Issaquah, Washington: The Nerve Center

The new Swedish Hospital in the Issaquah Highlands near Seattle serves a well heeled community whose residents include Google and Microsoft executives. The hospital and adjoining medical office building will be fully operating by the end of 2011. As envisioned by Senior Vice President Kevin Brown, the Issaquah facility will be an "ambulatory care center with beds out back." Patients with severe medical conditions are transferred to a downtown tertiary care facility. All other needs are served under one roof, from routine doctors' appointments to most types of surgery.

On the design team for the 4 years preceding the opening was a dynamic group of 25 community advisors, representing a spectrum of patient demographics from old to young, rich to poor. Four hospital leaders comprising the main design team recruited clinical and frontline experts from throughout the hospital system for guidance as the project progressed.

Chicken Soup for the Techie

One big early assumption fell hard: The core team assumed that this sophisticated, "techie" clientele would appreciate interacting with a computer kiosk upon entering the hospital. A series of screens and prompts would lead patients through routine questions, register them and tell them where to go next. The kiosk had been imagined as a marquee feature, a real draw.

The community advisors panned the idea.

"When techies get sick, they don't want a computer screen," said John Milne, MD, vice president for Medical Affairs. "They prefer the chicken-soup approach, with a human being to welcome them and talk to them. We had to rethink the entrance."

Thus, although IT is part of the hospital environment now, at Issaquah, it is very much in the background.

"We do have creature comforts, like an impressive patient entertainment suite. But we leverage the serious medical technology behind the scenes," said Milne. "Especially at the entrance, we want our look to be more like a Ritz Carlton than a Microsoft store."

The Command Center

Behind the scenes, technology is centralized in the Command Center, located between the trauma center and the OR (Figure 10.1). All operations and facilities are located here, including bed assignment, telemetry, security, staff scheduling, and operations for disaster. Patient flow can be monitored in real time.

Figure 10.1   The inside: Command Center at Swedish Hospital, Issaquah. Adjacent rooms monitor telemetry units, bed assignment, patient flow, staffing, and more. Located between the OR and trauma center, the Command Center is equipped to handle events ranging from a routine day to major disaster. (Photo by Naida Grunden, with permission from Swedish Hospital.)

"These functions are typically scattered throughout the hospital," notes Milne. "Having them all here makes communication across disciplines a matter of course."

Unifying communications and eliminating silos of technology align with Lean values by reducing waste, rework, and handoffs.

University of Pittsburgh Medical Center: Lean Thinking and the "SmartRoom"

The SmartRoom is an example of advanced, behind-the-scenes technology that merges Lean concepts with timely data from the electronic medical record (EMR) to create hospital units that allow caregivers to deliver safer care. The technology, developed under the auspices of the UPMC Center for Quality Improvement and Innovation, provides caregivers with relevant information in real time, as well as instantaneous documentation—all in the course of work. This technology is noteworthy because it was developed from day 1 using Lean design principles.

Donald D. Wolff, Jr., Center for Quality Improvement and Innovation

The Quality Improvement and Innovation Center at the University of Pittsburgh Medical Center (UPMC) provides quality improvement leadership, education, and support to healthcare professionals across the multihospital system.

The center began piloting SmartRoom technology to bring information to the bedside in 2004. The technology was developed from day 1 using Lean concepts for process analysis, problem solving, and design.

When David Sharbaugh became a quality director at UPMC, a large Pittsburgh hospital system, he had already spent 3 years pioneering Lean healthcare with a local nonprofit organization. His breakthrough work applying Toyota-based principles and streamlining care at an ambulatory care center was amply documented.[3,4]

Not long after arriving at UPMC, the quality team was confronted with an investigation into an adverse event. A nurse wearing latex gloves drew blood from a patient with a known latex allergy, prompting a severe allergic reaction in that patient. How had the nurse missed this crucial piece of information?

The investigation revealed an all too common workaround. As a shortcut on a harried day, the nurse had skipped a step: logging on to a computer and checking pertinent information before drawing blood. Because she had violated standard procedure and, particularly, because it resulted in patient harm, the nurse was verbally disciplined. And with that, the case was closed.

"That bothered me," Sharbaugh said of that long-ago day. "Nothing about disciplining the nurse was going to prevent the same thing from happening on another floor, with another nurse, the next morning."

If the computer knew of the patient's latex allergy, why did the nurse not know? The person who needed that piece of information did not have it when it was needed.

"Toyota uses the saying, 'Don't separate information from the product it describes,'" said Sharbaugh. He remembered, at a Toyota assembly line, seeing tags with a picture of a snowman affixed to the cars that required air conditioning—a visual cue to the technicians to install that equipment on this car. The snowman tag never left the car; the information and the product were always together, with no gap in time or place.

Sharbaugh came to the startling conclusion that "looking stuff up on the computer to double check whether you have all the information you need" is 100% waste. "If our computer system knew, it was as though the organization knew—down to the computer cables. It's almost as if the walls know, but the nurses don't. Why does the nurse have to run and get it?" he wondered.

Sharbaugh and his team recognized that when staff members enter a patient room, the information they need depends on who they are. Nurses need one set of information (vitals, last medication given, etc.), while house-keepers need another (this patient has glasses, dentures, and hearing aids, so make sure that they do not end up in the trash or tangled in the linens), and physicians need still another (labs, medications, test results, radiology images).

How many times does a nurse or aide collect vitals on a patient and then rely on recall or a cheat sheet to enter the data in the health record later as time permits? Get the information here and use it there, later, with time and technology separating events. Batching this way creates a gap in time and place and, along with it, room for error that creeps in when people rely on memory.

The most common, preventable forms of patient harm in American hospitals are pressure ulcers, falls, and hospital-acquired infection. There were well known routines for preventing these problems. Could they be woven into the decidedly nonlinear course of a caregiver's work? Could those routines be made easy so as always to do right?

Is Technology Always the Answer?

During their months of observation, Sharbaugh and his team came to the conclusion that technology can create the environment for vastly safer practices—for example:

- EMRs can create a consistent way to document patient care and provide continuity from place to place (if each place uses the same type of EMR).
- Computerized physician order entry (CPOE) eliminates errors of handwriting interpretation and nonstandard abbreviations.
- Bar-code medication administration (BCMA; a bar-code scanner) creates a reliable way to make sure that the right patient receives the right drug at the right time.
- Pagers, voice-activated devices, and computers on wheels (COWs) are all intended to streamline some part of the workload.

Technology is supposed to make work easier for workers and safer for patients. But while there have been undeniable improvements in error rates with innovations like EMR, CPOE, and BCMA, it cannot be said that they have been silver bullets. A study from the U.S. Department of Veterans Affairs confirms that, in some cases, staff members work around the EMR, "cutting and pasting" from some prior encounter rather than documenting correctly in real time. Incongruities between types of EMR software also can create new types of error.[5,6]

Says author Orzen:

> EMRs can create data saturation distorting information. Their unnecessary complexity adds process time to sift through the data to find what is truly needed. Because it's a puzzle (or perhaps a mosaic) of data—everyone sees and interprets it slightly differently and uses it in different ways—the EMR can actually undermine standardized work because it encourages interpretation and subjective practices.

For all the wonders of the EMR, nurses and doctors can feel overwhelmed by the amount and display of information. In the vernacular, it is a case of "TMI," or too much information. Of the 76 lines in one EMR, for example, nurses said they really only routinely used half a dozen. The rest they deemed distracting clutter—waste.

Regarding those bar-code scanners, Jeff Fee, CEO of St. Patrick's Health Center in Montana, noted, "We in hospitals have been congratulating ourselves for adopting 1970s grocery store technology. We haven't started asking, 'Is BCMA really streamlining the work?'" Clever nurses have been observed working around the BCMA, defeating its cumbersome safety features in the interest of getting their jobs done.[7]

Watch how BCMA technology is typically used. The medication cart usually remains in the hall. The nurse enters the room and with a handheld scanner (like those used to scan prices in retail stores) scans the patient's wristband to verify his identity. The nurse then returns to the cart and scans each medicine to make sure that it is the drug intended for that patient. Perhaps a medication is not on the cart, but is kept in an automated dispensing machine down the hall. The nurse travels there. Perhaps the patient needs a narcotic for pain. This entails another trip to the locked narcotics cabinet. Sometimes, finding the key to the narcotics cabinet can result in more delay. At last, minutes later, the drugs are assembled, put into a cup, and brought to the patient. Has technology made the nurses' work easier or the patients safer? This is an open question.

Overlooked in the zeal to automate is the real-world process into which this technological marvel has been summarily dumped.

"Hospitals have spent millions on EMR technology, and we're still writing things on paper," said Sharbaugh. "We're concentrating on making clever devices rather than on understanding the work. We're missing an opportunity to design high reliability into the work flow while we're implementing new technologies."

Adding more electronic devices and things to carry that do not correspond or "talk" to one another can create more confusion, work, and opportunity for error (Figure 10.2). Even in very advanced hospital systems with advanced technology, observations across many hospitals reveal a consistent theme: Frontline healthcare workers are asked to keep track of and remember a nontrivial amount of information about their patients—information that the computer information system is better equipped to manage.

Despite major advances, the truly "paperless" environment for documentation has yet to be achieved (Figure 10.3). One Kaiser-Permanente study suggests that documentation still takes 35% of a nurse's time, while patient care activities take just 19%.[8]

Ideally, technology will free nurses to use their higher critical thinking skills and give them more time to communicate with their patients. The rote

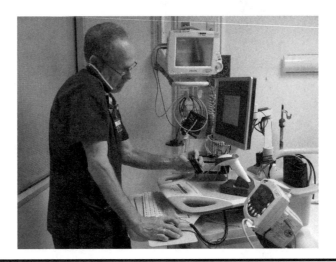

Figure 10.2 Technology is supposed to make work easier. Here, one nurse demonstrates why disjointed technology is no silver bullet. Not only is he "flooded" with information of questionable value, but also the ergonomics of the situation put him at risk of workplace injury. (Photo by Patrick R. Lee.)

"to do" lists and background information, such as latex allergies, current vital signs, I&O,[9] and so forth, would be available at all times. Perhaps more important, extraneous information would be removed.

Subtraction

In Sharbaugh's mind, the last thing that caregivers need is more work layered on with more electronic devices. In fact, he and his team decided to subtract distractions and extraneous bits from routine caregiving. Subtraction. In other words, waste reduction.

The goal was improved patient safety through Lean technological design of the patient room and the unit. The team would analyze work first and then help frontline workers design the Lean technology to support work flow, information, and documentation.

"We are finding ways to leverage technology to create a high-reliability organization," said Sharbaugh. "Getting things out of the way is the first step."

Activities: Prescribed, Derived, and in the Course of Work

Rule 1 of the Rules in Use (see Chapter 1) states that the activities of work shall be highly specified as to content, sequence, timing, and expected outcome.[10] In the constantly changing circumstances of healthcare, establishing that kind of order might seem nearly impossible.

Figure 10.3 Even "paperless" hospitals still rely on written records. (By permission, David Sharbaugh.)

Sharbaugh and his lead design nurse, Lucy Thompson, RN, who worked early on the SmartRoom design, began by analyzing the kinds of activities that caregivers are typically called upon to do. They classified them in three ways:

■ *Prescribed activities.* These are orders such as monitoring vital signs, specimen collection, or preparing the patient for a test.

■ *Derived activities.* All agree that routine tasks need to be done on time, every time; yet, they often fall notoriously through the cracks in a chaotic work environment. It may be time to reposition the patient to prevent skin breakdown. The patient's code status is not known. He or she needs a pain assessment, or pain medication is due, or the physician needs to be notified because the patient's condition is changing. It is time for hourly comfort rounds, when nurses and aides check to see if the patient needs water, blankets, or perhaps a trip to the bathroom. (Keeping unsteady patients from getting up by themselves is the best way to reduce falls.) A patient taking 10 medications or more should be considered for a bedside assessment by a pharmacist.

"Pressure ulcers, falls, medication errors, and gaps in dozens of routines cause patients a lot of suffering and cost hospitals an inordinate amount of money," said Sharbaugh. "We can make it easier to carry out important routines 100% of the time—right time, right place, right way."

■ *Activities built in the course of work.* Routines are far less likely to be overlooked when they are automated with thought, even when patient requests activate work such as filling water pitchers, adding blankets, or calling housekeeping for a cleanup. Staff members need to be able to document every task easily and quickly, at the point of work.

Defining "Ideal"

To define the "ideal" room meant flagging all three types of tasks for healthcare workers, making them hard to overlook and nearly effortless to document. Determining the "ideal" setup would mean identifying three dozen employee roles and discussing and thoughtfully considering the work activities in each role. What did they need to know and what did they need to share to provide the best and safest care customized to the needs of every patient? When and in what order should their tasks be done? How could they most easily be documented?

Nurses said that they always needed to know when the last medication pass had occurred, when the last pain medication had been given, when procedures were scheduled, and so on. Both nurses and aides wanted to know the schedules for routines like turning a patient or offering comfort rounds. Phlebotomists needed lab orders and allergy information. Housekeepers wanted a way to know when to clean a room. Dietitians wanted to know when to bring after-hours trays. And physicians needed many more details on demand from the EMR, in real time.

Of course, patients and families were consulted about what information they needed, how active a role they wanted in their care, and what other services they could use. Patients wanted to know who was entering their room. Was this the physician or the nurse, the aide or the housekeeper? With almost everyone dressed in scrubs, it was not always obvious. How in the world could the patient remember all those discharge orders and a whole new medication regime at home?

Using Lean principles, Sharbaugh and his team began to try to surround caregiver and patient with all the information they needed, exactly when they needed it. With Lean as the guide, the SmartRoom was born.

The Patient's Experience

SmartRooms do not seem exceptional at first. Patients may notice the large-screen TV monitors in their rooms—one for the patient and one for the caregiver (Figure 10.4). Every healthcare worker wears an ultrasound tag, the size

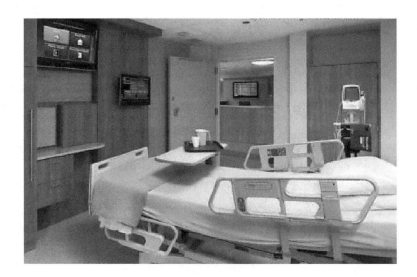

Figure 10.4 SmartRooms do not look much different from traditional rooms. (Courtesy UPMC.)

of a small pager, clipped to his or her identification badge; this activates sensing devices in the rooms. When the caregiver enters, his or her name and title appear in large letters on the screen. Patients immediately know whether this is a nurse, a physician, the physical therapist, or the housekeeper.

When the patient monitors the SmartRoom mode on the television, the message on the screen changes frequently, and includes the weather report, time of the next pain medication, names of the care team members, and so forth. Patient safety information also appears; for example, the screen may display a message that says, "Don't risk a fall. Please press your call button if you need to get out of bed."

Patient education modules feature prominently in the design, including information about the patient's diagnosis, upcoming tests, discharge, and recovery. Prompts at the end of the videos check for understanding and cue the caregivers if there are additional questions.

The Healthcare Worker's Experience

When a clinician is in the room, the monitor displays the "HIPAA screen," which includes the information on the patient's ID band (name, length of stay, allergies, age, gender, date of birth) plus safety information such as allergies and fall risk. From the cover screen, the clinician quickly brings up the customized screen. For example, the nurse screen includes the names of everyone on the medical team, the patient's emergency contact information and code status, oxygen levels, lab results, medications due or overdue, and whether the patient is allowed anything by mouth. Other screens contain lab orders and results, vitals, input and output, wheelchair status, and dietary requirements.

Physicians receive much of that information, plus the full list of medications, labs, and other desired information, through a feed from the EMR. They can access "bundles," or clusters of evidence-based activities known to improve outcomes.

Housekeepers, physical therapists, dietitians, and other workers have pop-up screens depicting all of and only the information that they need.

The system helps direct the flow of work on the unit and can even tell the worker which patient needs to be seen next and why. The object is to cut down on unnecessary travel and duplicate effort, while keeping care optimal.

Content, Sequence, Timing, and Expected Outcome

"The interface with the EMR is clever," said Sharbaugh. "The 'smart' part is orchestrating all the other things that need to happen."

SmartRoom technology greatly reduces reliance on fallible human memory. It remembers the routine that is due now in the right order, escalating tasks as they become due. It is a self-refreshing electronic checklist that, according to Sharbaugh, "takes a lot of the burden off the nurses' minds and builds high reliability in. It provides the 'how,' gives overtaxed brains a break, and makes it easy always to do the right thing at the right time."

If a patient needs to be turned every 2 hours, for example, the system activates a page for the nurse or aide who needs to do it and highlights it on an electronic white board, located at the nurses' station (Figure 10.5). Dozens of extraneous pager distractions—the bane of many a staff member's existence—are subtracted in this process.

While the IT wizards created the algorithms behind the task list and back-end analytics, the affected caregivers (nurses, doctors, therapists, housekeepers, and so on) designed the way that it should look and act up front. They used Lean process mapping to rank the tasks in each situation according to best practice, hospital policy, and experience.

One of the most significant bits of "subtraction" happens with documentation. Most routine tasks done for the patient are instantly recorded on the touch screen, in full view of the patient and family members. This enables the existing EMR to be "real time" because documentation is done in the course of work, at the bedside, with minimal keystrokes. Gone are the scraps of papers in nurses' pockets with last hour's vitals.

Figure 10.5   An electronic white board displays what nurses need to know. (Courtesy UPMC.)

This is rule 1 writ large: content, sequence, timing, and expected outcome of the work that needs to be done now.

Results to Date

The SmartRoom experiment picked up steam when UPMC decided to transition its South Side Hospital from an acute care to an ambulatory facility and clinic. Part of the transformation included creating a dozen-room simulation center for the UPMC Center for Quality Improvement and Innovation.

Currently, 130 beds at the urban UPMC Montefiore Hospital have been converted to SmartRoom technology. The rest of the building will be completed in the coming months and all 244 beds will have SmartRooms.

The team studied the ways in which 30 typical tasks were done in 10 rooms (Figure 10.6). Real-time charting in the SmartRoom reduced overall documentation time by 57% and vital sign documentation by 82%, as compared to batching the information and entering it at the end of the shift or charting it on a COW between patients.

The SmartRoom also produced a 69% reduction in time needed to document activities of daily living (ADLs). Waste reduction included:

■ There is zero documentation rework. Information in the EMR is always up-to-date.

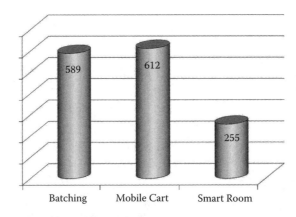

Figure 10.6 Real-time documentation (in seconds) took far less time than batching or running back and forth to the mobile cart. (Courtesy David Sharbaugh, UPMC.)

- Travel is reduced. Nurses walk 15% less per 12-hour shift, as measured by their pedometers.
- People do their assigned tasks appropriate to their skills.
- Patients receive routine care on schedule. Documentation for timely turning of patients to reduce pressure ulcers increased from 12% to 89%.

Follow-up surveys show that nurses are more satisfied and productive and have more time for patient care.

Says Sharbaugh:

> In medicine, there are always surprises. Let's let the surprises be hard. But let's make the routine things be easy. We know now that we can improve the quality of care by providing information directly to the bedside—where it's needed most—not to a computer in the hallway or to a workstation at the nursing desk. The less nurses have to focus on mundane, predictable tasks, the more they can focus on the human, compassionate side of patient care.

Summary

Two distinct approaches to information technology emerge in this chapter: (1) Seattle Children's Hospital, which prefers to use low-tech at every opportunity until the need and efficacy of a high-tech solution presents itself; and (2) the University of Pittsburgh Medical Center, which has devoted a research arm to developing better, more patient-centered software and using Lean concepts to design it.

Whether hospital leaders love technology or hate it, it is becoming part of healthcare, and as such it affects design and building of facilities. IT itself deserves careful design.

Discussion

- Is technology the answer? Why or why not? When and when not?
- How can technology selection affect the design of a new or remodeled facility?
- How can IT enhance the patient experience? The staff member experience? How can it degrade them?
- What advantages might there be to using Lean design concepts to develop software and IT solutions?
- When should hospitals use IT and when should they revert to "cans and strings"?

Suggested Reading

Bell, S., and Orzen, M. 2011. *Lean IT: Enabling and sustaining your lean transformation.* Boca Raton, FL: CRC Press.

Notes

1. Isaacson, W. 2011. *Steve Jobs.* New York: Simon and Schuster.
2. Bell, S., and Orzen, M. 2011. *Lean IT: Enabling and sustaining your lean transformation.* Boca Raton, FL: CRC Press.
3. Grunden, N. 2008. *The Pittsburgh way to efficient healthcare: Improving patient care using Toyota-based methods,* Chapter 3. New York: Productivity Press.
4. Spear, S. 2005. Fixing healthcare from the inside, today. *Harvard Business Review* 83 (9): 78–91, 158.
5. Hammond, K., Helbig, S., et al. 2003. Are electronic medical records trustworthy? Observations on copying, pasting and duplication. *American Medical Informatics Association Annual Symposium Proceedings,* 2003.
6. Koppel, R. 2011. EMR entry error: Not so benign. AHRQ M&M, April 2011. http://www.webmm.ahrq.gov/case.aspx?caseID=199 (accessed May 11, 2011).

7. DiConsiglio, J. 2008. Creative "work-arounds" defeat bar-coding safeguard for meds: Study finds technology often doesn't meet the needs of nurses. *Materials Management in Health Care* 17:26–29.

8. Hendrich, A., Chow, M., Skierczynski, B. A., and Zhenqiang, L. 2008. A 36-hospital time and motion study: How do medical-surgical nurses spend their time? *Permanente Journal* 12 (3): 25–34.

9. I&O refers to "input and output" of fluids that a patient is given.

10. Spear, S., and Bowen, H. K. 1999. Decoding the DNA of the Toyota production system. *Harvard Business Review* 77 (5): 97–106.

CONCLUSION AND RESOURCES

5

Chapter 11

Looking to the Future

Never before has the pressure to find innovation been greater in both construction and healthcare.

—Architect David F. Chambers
Efficient Healthcare: Overcoming Broken Paradigms[1]

Building a hospital may be one of the most complex tasks a society conducts.

"Well, okay," said one rogue physician, "maybe the space program is more complex. But, really, what is more complicated than a hospital?"

A hospital represents the confluence of two of society's most esteemed and advanced disciplines: the delivery of medical care to people and the design and construction of the building in which that care is delivered. For too long, the practice of architecture has been asked to proceed without crucial prerequisites: namely, the development of stable healthcare processes and the work flow that supports them.

"We need to understand processes and work flow so we learn what the architectural support should be, before we cast it in concrete," said David Munch, MD, a former hospital executive and chief clinical officer for a Lean healthcare practice.

The financial realities of the future tell us that healthcare cannot count on a steady or continuously increasing stream of money. In fact, the advent of accountable care organizations invites us to look differently at the way we deliver care—as a continuum instead of a batch of discrete services. Uncertainties abound with Medicare and declining compensation. Changing federal and state programs will continue to upend the payment system.

On top of that, the practice of medicine itself is morphing. Lines are blurring between inpatient and outpatient care; between the services of physicians and physician extenders, like nurse practitioners, physician assistants, and even pharmacists. New medicines for diseases like cancer and AIDS are blurring the lines between critical and chronic care. Public attention is slowly returning to the prevention of disease, rather than solely its treatment. The continuing information technology revolution is extending the reach of critical care specialists, blurring the line between urban and rural, crossing international boundaries. Change is the "new normal."

In the face of this new reality, hospitals cannot afford to build one square foot that is not needed or will not be used, remodel a dysfunctional space that was added just a couple of years ago, or take on large amounts of new debt. Then where will the money come from for needed extensions and renovations to the nation's 5,000+ hospitals?

It will have to come from the extraction of waste from the current systems of healthcare and design–bid–build.

"There is enough money in the American healthcare system right now to fund basic healthcare for every man, woman and child in the country," said former Treasury Secretary Paul O'Neill. "We need to wring the waste out of the system to find it."

We know that lack of stable, standard processes creates vast amounts of waste and harm in healthcare that can be alleviated through the discipline and leadership of Lean. We know that hospitals can be built faster, better, and less expensively when disciplines collaborate, such as when integrated project delivery works well.

How can the hospital of the future thrive? Patient experience will govern healthcare; any effort that does not speed the patient back to health will be recognized as waste. The hospital will use 100% of its space, 24 hours a day. It will be smaller. Spaces will flex among services. Processes will remain nimble and continuously improve. Costs and time lines for design, construction, and operation will decline precipitously. Collaboration between frontline healthcare workers, hospital executives, architects, and construction experts will be established from day 1 of any construction project, and it will remain vigorous through move-in. No longer a "fashion statement," Lean process thinking will be interwoven into every aspect of work, a prerequisite to excellence.

One hospital in the South undertook the Lean-led design of its new bed tower. Lean as a wall-to-wall process improvement strategy was in its infancy, and it was hoped that the new bed tower would accelerate the Lean effort across the organization, as well as attract more clients.

The collaboration was fabulous. Architects and frontline staff worked together to describe processes in a way that had not been done before. The design included point-of-service closets in alcoves leading to each room, along with small computer stations. Lines of sight to the patient were maintained. Bathrooms were on the headwall, so patients never crossed the floor without a handrail. Infection-control practitioners and housekeepers were delighted with the seamless, floor-to-ceiling sink modules in each room that were easy to clean. Leaders were thrilled with the process improvements revealed at every step, along with the utility of the design. Design was driving a culture shift in the right direction. Move-in was just around the corner.

Then the unthinkable happened.

In a one–two punch, the hospital declared bankruptcy and the CEO resigned. A new leader came in to straighten things out. The first casualty was the Lean initiative, which, by then, was considered unnecessary fluff.

When move-in day came, the point-of-use closets were filled with ad hoc supplies, linens, and things. There was no 5S or visual management or kanban replenishment system. In fact, complaints arose from the environmental service staff about the burden of having so many closets to fill. There was no system for it.

"Organizations don't adopt Lean in an all-out, system-wide way just because it's a good idea," said architect David Chambers. "They do it because they have to. American healthcare is on a burning platform. Lean will become a way of life when people finally smell smoke."

Within a year, the next turnaround expert was installed as CEO at this hospital, and this one knew the potential of Lean. She recognized the careful design that had been put in place in the new bed tower to support Lean process improvements. Under her thoughtful direction, with medical staff championing the work and the entire staff engaged, hospital performance improved and the bed tower began to reach its full potential.

Even the most beautiful Lean-led design and even the most penetrating process improvements are only as good as the leadership that guides and reinforces them. Lean is perishable; leadership is the key.

How big a leap of faith is this new way of Lean thinking? How can leaders, with so much at stake, trust that this new and different way will work?

We hope that the robust case studies shown in this book demonstrate that massive savings, better facilities, and continuously improving processes are possible. The Lean hospital is not a building, but rather a state of mind that constantly reduces waste and increases value.

Can we afford to try? We cannot afford not to.

Note

1. © David Chambers, 2011.

Appendix A: A Little History

Hospitals acquire their own identities, reinforced by architectural features and interior furnishings. Each composite personality, moreover, rests in great measure on traditions and staff behavior.

—Guenter B. Risse
Mending Bodies, Saving Souls: A History of Hospitals

Introduction

This book is about the way in which hospitals could be built in the future. It is a more complicated subject than it may seem because the hospital—as a place and as an institution—interweaves so many strands of American life.

First and foremost, hospitals are places of healing, where the heroes of healthcare perform daily miracles in their attempts to restore their fellow citizens to health, in an often chaotic environment. But hospitals are also institutions where civic pride, medical advances, social expectations, legislative requirements, and business trends intersect and, sometimes, collide.

Now, against this complex backdrop, hospital leaders and architects must find a way to house both the functions and ideals of "hospital" in a new building, wing, or unit; find a way to make the form enhance the function; and find a way to make the building relevant for future decades, where unknowable changes lurk. Above all, the challenge is to find a way, through design, to show respect for patients and staff, the community served, historical preservation, sustainable materials, and the incorporation of nature in the healing environment.

Perhaps before some new ways to think about the future of hospital architecture are proposed, a brief look at its history is in order. Two fine volumes have served as the framework for this appendix: *Healthcare*

Architecture in an era of Radical Transformation by Stephen Verderber and David Fine (2000)[1] and *Innovations in Hospital Architecture* by Stephen Verderber (2010).[2] This appendix cannot do justice to their in-depth inquiry; rather, the following thumbnail sketch of the history of hospital architecture is meant to provide a backdrop for discussion.

Early History

The Ancients[3]

From earliest recorded history, societies have devised places to care for the sick and dying:

- Neolithic drawings show that sick and dying people were segregated in special caves, where caregivers came and went.
- The Chinese cared for their ill family members in their multigenerational homes.
- In Europe, the poor and indigent were cared for in sick houses or death houses.
- Institutions for the sick emerged comparatively early in Iraq, Iran, Egypt, and Turkey, with separate quarters for men and women and a central prayer center.

Middle Ages

After the fall of Rome in the fourth century, the Catholic Church filled the role in healthcare, extending across Europe through the late fourteenth century. These were horrific times, typified by the bubonic plague, which swept across the continent and decimated whole communities. The charitable work of caring for the sick fell to the monasteries.

Patients were treated in large, open wards, where they heard mass each day, since faith remained the main healthcare offering. Inquiry about other causes of disease, along with considerations like light, ventilation, cleanliness, and view, fell by the wayside.

Two European developments in the Middle Ages might strike modern sensibilities as "progressive": hospices as compassionate places for the dying and environmental sustainability. Inside the walled compounds, people had to grow what they ate and make what they used. Some places devoted thousands of acres to agriculture and livestock.

Comparatively speaking, facilities in the Middle East advanced more quickly during the Middle Ages. By the eighth century AD in Iraq, free public infirmaries stood adjacent to every mosque. Cairo had a relatively luxurious, 100-patient "teaching" hospital (with a school attached) with an ophthalmology department, pharmacy, library, and mosque. These facilities were prominent structures, meant to be noticed and integrated as part of the larger community.

Renaissance

The Renaissance renewed scientific inquiry into human anatomy and the origin of disease. The discovery that the heart pumped blood, for example, gave rise to the idea of interdependent organ systems within the body. The fifteenth century invention of the printing press ensured wide dissemination of these findings. Renaissance hospitals included daylight, fresh air, fireplaces, and gardens.

Florence Nightingale Movement: 1860–WWII

In London in 1860, Florence Nightingale established one of the first secular nursing schools in the world.[5] In addition to her revolutionizing the role of the nurse as a medical professional, Nightingale's profound influence on hospital architecture can still be felt. She favored large, open wards, with two or three dozen beds and access to fresh air, water, daylight, and excellent sanitation.

Semmelweiss, Pasteur, and Lister all promoted the germ theory, which held that microscopic organisms caused disease, but its acceptance was slow. The prevailing idea held that "miasma," or bad air, caused disease. And although Nightingale held to the miasma theory, she still insisted on sanitary techniques and conditions in medical facilities. Nightingale's work led to several principles of modern hospital planning that are still relevant:

> [She] emphasized function above form some two decades before the phrase "form follows function" was coined by Chicago architect Louis Sullivan to epitomize the new epoch of modern architecture…[and] developed guidelines on width and length of a ward, size of windows and their placement, overall ambiance, ventilation and heating, use of bright white walls and polished hardwood floors.[1]

Figure A.1 The barracks hospital at Scutari during the Crimean War (1853–1856).
Florence Nightingale's design and sanitary practices revolutionized healthcare. Note
access to air and light in this multiple-bed ward—attributes today noted as "evidence-
based design." (Getty Images.)

Nightingale devised the long, straight ward, with a supply spine for efficient circulation of people and supplies. Early VA hospitals in the United States were designed this way.

Lack of sanitation in urban environments from London, England, to Memphis, Tennessee, led to outbreaks of diseases, including yellow fever, malaria, typhoid, and cholera.[6] The health emphasis on pure air and water led to increasing popularity of health spas and mineral baths. Tuberculosis sanitariums also emerged as healing natural havens. The spa movement for the masses ended during the Depression, as the economy declined and public health and sanitation improved. Elite sports medicine retreats and resort spas are today's descendants of those early spas.

An American Chronology

The rest of this appendix describes events within the United States. Of necessity, the highlights here are compact and summarized.[7]

1900–1940

With the acceptance of germ theory, the practice of surgery increased. The invention of x-rays as diagnostic tools created the need for higher skills and specialized hospital space. The radiology department had arrived—the first of many departments.

1900–1940 Snapshot

- Legislative
  - The Flexner Report issued and has far-reaching impact on medical schooling.
- Social
  - Racial and ethnic segregation exists.
- Medical
  - Marie Curie discovers radium.
  - Roentgen discovers x-rays.
  - First successful blood transfusion occurs.
  - Early electrocardiograph is made.
  - Vitamins are understood.
  - Role of insulin is understood.
  - Vaccines for diphtheria, pertussis, tetanus, tuberculosis, and yellow fever are developed.
  - Alexander Fleming discovers penicillin.
- Architectural
  - Ochsner proposes first high-rise hospital.
- The single-bed ward is introduced in the United States, but rejected in Europe.

Legislation

A survey of American medical schools by Abraham Flexner found them far below European standards. Many were little more than 2-year trade schools, their quality especially poor when compared against the best performers such as Johns Hopkins. As a result of the Flexner Report, medical school standards were established that remain relevant today. In the first three decades of the twentieth century, about half of American medical schools were closed.[8] In their place emerged postgraduate medical education and specialization.

Social Backdrop

Religious communities exerted their influence. Catholic hospitals, with their deep roots in charity for the sick, had been operating in America since about 1663.[9] Priests and nuns played heroic and pivotal roles in healthcare crises, such as cholera outbreaks[10] and the Memphis yellow fever epidemic of 1878.[11]

Between 1850 and 1950, Jewish communities across the country found their sick and indigent denied treatment in local hospitals and their physicians denied the right to practice. Jewish groups in 24 cities eventually founded their own acute-care hospitals. "These institutions were often the local Jewish community's most visible and impressive charitable enterprise."[12] In addition to providing care for members of their communities, Jewish hospitals opened their doors to others, seeking to combat stereotypes and increase acceptance.

Likewise, hospitals for African Americans were segregated, and black physicians were denied privileges. Several hospitals were established by whites to serve blacks as early as the 1890s. In the 1920s, the National Hospital Association was formed to ensure proper standards in black hospitals. Black-founded hospitals, like Homer G. Phillips in St. Louis, which opened in 1937, helped train black physicians. The Veterans Administration did not desegregate its wards until after the Second World War.[13]

Architecture

Advances in structural engineering and materials had begun to make the skyscraper feasible in space-constrained American cities. The first high-rise urban hospital was proposed in 1905 by Chicago surgeon Albert Ochsner. In proposing this 5-acre, 500-bed, 10-story concept, with a Nightingale ward on each floor, he anticipated improved efficiency in "space, heating, supervision, housekeeping, materials management, and staff travel distances."[2] Hospitals built today usually seek to maximize these very things.

In 1913, architects John A. Hornsby and Richard E. Schmidt recommended several stock footprints for American hospitals.[14] They advocated more single rooms and wards of between three and ten beds, rather than the European model, which kept the larger Nightingale ward.

After World War II, the United States moved away from large wards toward two-, four-, or six-bed rooms and since has moved to a standard of all-private rooms.[15] In Europe, however, planners still favor a block plan with a mix of one-, two-, and four-bed rooms.

Early multistoried urban hospitals adopted innovations like central air conditioning systems, which emerged in the 1920s, along with specialized departments and equipment to serve a growing population. Most of the skyscraper hospitals built between 1910 and 1940 are gone now, leaving many wondering whether demolition or preservation and repurposing would be the better way to deal with the rest.

1940s

Legislation

With the passage of the landmark Hospital Survey and Construction Act (Hill–Burton Act) of 1946, the federal government funded the building of hospitals to improve access to healthcare in rural and poor areas. Coinciding with the end of World War II, it also helped to accommodate returning GIs.

1940s Snapshot

- Legislative
  - The Hospital Survey and Construction Act (Hill–Burton Act) of 1946 is passed during the Truman administration.
- Social
  - World War II ends and GIs return. A building boom includes utilitarian hospitals. The New Deal era ends and the urban renewal era begins.
- Medical
  - Streptomycin is discovered and used to treat tuberculosis.
  - Penicillin is mass produced.
  - Blood and plasma become more available.
  - The Framingham Study of 28,000 subjects begins (and continues today).
  - It is discovered that some cancers (prostate, breast) are influenced by hormones.
  - The first heart–lung machine is developed.
  - The first linear accelerator is produced.
- Architectural
  - The megahospital becomes the center of the community.
- Reliance on machinery and specialization increases.

The idea behind the legislation was to create a "matrix of care," with a teaching hospital at the core for the critically ill and circles of community clinics radiating out into rural areas, providing public health, preventive care, and mental health services. Ultimately, Hill-Burton included facilities for the urban poor as well.

Hill–Burton marked the last extension of New Deal legislation of the 1930s. The funding of strictly utilitarian hospital buildings was the federal healthcare legislation of its time. The result was a hospital building boom that lasted 40 years.

Social Backdrop

World War II was fought and ended in this decade. As with wars past, hard-won medical advances were brought back from the battlefield—breakthroughs like antibiotic therapy, a better understanding of blood transfusions, and technological advances in radiology and other disciplines. This new knowledge would now enter mainstream medicine.

Architecture

Hill–Burton sought to set minimum standards of care by creating preset floor plans. Initially, those included rooms on both sides of long corridors with nursing stations at the end. They even suggested layouts for diagnostic and treatment areas and patient rooms.

Most of the new hospital buildings were of a utilitarian, minimalist style called the international style. At the time, that futuristic style seemed to reflect the new kind of medicine being practiced inside. These hospitals grew over time into megahospitals and became sources of community pride.

As they grew bigger, hospitals also grew more specialized, housing new departments with distinct identities. Each zone required "unique functional planning—diagnosis, imaging, treatment, surgery, meal preparation, administration and support functions."[2] In other words, hospitals began to fracture into functional silos.

Built in blocks, the megahospitals largely ignored Nightingale's guidelines. Long corridors and windowless rooms, with sealed HVAC systems, dominated the plans. "Efficiency" meant creating a hospital that would require fewer employees. The emphasis began to shift toward machinery and medical wizardry, and away from the patient's experience. Patients began to feel that the practice of medicine centered more around the machines and less around them.

1950s

Legislation

The Hill–Burton Act began to fund nursing homes and rehabilitation centers.

Social Backdrop

New Hill–Burton funding for hospitals in poor urban areas coincided with urban renewal, an experiment that reconstructed the urban cores of cities in an attempt to eradicate slums, replace them with safer and more attractive high-rise, low-income housing, and attract new development and business to the city center. But the architecture for replacement housing was drab and monotonous, involving blocks of boxy high-rises with patches of green in between.[16]

1950s Snapshot

- Legislative
  - The Hill–Burton Act expands to include nursing home and rehabilitation centers during the Eisenhower administration.
- Social
  - Urban renewal begins in earnest. City cores are transformed. Hill–Burton finances hospitals for the urban poor.
- Medical
  - DNA is discovered.
  - More antibiotics are synthesized.
  - Shock is used to restart the heart of a patient in cardiac arrest.
  - Open-heart surgery takes place; the pacemaker is developed.
  - A vaccine for polio is produced.
  - The first artificial hip replacement is performed.
  - Coronary angiography is developed.
- Architectural
  - The megahospital remains the center of the community.
  - "International style" deemphasizes nature, views, etc.
- Bigger is better. Continuous building is seen as a sign of fiscal health.

While some urban renewal projects met with success, many met with unintended consequences. Fracturing neighborhoods, relocating businesses, and demolishing old structures decimated inner cities' sense of identity. The new development did not necessarily attract the desired business. Urban renewal did not consider land use and environmental consequences. The mass relocation resulted in what later would be called "suburban sprawl" as developers moved away from the city core. Transportation and traffic problems resulted.

Architecture

Urban renewal also meant the demolition of many old, inner-city hospitals, ostensibly to make way for new ones. "The loss of a hospital to city core was like the loss of a beloved church or other institution. The fabric of inner city neighborhoods was decimated."[2]

When plans came through with new, state-of-the-art hospitals in the urban core, they tended toward sterile, "modern" architecture. The reconstituted neighborhoods in the area did not feel the same type of ownership toward these hospitals.

With suburban sprawl came the suburban hospital, where the formula for community success, vitality and pride came to be equated with constant hospital expansion. Bigger was definitely better. Growth was a responsibility.

1960s

Legislation

The Hill–Burton Act came to its sunset during the 1960s. In 1965, Lyndon Johnson signed two amendments to the Social Security Act, creating Medicare (Title XVIII) and Medicaid (Title XIX). With the passage of these amendments, the federal government moved away from funding construction and into funding health programs. Medicare and Medicaid were conceived as small programs that would keep seniors and poor people from being ruined financially due to medical costs. Since then, costs for these programs have grown to the point of concern.[17]

Social Backdrop

Social upheaval in the 1960s gave rise to a reexamination of societal assumptions, such as the rights of minorities and women, and concerns about the environment, social awareness, education, and the role of the military. "The Great Society" antipoverty program competed for funding with the Vietnam conflict.

1960s Snapshot

- Legislative
  - The Hill–Burton Act sunsets.
  - The 1965 Social Security Amendments create Medicare and Medicaid during the Johnson administration.
- Social
  - Upheaval and protest accompany involvement in Vietnam. "Great Society" programs seek to eliminate poverty. There is new awareness of environment, equality, and patient rights.
- Medical
  - The first human heart, lung, and liver transplants are made.
  - An intra-aortic balloon procedure is developed.
  - Coronary artery bypass graft surgery takes place.
  - Oral contraceptives become widely available.
  - Chemotherapy for cancer treatment becomes more available.
- Architectural
  - There is a turning against the megahospital and toward residential design.
  - The racetrack plan with its variants is developed.
- Hospitals continually add or renovate space.

New attitudes led to a rejection of urban renewal and an acknowledgment that social and environmental sciences would need to be considered in future design and building. The era of the sterile-looking megahospital would, in coming decades, give way to more "human-scaled" buildings that resembled residences more than institutions. Likewise, the semiprivate and private room would supplant open wards.

Architecture

Hospitals still built large and added on. But architects experimented with several variants on the sterile international style, with pinwheels, triangles, and sawtooth-shaped units opening to a central core. Consideration was once again given to views from the patient rooms.

During this time, the "racetrack" plan appeared. Rather than having one long corridor with rooms on either side and a nursing station at the end of the hall, the racetrack model widened the hall and placed nursing and support functions in the center. In this model, all rooms opened toward the nursing station. The addition of equipment tended to expand the length of the core, increasing nurse travel. Nevertheless, the racetrack model became a standard. "A criterion dating from the earliest cross-ward monastic hospitals of the Middle Ages continued to exert an influence on the modern hospital: the need to control the largest number of patients with the fewest number of staff."[2]

The 1960s saw the founding of the first two for-profit hospital ventures: Hospital Corporation of America (HCA) and Humana. Viewed at first with distrust, these corporate hospitals gained acceptance by building in underserved areas, mainly in the South, and by working with other local hospitals so that they would not duplicate services. They also spurred breakthroughs in:

> ...management and staff efficiency, new construction techniques such as fast-tracking, innovations in equipment design in cooperation with equipment suppliers, construction management and lower-cost product to the patient as a result of their national scope as purchasers and sellers of services. This translated into standardized construction and operating methods, and mass purchasing.[2]

The hospital was firmly entrenched as the central institution of American healthcare. By the end of the decade, hospitals were expanding into "health systems," serving entire regions instead of individual neighborhoods. Duplication of services and machinery was not yet considered.

1970s

Legislation

Two consequential health bills passed during the Nixon administration:

■ The Health Maintenance Organization Act of 1973 proposed that employers with 25 or more employees must offer a health maintenance organization (HMO) as an insurance option.
■ The Health Planning and Resources Development Act of 1974 required certificates of need for hospital construction.

1970s Snapshot

- Legislative
  - The Health Maintenance Organization Act of 1973 and the Health Planning and Resources Development Act of 1974 are passed during the Nixon administration.
- Social
  - There is a move to patient-centered care, as seen in the Planetree movement. Natural childbirth and hospice movements gain acceptance.
- Medical
  - CAT and PET scanners are introduced.
  - The first baby is born using in vitro fertilization.
  - Vaccines are developed for rubella, chicken pox, pneumonia, and meningitis.
  - Smallpox is declared eradicated worldwide.
  - Oncogene is discovered.
  - l-Dopa relieves Parkinson's symptoms.
- Architectural
  - The hospital building boom ends; the rise of the master plan begins.
- Investor-owned hospitals and managed care lead to attempts to make hospitals less barren and more appealing and home-like.

Social Backdrop

The sometimes raucous social inquiry of the 1960s ultimately won acknowledgment of the rights of minorities and women, and consideration of the environment. Two important movements—hospice and natural childbirth—heralded a shift in medical care from provider centered to patient centered. Rather than passive recipients of care, patients would increasingly become partners. "Antihospitalism" caused patients to seek alternatives; hospitals would seek to address the need.

During this decade, a new trend called for the release of many mental patients from institutions, stemming from the belief that many patients had been diagnosed inappropriately and merely warehoused and could be cared for adequately in the community.[18] Community-based clinics increased in importance. Medical care became decentralized, with the hospital focus shifting toward care of the critically ill. The emergence of technology, such as computerized axial tomography (CAT) scans, sealed the American hospital's reputation as the high-tech medical delivery center.

Architecture

Push-back from consumers in the form of the hospice and natural childbirth movements, the emergence of corporate hospitals and managed care, and the end of Hill–Burton funding led hospitals to look for ways to humanize the dull, intimidating high-tech hospital. Constant building and remodeling had left many megahospitals disfigured and less than functional, even as they continued to add space and equipment. For patients and practitioners alike, finding the way in these facilities became difficult and stressful. Even boldly colored floor stripes, in the end, were not always the best answer. "Critics of the modern hospital claimed that more than 40 percent of the U.S. health budget went toward sophisticated but not always useful diagnostic and treatment procedures, and to the construction of complex clinical spaces for an ever-expanding battery of machines."[2]

Constructed in 1980, 1,000-bed VA hospitals in Houston and Los Angeles, portended the end of the megahospital and a move toward more human-scaled, "residentialist" design. The megahospital would diminish in dominance. Community-based services, accessible to more people, would emerge in its place.

Without Hill–Burton's funding stream, hospitals needed to take a much longer view in prioritizing changes and sequencing improvements to their buildings. The 1970s saw the rise of the master plan, a way to look long term at building priorities and budgets. (See Chapter 2 for a fuller discussion.)

Hospital designers and equipment manufacturers looked at ways to make space more flexible over time, reducing the difficulty and expense of remodeling. Modular furnishings and equipment emerged as a new option during this time.

Wealthy communities set different standards for the well insured. In Palm Desert, California, the Eisenhower Memorial Hospital featured a soaring atrium, a pool and sauna, excellent food, and single rooms with upscale, home-like furnishings. "These were the vanguards in a movement toward the lavish home or resort-type hospital, and it set off a trend that would continue for another 20 years."[2]

1980s

Legislation

The 1983 Tax Equity and Fiscal Responsibility Act (TEFRA), passed during the Reagan administration, created diagnosis-related groups (DRGs)—a way of grouping patients (and paying medical providers) by type and severity of illness. The idea was to cap prices in categories of care. The effect was to reduce patients' length of stay.

1980s Snapshot

- ■ Legislative
  - – The 1983 Tax Equity and Fiscal Responsibility Act (TEFRA) is passed during the Reagan administration, as is the 1986 Emergency Medical Treatment and Labor Act (EMTALA).
- ■ Social
  - – Urban renewal ends and social programming is reduced. There is a move to control healthcare costs by establishing diagnosis-related groups. Deregulation and competition mean an end to certificates of need. Hospital mergers begin.
- ■ Medical
  - – The first MRI scanner is developed.
  - – The AIDS/HIV epidemic begins.
  - – Antibody testing and the first antiretroviral drugs are developed.
  - – Vaccines for hepatitis A and B and leprosy are produced.
  - – Bedside computerization begins.
  - – Cardiac stents keep vessels open after angioplasty.
- ■ Architectural
  - – The "residentialist" movement begins in earnest.
  - – There is a more "human" scale to hospitals; they are not so large and imposing.
  - – The atrium is used as a welcoming area.
  - – A healing environment, not machinery, is now the marquee.
- ■ IT is first used at bedside.

TEFRA also repealed the federal requirement for a certificate of need (CON), deregulating the building of hospitals and relying on the free market to right-size supply. (Certain states still require CONs.)

The 1986 Emergency Medical Treatment and Labor Act (EMTALA), the "anti-patient-dumping law," gave every person in the United States the right to emergency medical care. Emergency rooms could no longer refuse or reroute uninsured or indigent people. This was an unfunded mandate.

Social Backdrop

In her seminal 1979 essay, "How Modern Hospitals Got That Way," University of California, Berkeley, architecture professor Roslyn Lindheim summarized the quandary of the hospital:

> Indeed a look at the modern hospital speaks not of human healing, but of awe of technological process, not of caring but of increase in the GNP, not of generating health but of saving jobs and institutions...the paramount architectural issue was not the most caring way to accommodate the needs of the sick but how to build flexible forms to house constantly changing medical technology...
> With the advent of Medicare and Medicaid in 1965, reimbursement rates favored development of increasingly more complicated treatments and institutions to house them. Studies preceding the Hill–Burton legislation had anticipated and recommended decentralized medical care in a so-called "coordinated hospital system." Ideally, there would be one large, central hospital and teaching center, several secondary district hospitals, and many small neighborhood clinics providing people with primary care near their homes. Instead, in larger cities, medical facilities began to cluster around more expensive, complex services, and we began to have "Pill Hills" depleting the rest of the city and the outlying areas of available medical care...the larger, more technological hospitals absorbed the smaller ones and resulted in institutions of enormous size, confusion and complexity."[19]

With the advent of the AIDS epidemic, calls grew louder for more humane, local treatment for all people suffering from serious or terminal illness. Planetree, founded in San Francisco, advanced a more patient- and consumer-driven approach and a demand for practitioners and hospital leaders to acknowledge the voice of the patient. The patient's state of mind, formerly ignored in the field of hospital architecture, regained importance.

Architecture

The era of postmodernism had arrived, bringing a more understated approach to hospitals. The buildings were smaller, "human scale," with a more friendly appearance that was less intimidating to patients. Back came Nightingale's healing environment—light, nature, color, air, and water—shifting away from the emphasis on high-tech machinery.

The new, friendlier hospital appealed not only to patients and staff members, but also to hospital business planners. As investor-owned hospitals expanded and hospitals began merging, attractive architecture became a competitive advantage.

The extremes of the decade were exemplified in the soaring atrium. For many older hospitals, creating an atrium in the middle of disparate, built-on wings of a hospital provided unity and direction. Atria provide people with views of where they needed to go and make it easy to find the cafeteria and gift shop. Atria made hospitals seem more hospitable, like hotel lobbies or shopping malls. (Indeed, the Swedish Hospital and Medical Office Building in affluent Issaquah, Washington, which opened in late 2011, features a four-story atrium complete with retail spaces, high-end coffee shop, grand piano, five-star restaurant, day care, a yoga center, and a desk for the healthcare concierge. The idea is for this lobby to be a community wellness center.)

In trying to rein in costs by creating DRGs, the TEFRA act created another consequence: reducing the amount of time patients spent in the hospital. Reducing length of stay (LOS) meant that more people would be treated as outpatients. Outpatient surgery units, MRI and mammography clinics, and birthing centers proliferated. Suddenly, smaller was better. Care that had been given only in hospitals before was now given in other facilities, and patients who needed admission to the hospital were sicker than before.

The first serious information technology (IT) applications for healthcare also arose at this time, heralding a profound change in the way in which records would be kept. Systems that could document care at the bedside came into use at the end of the decade.

Caring for sicker patients required more room. As hospitals moved from general care toward critical care centers, room sizes grew nearly 25% to accommodate movement of equipment into and out of the room. This way, regular med-surg rooms could double as critical care rooms if the need arose. The acuity-adaptable room, or universal care unit, minimized patient transfers and, in most cases, made safety sense.

As funding shrank, flexible design became more important. Hospitals were now being designed to be rearranged, expanded, or remodeled as new technologies arrived. Architects looked at new ways to "shell" spaces or create logical ways for expansion to occur in the future.

1990s

Legislation

Addressing privacy concerns attendant with the rise of electronic information technology, the Health Insurance Portability and Accountability Act (HIPAA) of 1996, passed under the Clinton administration, sought to protect private health information and give patients the right to direct its use.

1990s Snapshot

- Legislative
  - The Health Insurance Portability and Accountability Act (HIPAA) of 1996 is passed during the Clinton administration.
- Social
  - The Internet begins to put more information in consumers' hands—including healthcare consumers. Healthcare IT increases. The era of patient as partner rather than passive recipient has begun.
- Medical
  - The Human Genome Project is created.
  - Gene therapy for cancer is developed.
  - The first animal is cloned.
  - A vaccine to treat Lyme disease is produced.
- Architectural
  - Functional deconstruction looks at each component, each service, and each site.
  - There is a reappraisal of "mother ship" hospital and community hospitals and the services in each.
  - Ambulatory surgicenters and hospitals as critical care centers are on the rise.
  - Evidence-based design looks at what makes the patient experience easier.

Social Backdrop

In its seminal 1999 report, *To Err Is Human,* the Institute of Medicine placed the number of deaths from medical error at 100,000 Americans. Subsequent data from the Centers for Disease Control and Prevention (CDC) indicated that another 100,000 Americans also die each year from infections they contract while in the hospital,[20] making them the fourth leading cause of death, behind heart disease, cancer, and stroke. The ensuing uproar kicked off a national patient safety movement, which intensified over the succeeding decade.

Architecture

By financial necessity, fewer hospitals were built from the ground up. Restructuring and remodeling provided a way for hospitals to modernize, humanize, and make way for new equipment.

The exception was the stand-alone specialty center, such as the surgicenter, imaging center, sports medicine facility, and others. With these services now disseminated out into the community, fewer people had reason to get their care at the hospital "mother ship." Smaller, decentralized facilities actually aligned with Hill–Burton as originally envisioned.

Traditional hospitals provided mainly acute care in what were now large, awkward, overbuilt facilities. Mergers and acquisitions began—by one count, over 1,300 of them from 1989 to 1993, with many more since.[2]

Every aspect of caregiving was dissected during this time of "functional deconstruction." Architects and planners looked at moving more services into the community, downsizing and reconstituting the "mother ship" hospital, and at every aspect of care to determine how to provide it in the best, most cost-effective way. Hospitals looked at pooling resources and technologies and managing ever increasing volumes of health information. Strategic plans were done regionally; for example, if the region already had three cardiac care units, did it need one more? Functional deconstruction, in essence, accomplished much of what had been intended with CON legislation by streamlining offerings, lowering costs, and reducing redundancy.

"Residentialism"—finding ways to make the hospital room more homelike, through the use of natural materials, increased privacy, and reduced noise—became the dominant theme. Research emerged on "evidence-based design," which developed data to show that considerations on things like one's way in the hospital, privacy, noise, sanitation, fresh air, and a view of nature (many ideas in line with Nightingale's original recommendations), did indeed help reduce patient stress and improve healing. Ultimately, the evidence would also show cost savings.[21]

2000s

Legislation

The Patient Protection and Affordable Care Act of 2010, passed during the Obama administration, makes health coverage available to more Americans and creates "accountable care organizations" (see Chapter 1) to integrate care given for Medicare recipients as a way to reduce costs. It also mandates greater use of electronic medical records.

2000s Snapshot

■ Legislative
  – Patient Protection and Affordable Care Act of 2010 is passed during the Obama administration.
■ Social
  – Patient safety becomes a movement, with disclosures that 100,000 Americans die each year from medical error and another 100,000 from hospital-acquired infection. Patients move to become informed partners in their care.
■ Medical
  – The human genome is sequenced.
  – Stem cell research advances.
  – The first robot-assisted laparoscopic surgery takes place.
  – HPV and shingles vaccines are developed.
■ Architectural
  – "Green" building gains acceptance with LEED certification.
  – AIA, a self-assembled, nongovernmental group of architects, recommends single-patient room as "standard."
  – "Lean" healthcare shows that detailed process design can produce more useful and safer hospitals.
  – Conservation and reuse of historic hospitals is desirable.
■ Remote access and telemedicine are developed.

Social Backdrop

Patient safety entered the public lexicon and became a movement. Stories of death in the finest American hospitals began to appear in newspapers and the public consciousness—stories like the death of the toddler, Josie King, of dehydration at Johns Hopkins[22]; of reporter Betsy Lehman of a medication error at Dana Farber Cancer Institute[23]; and of skydiver Josh Nahum, who survived a skydiving accident only to succumb to multiple hospital-acquired infections.[24] Each of these devastating events kicked off a major movement, led by patients' families, to end avoidable mortality in the nation's 5,795 hospitals.[25]

In response to this growing awareness, organizations like the Agency for Healthcare Research and Quality (AHRQ) acted. The AHRQ introduced "never" events: a list of medical errors that should never happen. They include wrong-site surgery, postoperative complications, medication errors, and patient falls. Eventually, the Centers for Medicare and Medicaid Services (CMS) stopped paying when these events occurred and private insurers followed suit.

The shift from provider-centered care to patient-centered care continues. The availability of information on the Internet has armed consumers with the information they need to become partners in their own healthcare.

As public awareness of medical hazards grew, experiments began on both sides of the country in the use of Toyota-based industrial principles in the American hospital. In the 1990s, executives at Virginia Mason Hospital in Seattle teamed with Boeing engineers, schooled in the Toyota Production System. Together they applied Lean principles to make the hospital run more efficiently and safely. In 2000, Alcoa CEO Paul O'Neill[26] headed a business consortium in Pittsburgh. He was convinced that the Toyota-based system used at Alcoa could benefit hospitals too. Through the nonprofit Pittsburgh Regional Health Initiative,[27] O'Neill and cofounder Karen Wolk Feinstein, PhD, assembled a team that spearheaded pilot projects using Lean methodology in some 40 hospital units across southwestern Pennsylvania.[28] These early experiments proved that industrial principles could be applied in any system—including hospital systems.

Architecture

The introduction of industrial systems thinking to healthcare raised intriguing questions for architects. Could hospitals be designed to be safer? What if safety were the primary determinant of design? Hospital leaders like John Reiling believe that hospital buildings can be designed to reduce latent failures greatly, making events like falls, pressure ulcers, and infections far less likely.[29]

Another group of architects began to look at which design features could be justified by evidence of safety and cost benefit.[30] Evidence-based design focuses mainly on amenities like light, air, view, noise reduction, task lighting, and installation of ceiling-mounted patient lifts. For each intervention, improved safety and reduced cost are shown.[21,31]

In 2006 the professional organization American Institute of Architects called for single rooms in all new hospital construction. A 2008 article in the *Journal of the American Medical Association* stated the American view:

> In the last half of the 20th century, new hospitals were built featuring mostly single-, double-, and 4-bed rooms. It is likely that these hospitals may not be able to adequately provide safe patient-centered care over the next 50 years of their life span. Most modern hospitals have public value statements regarding safety, dignity, privacy, and patient-centered care. A tangible way to show commitment to these values would be to give patients their bed with their own bathroom in a single-patient room.[32]

Also of increasing importance is the "green" hospital. Builders are moving toward using sustainable, local materials in hospital buildings. In April 2011, the U.S. Green Building Council launched a green building rating system called Leadership in Energy and Environmental Design, or LEED, for healthcare. They encourage green building design focused on energy savings, water efficiency, CO_2 emissions reduction, improved indoor environmental quality, and stewardship of resources and sensitivity to their impacts. Hospitals increasingly fold LEED considerations into their plans.

Environmental impact is also being considered in the demolition of hospitals. A growing cadre of architects believes that the landmark old hospitals deserve a second look for reuse as nursing homes, residential care and low-income housing, and even, in some cases, gentrified condos: "The high cost of replacement facilities, their rock-solid construction, and prime locations, often in redeveloping neighborhoods, would warrant high ratings in any due diligence analysis of their reuse potential."[2]

Another key development is integrated project delivery, or IPD. With IPD, the work is done under a single contract covering the owner, architect, contractor, subcontractors, and others. IPD provides a way to collaborate and align the team in pursuit of the project goal. Toyota/Lean philosophy is catching on as an operating system in the building trades.

New building information management (BIM) software fosters collaboration and information sharing by tracking every aspect of the project in real time. For example, it can detect potential clashes of the heating and electrical systems and track budget consequences of each change. In the case of Seattle Children's Hospital's new outpatient facility, the use of IPD and BIM reduced construction costs by $10 million and also enabled the facility to achieve LEED certification.

Conclusion

> The distance medicine has traveled [since the 1930s] is almost unfathomable…We now have treatments for nearly all of the tens of thousands of diagnoses and conditions that afflict human beings…
>
> [In times gone by] we were craftsmen. We could set the fracture, spin the blood, plate the cultures, administer the antiserum. The nature of the knowledge lent itself to prizing autonomy, independence, and self-sufficiency among our highest values, and to designing medicine accordingly. But you can't hold all the information in your head any longer, and you can't master all the skills… The revolution that remade how other fields handle complexity is coming to health care…[33]

The information age has helped to raise public awareness of the avoidable deaths and injuries that occur within hospital walls. Safety is supplanting aesthetics and comfort as the most important design consideration that hospital architects face.

Achieving safety means creating a more efficient workplace and more efficient processes within that workplace. Historically, efficiency meant overseeing the largest number of patients with the smallest number of staff, cutting staff, and cutting supplies, with safety a secondary consideration. Adding to that perception was the assembly line nature of the way in which healthcare was delivered in these institutions—for example, babies in the nursery lined up for examination by the physician for the convenience of the physician, rather than of the parents or patients being moved, assembly-line style, from service to service.

Today, the very meaning of efficiency has changed. Efficiency means respect for workers and patients. It means redesigning work to be less difficult, less overwhelming, and easier to do right every time. It means helping people on the front line to improve the way in which they work.

Respect also encompasses respect for the patient, out of which flows the carefully planned, healing environment with natural ventilation, daylight, view, landscaping, human building scale, and so forth.

Respect also encompasses the conservation of historic buildings and the use of local and sustainable materials.

Infusing hospital architectural programs with Lean thinking from the start is something entirely new. The chapters in this book discuss this revolutionary approach.

Summary

This appendix gives a broad overview of the evolution of the American hospital, from ancient times to today. The hospital as an institution is tied to the social, legislative, and medical climate and does not exist by itself.

Postwar America used federal dollars to construct hospitals. The sign of a healthy hospital was one that was under construction. Federal dollars switched from buildings to programs with the passage of Medicare/Medicaid in the 1960s. Miraculous new medical machinery meant regular changes to hospital floor plans.

In today's more constrained budgets, every healthcare dollar is being maximized. The idea of building strategically, looking at process first, is gaining in importance.

Discussion

- How do social programs, medical advances, and legislation work together to influence the design and function of American hospitals?
- What was the significance of the Hill–Burton Act?
- How did the discovery of new medical techniques affect the hospital layout?
- How did urban renewal of the 1950s and 1960s change the hospital landscape?

- What were some of the effects of the introduction of Medicare? How were hospitals affected? Did it affect hospitals' physical layout?
- What financial, medical, and social constraints and opportunities do hospitals face today?
- Discuss the "things to consider": (1) a building is not an excuse, (2) build only if you must, and (3) be prepared to invest up front.

Suggested Reading

Risse, G. 1999. *Mending bodies, saving souls: A history of hospitals*. New York: Oxford University Press.

Rosenberg, C. 1987. *The care of strangers: The rise of America's hospital system*. Baltimore, MD: Johns Hopkins University Press.

Starr, P. 1949. *The social transformation of American medicine: The rise of a sovereign profession and the making of a vast industry*. New York: Basic Books.

Thompson, J., and Goldin, G. 1975. *The hospital: A social and architectural history*. New Haven, CT: Yale University Press.

Verderber, S. 2010. *Innovations in hospital architecture*. New York: Routledge, Taylor & Francis.

Verderber, S., and Fine, D. J. 2000. *Healthcare architecture in an era of radical transformation*. New Haven, CT: Yale University Press.

Notes

1. Verderber, S., and Fine, D. J. 2000. *Healthcare architecture in an era of radical transformation*. New Haven, CT: Yale University Press.
2. Verderber, S. 2010. *Innovations in hospital architecture*. New York: Routledge, Taylor & Francis.
3. Thompson, J., and Goldin, G. 1975. *The hospital: A social and architectural history*. New Haven, CT: Yale University Press.
4. The four humors were black bile, yellow bile, phlegm, and blood. Illness was thought to be due to an imbalance of these four substances in the body. Early medicine in Greek and Roman times developed under this theory.
5. The world's first secular nursing school was established in Lausanne, Switzerland, in 1859. See Nadot, M. 2010. The world's first secular autonomous nursing school against the power of the churches. *Nursing Inquiry* 17 (2): 118–127.
6. Today, although these diseases are called "tropical diseases," they are associated with poverty and its attendant lack of sanitation, rather than with climate.
7. Verderber and Fine (2000) and Verderber (2010) have fuller discussions of hospital architecture in the United States and across the world.

8. Starr, P. 1949. *The social transformation of American medicine: The rise of a sovereign profession and the making of a vast industry.* New York: Basic Books.

9. Today there are more than 400 Catholic hospitals in the United States, serving about half a million patients annually. Catholic Health Association of the United States Fact Sheet January 2009.

10. Rosenberg, C. 1987. *The cholera years: The United States in 1832, 1849, and 1866.* Chicago: University of Chicago Press.

11. Crosby, M. C. 2006. *The American plague: The untold story of yellow fever, the epidemic that shaped our history.* New York: Penguin Group.

12. Katz, R. 2008. Continuing their mission, Jewish hospitals reinvest in philanthropy. *The Jewish Daily Forward,* June 18, 2008. http://www.forward.com/articles/13591/"\l "ixzz1HOAD6Rzh (accessed May 30, 2011).

13. Johnson, L. *Black physicians and black hospitals,* Chapter 6. http://medicine.missouri.edu/ophthalmology/faculty/johnson-l/book/ch06.pdf (accessed May 31, 2011).

14. Hornsby, J., and Schmidt, R. 1914. *The modern hospital: Its inspiration: Its architecture: Its equipment: Its operation.* Philadelphia: W. B. Saunders Company.

15. The private, nongovernmental American Institute of Architects (AIA) recommended the private patient room as standard in all new construction in 2006.

16. Perhaps the most infamous example of this sterile housing dating to urban renewal was the Cabrini-Green housing development in Chicago. The development became synonymous with crime and drugs, the residents a symbol of hopelessness. The last of its high-rises was demolished in March 2011, to make way for new, upscale development. http://abclocal.go.com/wls/story?section=news/local&id=8042787 (accessed June 1, 2011).

17. According to the Office of Management and Budget, by 1971, Medicare costs consumed 0.7% of the GDP; by 2010, the share was 3.6%. In 1971, Medicaid required 0.3% of the GDP; by 2010, the share was 1.9%. Source: Congressional Budget Office, Office of Management and Budget. Budget and Economic Outlook: Historical Budget Data, Table E-10, January 2011. http://www.cbo.gov/ftpdocs/120xx/doc12039/HistoricalTables%5B1%5D.pdf (accessed May 29, 2011).

18. Lyons, R. 1984. How release of mental patients began. *New York Times,* October 30, 1984.

19. As quoted in Verderber (2010).

20. Klevens, R., Edwards, J., Richards, C., et al. 2007. Estimating health care-associated infections and deaths in U.S. hospitals, 2002. *Public Health Report* 122 (2): 160–166.

21. Sadler, B., Berry, L., and Guenther, R. 2011. Fable hospital 2.0: The business case for building better health care facilities. *The Hastings Center Report* 41 (1): 13–23. http://www.thehastingscenter.org/Publications/HCR/Detail.aspx?id=5066&page=7 (accessed June 22, 2011).

22. Josie King Foundation at BCF. http://www.josieking.org/

23. Betsy Lehman Center for Patient Safety and Medical Error Reduction. http://www.mass.gov/?pageID=eohhs2terminal&L=5&L0=Home&L1=Governme nt&L2=Departments+and+Divisions&L3=Department+of+Public+Health& L4=Programs+and+Services+A+-+J&sid=Eeohhs2&b=terminalcontent&f= dph_patient_safety_g_betsy_overview&csid=Eeohhs2

24. Safe Care Campaign: Preventing health care and community acquired infections. http://www.safecarecampaign.org/

25. American Hospital Association (AHA). Fast facts on U.S. hospitals, © 2010 Health Forum, LLC, an affiliate of the American Hospital Association. http://www.aha.org (accessed June 1, 2011).

26. O'Neill was to become the secretary of the Treasury under President George W. Bush. His visibility in the role increased interest in the Toyota work in Pittsburgh hospitals.

27. Conducted under the auspices of the Jewish Healthcare Foundation and its president, Karen W. Feinstein, PhD.

28. Grunden, N. 2008. *The Pittsburgh way to efficient healthcare: Improving patient care using Toyota-based methods.* New York: Productivity Press.

29. Reiling, J., ed. 2007. *Safe by design: Designing safety in health care facilities, processes, and culture.* Oakbrook Terrace, IL: Joint Commission on Accreditation of Healthcare Organizations.

30. Center for Health Design. http://www.healthdesign.org/

31. Campbell, C. 2009. Health outcomes driving new hospital design. *New York Times,* May 18, 2009.

32. Detsky, M., and Etchells, E. 2008. Single-patient rooms for safe patient-centered hospitals. *JAMA* 300 (8): 954–956. doi: 10.1001/jama.300.8.954

33. Gawande, A. 2011. Cowboys and pit crews. Address to the graduating class of Harvard Medical School, posted in the *New Yorker* magazine blog, May 28, 2011. http://www.newyorker.com/online/blogs/newsdesk/2011/05/atul-gawande-harvard-medical-school-commencement-address.html (accessed June 1, 2011).

Appendix B: Nine Questions to Assess Your Organization's Lean State

This unique scoring system[1] is intended to help you understand where your organization is on its Lean journey.

Respondents are to consider each element and respond to the progression of their organization by considering the pathway as progressive. Check only the boxes for which your organization meets the standard described and has met the prior standards in the progression.

If, at any point along the way of assessing your organization on a particular element, you are unable to respond with a "yes," stop and move on to the next element.

Do not skip progressions in the element. For example, if for the "learning organization" element, I can respond "yes" to progression levels 1, 2, 3, and 5 but not progression level 4, I may only place check marks in columns 1, 2, and 3 (not column 5).

After scoring each question, add all your check marks and compare to the scale at the bottom of the page.

	Element	1	2	3	4	5
1	Establishment of a learning organization	There is no formal process for ensuring training on process standards or Lean principles.	Leaders have gained baseline knowledge of Lean principles.	There is a strategic plan to educate all levels of the organization.	Training systems include process standard work and Lean principles.	Individuals are evaluated on their progression through the completion of position-specific training. Competency (beyond clinical) is a component of determining compensation.
2	Decentralization of information	Information needed to make decisions about daily operations resides only with higher level leaders and not with frontline staff. Frequent clarification or direction from management is often required to complete fundamental processes.	Communications, notes, or other attempts to provide direction for staff are occasionally posted throughout the gemba but are inadequate for managing the flow of work.	Visual controls are prevalent throughout the gemba and are being effectively used by workers to queue work and allocate resources. Workers have the knowledge required to manage the flow of work.	Effective standards have been developed and deployed so that workers are empowered to make tactical decisions regarding process. Appropriate escalation points are identified. Teams are becoming self-managing.	Decentralization of process standards is an element of every improvement initiative. Rarely do staff-level employees have to consult their manager in order to do their work.

#		1	2	3	4	5
3	Demonstrated leadership commitment to Lean cultural transformation	There is no strategic plan for the Lean cultural transformation. There is no dedicated process improvement staff.	Leadership has committed resources and staff to lead the organizational development.	A full-time process improvement staff is in place. A comprehensive plan for Lean transformation is in place, reviewed regularly, and being executed.	Top-level strategic planning addresses Lean deployment throughout the organization. Lean deployment is a significant component of the performance evaluation process for top-level leaders.	All leaders in the organization deploy Lean to execute strategic initiatives.
4	Evidence of process versus outcome focused leadership	There is little or no proactive monitoring of metrics (outcome or process) by leadership. Almost all management activity is reactionary.	Leaders focus efforts on tracking monthly or quarterly reported metrics that are a function of many processes. There is often a significant delay in reporting of these metrics. There is little or no line of sight to the performance of the processes to deliver the outcome.	Leaders at all levels monitor "how" results are achieved rather than "what" results are achieved. Very few metrics have been created to track these behaviors.	Throughout the organization there is a consistent focus on identifying the behaviors required to achieve the organization's goals, and measurement systems are in place to manage these behaviors.	Appropriate process metrics are established for each key organizational initiative. These are tracked in near real time with appropriate countermeasures when appropriate. Leaders focus on these process metrics with confidence that outcome metrics will follow.

	Element	1	2	3	4	5
5	Use of standard work	Process standard work does not exist. There is significant variation in the way in which staff members perform routine tasks.	Some standard work for routine tasks has been developed, but adherence to this standard work is spotty.	Standard work for routine tasks has been created and is widely understood. But, this standard work is not used by leadership or management to evaluate work flow.	Standard work has been developed and is used by all care areas within the organization. Management uses standard work to evaluate work flow. This standard work is occasionally outdated.	Standard work has been developed and is used effectively by management. Deviations from standard work generate healthy problem-solving efforts. Standard work is updated regularly to reflect process changes or improvements.
6	Presence of effective problem solving and continuous improvement	Problems are contained and corrective actions are the focus. There is little or no effective root-cause solution to problems. Leadership is often solving the same problems repeatedly.	Problems are solved by individuals or small groups with little or no input from those who do the work. Solutions are driven by subjective opinion and experience.	Staff-level employees are involved in problem solving. But there is no documented formal method to ensure appropriate analysis, identification of countermeasures, and monitoring of effectiveness.	Staff-level employees are facilitated through effective problem-solving processes (such as A3) for problems that are identified by leadership. Corrective actions are championed by leadership.	Staff-level employees routinely identify process problems and begin the formal problem-solving process without leadership initiating. Each staff-level employee generates a determined number of improvement ideas annually.

		Level 1	Level 2	Level 3	Level 4	Level 5
7	Creation of a safe environment	Little trust is evident throughout the organization. Employees do not escalate known process failures due to fear of criticism or professional risk. This results in little improvement and lots of firefighting.	Trust is achieved in some areas. Employees are beginning to report problems or deviations from standard work. Some problem solving is occurring.	Leaders of all areas have formally announced a vision of problem solving by all employees reinforced by a culture where employees can report problems.	Employees are beginning to identify and escalate deviations from standard work. Due to lower levels of trust, this is not done in real time and is escalated through leadership after the deviation.	All employees regularly identify and intervene in real time, when deviations from standard work occur. Trust is high and employees do not experience professional risk when doing so.
8	Use of visual management systems	Leadership and management do not use a visual management system.	Visual management exists, but data are often not current. There are no targets or goals, and reasons for misses are not documented.	Visual management systems exist but are at a strategic level and do not effectively provide line of sight for employees working in the area.	Visual management system exists in all areas and provides "line of sight" for the workers in the area. This system is maintained by frontline staff.	Visual management systems are effective to empower staff-level employees to manage work. They allow every employee to understand how his or her performance affects the strategic initiatives of the organization. The system is used as a tool for problem solving and continuous improvement.

	Element	1	2	3	4	5
9	Achieving flow (patients, supplies, equipment, staff)	Pull techniques are not in place.	Some limited implementation of demand signaling and pull is in place, but there is still a strong reliance on batching and queuing of patients, supplies, and equipment.	A strategic effort is under way to eliminate the process obstacles that necessitate batching of patients, supplies, or equipment.	Fundamentals of flow are in place. Activities are initiated when a defined signal occurs. Processes flow in single-unit quantities.	Flow measurement is supported by a system of standards, andons, and responses. When a standard is exceeded, workers are empowered and expected to make process adjustments.

Score	Organization maturity level
0–13	Immature
14–32	Growing
33–45	Mature

Note: This abbreviated assessment tool was condensed and prepared by Jeff Wilson of Healthcare Performance Partners.

Note

1. This short-form scoring matrix is based on the comprehensive Lean organizational developmental matrix developed by Healthcare Performance Partners. Please note:
   - The abbreviated matrix in this appendix is not an all-inclusive list of criteria. Other factors should be considered.
   - The most important aspect of doing an assessment of this nature is to "go to gemba" (to the place where work is done) to find evidence of the progress.
   - This tool is intended to be used to assess the maturation of an organization directionally, but not to formulate a development plan.

Appendix C: Selecting the Right Design and Construction Team

The design team is more than just the architect. The team includes architects, engineers, contractors, interior designers, medical equipment planners, and many others. Frontline workers, leaders, and patients must be included in design sessions. In an IPD or IFD, construction managers and subcontractors are in the loop as well, looking for ways to design in "buildability." All members of the project team must work collaboratively, using Lean as the foundation, in order to eliminate the waste of defects and broken connections.

The word "Lean" has unfortunately become fashionable. Nevertheless, Lean discipline is not a fad. As with any discipline, the experience of the person applying it matters. Here are some questions to ponder when selecting a design and construction team.

What to ask	What to know	Why you need to know this
Do any of the proposed team members identify themselves as Lean black belt or Lean certified?	BEWARE: there is no nationally recognized Lean certification degree or program at this time.	"Certificate" or introductory courses are essential to building understanding. But learning is continuous with Lean. No one ever "arrives." (That is why there are no recognized "belts" in Lean.)

What to ask	What to know	Why you need to know this
Does the architecture firm/construction company incorporate Lean principles into its daily operations and business practices? If so, in what ways?	Architect/engineer/ construction firms need to walk the walk and talk the talk if they are to be effective facilitators of Lean.	It is essential to have Lean seen as a way to do business—an operating system, not the latest "thing" to add on.
Does the architecture firm/ construction company "go to the gemba" (go repeatedly to the point of work to observe) as an integral component of its design process?	The importance of on-site observation of actual work in the actual space cannot be overemphasized. It is THE basic tenet of Lean.	Those who make decisions about the work space without having seen it firsthand, up close, for a long period of time, will not understand the current condition and will come up with incorrect or incomplete conclusions.
Have the proposed design team members completed specific Lean training courses?	A few firms offer in-house Lean training. More commonly, they will send architects to introductory courses offered by experienced Lean trainers.	Architects must learn the Lean mind-set, which relies on observation and wisdom from the front line. They must incorporate this new wisdom in their design.
How has Lean thinking influenced the proposed team members' previous healthcare projects?	Architects with experience and understanding of Lean concepts such as pathways, connections, and standard work can help guide the team toward better solutions.	Even when the firm reports Lean design experience, it does not necessarily mean that each member of the proposed team has that level of experience.
How will the proposed design team facilitate the transition of your current processes into waste-free, future-state processes that can be integrated into the design of the new environment?	How will they actually apply their Lean knowledge to the design of a building that will foster continuous improvement?	Understand their facility with Lean tools and facilitation methodology. This is the most important question of all: How will they do it?

Note: This matrix was developed by Teresa Carpenter, RN, of Healthcare Performance Partners.

Appendix D: Voices from the Field

Doctors, nurses, engineers, pilots, scientists, architects—Lean healthcare practitioners emerge from many disciplines, equally committed to changing and improving the way American healthcare is delivered. The vision unites them, as does their commonsense approach of Lean thinking.

Only infrequently does the general public hear from Lean practitioners, who work in one hospital and then another in the interest of teaching and learning new and better ways to work. This collection of short essays compiles some of the most trenchant lessons from the front line of care, as seen through the eyes of the Lean consultant.

Special thanks to these contributors, whose distinctive voices add such value to this book:

- In his penetrating essay, *Mark Graban* challenges us to look at Lean as more than cheap window dressing, but rather as a way of work that brings respect and constant improvement to every transaction. Graban is a nationally known, Shingo Prize-winning author (*Lean Hospitals,* now in its second printing), consultant, and speaker on Lean healthcare who holds degrees in engineering and an MBA from MIT. He is a former executive with the Lean Enterprise Institute and now a principal in the KaiNexus consulting firm.
- *David F. Chambers,* RA, renowned hospital architect, takes on the topic of evidence-based design in hospital architecture. Is evidence always required? Can improvements be made without it? Is it a way station on the way to improvement, or is it a detour? Chambers is the director of strategic facility initiatives of the University Research Institute (URI). This is an excerpt from his book, *Efficient Healthcare—Overcoming Broken Paradigms,* for which he graciously offered permission for use.

- In his essay, *David Munch,* MD, describes what it takes to sustain the gains: namely, to imbue in the culture deep respect and the mentality of continuous improvement at each level of the organization. As executive vice president and chief clinical officer, Dr. Munch leads clinical and Lean healthcare engagements for Healthcare Performance Partners and speaks frequently on leadership effectiveness and Lean transformation. He formerly served at Exempla Lutheran Medical Center as chief clinical and quality officer.

- In his flawless essay, *Gary Bergmiller,* PhD, talks about the interplay of leadership and standard work. He has led Lean transformations for GE, Philips, and Cox corporations and worked with Toyota Way series author Dr. Jeffrey Liker to develop a Toyota Way academy healthcare workshop. Dr. Bergmiller received his doctorate in industrial engineering from the University of South Florida.

- A nurse with over 10 years' experience working at the front lines of architectural planning, *Teresa Carpenter,* RN, offers a witty assessment of what to do (and what not to do) with all the space that Lean planning will help you find. Carpenter is the director of Lean clinical and facilities design for Healthcare Performance Partners and brings a unique perspective to Lean healthcare as a registered nurse with extensive architectural design and facilities planning experience as well as move-in expertise. She assists hospitals and healthcare systems in all aspects of applying Lean to the master plan, design, and operational aspects of a facility design or clinical expansion.

- Watching a friend undergo a medical procedure reinforced RN *Maureen Sullivan's* belief that listening to the patient is the core value of Lean. Sullivan, an RN, has over 28 years of healthcare experience in Lean healthcare, clinical nursing, management, and quality leadership and is an expert in the application of 3P to healthcare. She successfully led the implementation of Exempla Lutheran Medical Center's Lean production system from 2004 to 2008, demonstrating improvements in clinical quality, employee engagement, and financial stewardship. She now serves as an associate with Healthcare Performance Partners.

Be Lean, Not L.A.M.E.

Mark Graban, MBA

Even with the clearly demonstrated benefits of Lean as an improvement methodology and a management system in multiple industries, including healthcare, there are a few problems that arise with the word "Lean."

One problem is that the everyday usage of the word "Lean" often has negative connotations, usually referring to not having enough money or resources to get things done. For example, headlines refer to living in "Lean times" or a "Lean economy" and we know they are not talking about the patient-centered and staff-focused Lean healthcare and Lean design that is described so wonderfully in this book. Yes, a professional fighter might be happy to be called "Lean and mean," but that rhyme does not usually sound good in the workplace. People hear Lean and they think of mean things (including layoffs), when the best Lean healthcare organizations, like ThedaCare and Avera McKennan, actually have "no layoffs due to Lean" philosophies.

The second problem is that any leader in any organization can do anything and then label it as "Lean." While there is a wealth of published knowledge about Lean management and the Toyota philosophy, too many organizations try to use a single Lean tool or concept in the context of their traditional and dysfunctional culture. To borrow a common refrain, an organization might know "just enough about Lean to be dangerous." Organizations like the Lean Enterprise Institute do not put a stamp of approval on efforts labeled as Lean, nor do they sue organizations that misuse the term or Lean concepts.

A few years back I coined an admittedly awkward acronym: L.A.M.E. The acronym has a few different variations, including:

- Lean as mistakenly executed.
- Lean as misguidedly explained.

The acronym was inspired by reading a steady stream of articles that described practices as "Lean," but seemed to stray far from the true north of stated Lean and Toyota Production System principles. For example, if a writer described Lean as being "dehumanizing" or "turning people into robots," it was likely a case where the writer had the completely wrong idea about Lean. Or, the writer was describing a sad scenario where, perhaps, Lean tools were being used with traditional and dysfunctional command-and-control mind-sets. There are cases where L.A.M.E. has given Lean a bad name.

The two pillars of "The Toyota Way" management philosophy are:

- Continuous improvement.
- Respect for people.

For practices to be truly Lean, leaders must practice both of these pillars. Former Toyota leader Gary Convis made it clear when he said that an environment for continuous improvement can "only be created where there is respect for people." Ignoring the "respect for people" principle is what usually leads to the problems described as L.A.M.E.

As author and professor Bob Emiliani writes, "Real Lean [is a] non-zero-sum principle-based management system focused on creating value for end-use customers and eliminating waste, unevenness, and unreasonableness using the scientific method." Emiliani also emphasizes that you must practice both pillars of the Toyota Way for the benefit of all stakeholders.

Hospital leaders have, sadly, relied on layoffs and old-fashioned cost cutting for a long time, and their efforts might get described in the news as "getting Lean." Yet these measures have nothing to do with the adoption of Toyota management methods. Or, hospital leaders might unfortunately use productivity improvements directly to drive layoffs—a result that is clearly a zero-sum game (the organization gains in the short term, while the employees lose).

When organizations use Lean methods to drive layoffs, this would be an example of L.A.M.E., not real Lean. Since Lean is based on Toyota's practices and philosophies, we should compare practices described as Lean to that dual ideal of continuous improvement *and* respect for people.

As part of its "respect for people" philosophy, Toyota values its employees and chose not to lay off any permanent employees during even the worst of the postfinancial crisis recession. Instead of taking short-term cost savings from layoffs (since, after all, the company did not need people to build cars and trucks for a period of time), Toyota invested in its employees by paying them for training, education, and volunteer work in the community. Taking a long-term, win–win perspective, Toyota was not being charitable; rather, it was investing in the future success of its factories and the company as a whole. After the 2011 earthquake and tsunami disaster in Japan, GM laid off employees (L.A.M.E.), but Toyota invested in them (Lean), even though both companies have roughly the same amount of money in the bank.

Another way in which so-called Lean might really be L.A.M.E. is if changes are forced on people in a top-down way. A variation on this L.A.M.E.-ness can be found when the Toyota concept of "standard work" is somehow translated into an inflexible, unchangeable "standard operating practice" that is forced on people by managers or outside experts. Taiichi Ohno, one of the creators of the Toyota Production System, wrote that people should create their own standardized work. This is quite a break from the old approach of procedures being written by the boss or an expert (an idea that traces back more than 100 years to Frederick Taylor). A truly Lean environment is one where every employee has a voice in defining his or her standardized process in a way that best meets customer (patient) needs. Additionally, a truly Lean environment is one where everybody has a voice in improving the way in which work is done.

Look, for example, at the use of checklists to prevent surgical errors or central line infections, as demonstrated and advocated by Dr. Atul Gawande, Dr. Peter Pronovost, and the World Health Organization. Similar work was pioneered by Dr. Richard Shannon using Toyota and Lean methods as the model. The effective use of checklists has been demonstrated to virtually eliminate central line infections, but this success is characterized as a combination of the tool (the checklist or standardized work) and culture (how it was created and used). Checklists, as a close parallel to standardized work, can be utilized in a way that demonstrates respect for people or, unfortunately, in a way that does not.

Checklists might be L.A.M.E (or its close equivalent) if they are forced on physicians by senior leaders. The Lean way would be to engage physicians and other team members in the creation of their own checklists. I know one commercial airline pilot whose consulting group teaches hospitals how to guide people through the process of writing their own checklists. Not only does this demonstrate respect for people, but it is also more effective because people have a greater sense of ownership over something they have created. My pilot friend complains that a competing consulting firm will basically sell a hospital a prewritten checklist. It might seem like a reasonable time saver not to reinvent the wheel, but how do you think an off-the-shelf checklist that is forced on people is likely to be received? Which approach is more likely to have clinicians and caregivers fully engaged in continuous quality and patient safety improvement?

Another example of L.A.M.E. is the use of Lean tools to address things that are not the most pressing problems for patients or staff members. It has been demonstrated that a truly Lean environment can improve patient outcomes and quality while reducing length of stay and creating a calmer, more fulfilling workplace for healthcare professionals. Lean methods should be used to solve important problems, of which hospitals have many.

One news story, from a few years back, featured complaints from nurses who said that they were trying to engage their leaders in improving patient safety, yet were having their nurses' station micromanaged by managers and a central Lean department. The nurses were told that they could have only two pens and two pencils at their desk, likely being told that anything more was "waste." It is inexcusable to focus Lean "5S" practices on something as insignificant and inexpensive as a few pens, while patients are being harmed due to preventable falls and medication errors. This example illustrates the use of a tool, done in a top-down way, that "solves" something that was not a big problem to begin with—a perfect illustration of L.A.M.E., not Lean. Instead of starting with "What Lean tools should we use?" the question should be "What problems do we need to solve?"

Another indicator of L.A.M.E. would be cases where "hands-off" senior leaders think that Lean is just a method that can be delegated to a quality department or that Lean methods only apply to frontline staff. Impressive and sustainable Lean results come from organizations where the CEO and leaders at all levels embrace Lean as a way of managing and a way of guiding daily decisions and improvement activities. Organizations like ThedaCare and Virginia Mason Medical Center have transformed their culture because Lean was not just a set of tools or just a bunch of projects.

As Lean becomes more popular in healthcare, there is a risk that the term will become a buzzword and a marketing tool without much depth behind it. At this stage, I would bet that most healthcare architects and construction companies would answer "yes" if asked by a client or owner, "Do you utilize Lean design and construction methods?" I have heard complaints from some hospitals that their architects could throw around the buzzwords, but then utilized the same old traditional design process. At the same time, I have heard an architect rightfully complain that some hospitals want him to design a "magically Lean building"—something that is not possible without the right effort from the hospital. As with checklists, Lean design has to be used in the right way—keeping "respect for people" at the forefront.

After the publication of this book, we will likely have reports of "L.A.M.E. design" instead of truly "Lean design." This will not be the fault of this book's authors, as those who read this book are far more likely to understand real Lean than those who just hear the phrase. Lean design has to engage frontline staff to understand fully how they work and what they need to provide the best patient care. Lean design must also include patients and families within the boundaries of "respect for people," involving them in the design process as well. Lean design must be an iterative process (using the Lean approach of plan–do–study–adjust), and the space and work flow design must utilize Lean principles such as point-of-use inventory, minimized walking distances (for staff and patients), and having as close to "single-piece flow" as possible.

Can we absolutely determine if something is Lean or L.A.M.E.? There are some clear-cut cases where the approach described as Lean violates a core principle or belief of the Toyota-based Lean approach. Sometimes, however, it is a judgment call based on experience and there is room for disagreement. When is something L.A.M.E.? Repurposing a quote from the late US Supreme Court Justice Potter Stewart, "I know it when I see it."

Evidence Based Design: Boon or Boondoggle?

Excerpt from Efficient Healthcare, Overcoming Broken Paradigms:
A Manifesto by David Chambers (by permission of the author)

This manifesto argues that optimized work flows provide for dramatically improved patient safety and delivery of high quality care; they produce great outcomes and promise significant cost reductions in delivering that care. Work flow based solutions draw on the deep connection between the design of the space and the cultures of care in an organization.

Initiatives such as "evidence based design" (EBD) have been gaining ground in addressing key aspects of service delivery in health care, lately in the field of medical architecture and design. While I can understand the dissatisfactions and concerns (and the real failures and weaknesses) of health care design practice that have given rise to the EBD initiative, I am not an enthusiast of the movement. I would instead invite others to join me in thinking more deeply about health care design and what EBD may be bringing to it.

I know that that the movement, in part, stands in opposition to shallow architectural and design sensibilities that have had too large a place in our field for too long. I endorse that concern. I also understand that this movement is following another "evidence based" movement in medicine itself. The visionary work of great physicians, like Don Berwick, MD, MPP, FRCP, and President and CEO of the Institute for Healthcare Improvement (IHI), has contributed immensely to crucial policy advances in acute health care and public health policy, and has generated evidence based on thousands, even millions, of outcomes from clinical actions. The IHI's work has been instrumental in helping us know that change is not only desirable but essential. It is also deeply attentive to the *cultures* of care that cause harm, more so than the *buildings* of care that EBD attends to.

Yet, the collection of evidence is not sufficient in and of itself. Sometimes care providers must act in heroic ways to upturn the current wisdom (which is also based on the evidence of the time) and create entirely new databases of evidence in support of vital health strategies. Paul Farmer, an American anthropologist and physician who is one of the founders of Partners in Health, literally transformed the way that countries treated multi-drug-resistant tuberculosis (MDRTB) and strongly affected the protocols adopted by the World Health Organization to treat MDRTB. Men like Berwick and Farmer not only use evidence based medicine, but generate measures of efficacy based on that evidence to empower others to change policy and thereby save countless lives.

Form for the sake of form, without deep concern for what that form does to the people who live and work in the spaces we design, is tragic. As Winston Churchill warned us, "We shape our buildings and afterwards our buildings shape us." No doubt the generations that follow will charge us with responsibility for the waste, ineffectiveness, and wrongheaded orientations of our age—and they will be right. But EBD is not the solution for the simple reason that EBD is not moving in the revolutionary tradition of "evidence based" medicine described above.

Perhaps the problem is with the term *evidence based*, which strikes me as offensive, a hidden accusation that anyone who does not work in the way that the speaker likes is somehow indifferent to evidence. Who among us—and here I speak to other architects participating in the great adventure of inventing futures and spaces for people to live in, learn from, and be inspired by—has ever taken the position that we don't want to listen to the evidence? Who among us is committed to dismissing the world around us and the need to do our homework before making our proposals? It must be said, however, that not heeding the "evidence" is far different from not heeding the boundaries imposed on some of the greats in our field by their contemporaries and their traditions. Albert Einstein's words, "The only thing that interferes with my learning is my education,"[1] speak to the dangers of establishing overly rigid traditions. Yet Roger Ulrich and Craig Zimring appear to be doing precisely that when they state:

> Just as medicine has increasingly moved toward "evidence-based medicine," where clinical choices are informed by research, healthcare design is increasingly guided by rigorous research linking the physical environment of hospitals to patients and staff outcomes and is moving toward "evidence-based design" (Hamilton, 2003). This report assesses the state of the science that links characteristics of the physical setting to patient and staff outcomes:
>
> ■ What can research tell us about "good" and "bad" hospital design?
> ■ Is there compelling scientifically credible evidence that design genuinely impacts staff and clinical outcomes?
> ■ Can improved design make hospitals less risky and stressful for patients, their families, and for staff?[2]

Clearly, from the outset the authors are telling us they know "good hospital design" versus "bad hospital design." Evidence is already becoming dogma even before it is substantiated. (I should note that this white paper is written by some of the icons of the EBD movement. It is thus a centerpiece of the movement's position and represents the thinking of its founders. This is one of the key reasons I have used it in my argument.)

I have been surprised by the lack of resistance in the medical field to exhortations that it adopt "evidence based" medical practice. For well over a hundred years, good medicine has been grounded in the sciences. I am fond of medical educator Kathryn Montgomery's book *How Doctors Think,* in which she claims that the old saw about medicine being half science and half art is wrong on both counts. She insists, and I find her argument persuasive, that medicine is fundamentally about the exercise of clinical judgment.[3] Doctors must be deeply steeped in science, and hence what they do is indeed obviously "evidence based." To ask them to *start* basing their judgments on evidence is as patently offensive as asking architects—whose work, when well done, is deeply steeped in science and engineering—to do the same.

Furthermore, not only is the whole movement wrongheaded, but the literature of EBD and related initiatives such as Evidence-based Design Assessment and Certification (EDAC) is rooted in very poor (almost nonexistent) science and is applied to only the most limited, highly specific design elements. Looking at a few examples from the Ulrich and Zimring paper, we can begin to see a pattern emerge. First, studies are pursued to build evidence for what we know by common sense and basic observation to be true:

> The research team found rigorous studies that link the physical environment to patient and staff outcomes in four areas:
>
> 1. Reduce staff stress and fatigue and increase effectiveness in delivering care
> 2. Improve patient safety
> 3. Reduce stress and improve outcomes
> 4. Improve overall healthcare quality[4]

Who among us would disagree that reducing noise would reduce stress (and assess that this is a good thing) or that fewer transports would improve patient safety? I have contended this myself throughout this manifesto.

The problem is that the authors' conclusions do not point to revolution-ary improvements in design. If EBD is to have value, it must lead to *real* design changes, not incremental improvements to a broken model. This is my fundamental concern: EBD doctrine is becoming the "bible" of health care architecture, fixing only the existing paradigm and effectively killing innovation.

The authors further contend that they have used rigor in their investiga-tions, but they have not substantiated this. Laced throughout the white paper are expressions such as "there is convincing evidence," and "evidence from many studies leaves no doubt." These statements are qualitative. No actual measures (nor the means for collecting and assimilating them) are included for the reader's critical assessment. Statements without measures and without clear descriptions of how those measures were collected have little or no grounding in real science.

Another significant problem with EBD becomes apparent when the authors go on to say that single-bed rooms lower nosocomial infection rates (these are infections as a result of treatment in a health care service unit that are secondary to the patient's original condition), but conclude only that we should design single-bed patient rooms. What about all the other environ-ments patients experience before they get to the room? The problem is one of faulty synthesis of the knowledge base. The authors write:

> To summarize briefly, there is a convincing pattern of evidence across many studies indicating that single-bed rooms lower noso-comial infection rates. Singles appear to limit person-to-person and person-surface-person spread of infection in part because they are far easier to decontaminate thoroughly than multibed rooms after patients are discharged. Also, single rooms with a conveniently located sink or alcohol-gel dispenser in each room may heighten hand washing compliance compared to multibed rooms with few sinks. Finally, single rooms are clearly superior to multibed rooms with respect to reducing airborne transmission of pathogens.[5]

Many patients move through a significant number of spaces and depart-ments and are cared for by many caregivers well before they are delivered to the patient room. Even once they get to the inpatient bed, patients may be transferred to several discrete services during the course of their inpatient stay. The conclusion stated above ignores these steps and therefore pro-vides limited value in its overall assessment. Were the inpatient stays for the

specific patients studied relatively simple stays with little movement throughout the diagnostic and treatment services within the facility? What were the
environmental characteristics of the stations where movement did occur
or was required? Is the inpatient room the primary location where patients
may acquire these infections? Without addressing these and other reasonable questions, no conclusion reached by the authors adds real value to the
conversation.

A better conclusion might be that departmental handoffs and unnecessary patient movement (involving person-to-person or person-surface-per-
son interfaces) may be the real culprit as regards the spread of infections,
whether they occur in a multi-bed room, a single-bed room or a surgical
prep ward. Later in the paper, the authors even acknowledge these movements as a potential source of errors and so draw another conclusion that
(again) claims to be based on evidence:

> There is mounting evidence that the transfer of patients between
> rooms or different units is a source of medication errors (Cook,
> Render, & Woods, 2000). Reasons why errors plague room transfers
> include delays, communication discontinuities among staff, loss of
> information, and changes in computers or systems. The solution
> implied is to create an acuity-adaptable care process and patient
> rooms that substantially reduce transfers.[6]

I don't disagree with the authors' essential conclusions that single-bed
and acuity-adaptable rooms are superior to multi-bed wards and excessive
patient transfers. The issue is that the justification in this white paper relies
on claims of methodological correctness combined with weak evidence
rather than careful arguments built with attention to the overall logic of
the design. Furthermore, the paper does not take its conclusions nearly far
enough. If we limit ourselves to addressing the inpatient environment, we
are missing the opportunity to do a great deal more, such as addressing the
behavior of medical professionals, the organization and behaviors of the
institutions involved, and the pervasive and difficult-to-change habits of staff
working in obsolete and even, in the nosocomial infections case, dangerous
ways.

By examining this iconic text, it becomes possible to see how the advo-
cates of EBD are frequently busy with details but miss the opportunity and
challenge of producing a real sea change. For example, if acuity adaptability
provides the benefits articulated in this paper, why aren't we engaged in a

much greater debate over the way patients flow into the inpatient environment? The substantial complexities of patient flow were demonstrated in the earlier chapters of this manifesto. Architects need to be committed to eliminating unnecessary patient movement for many reasons and not just because of this oversimplified metric. In addition to increasing infections or causing medication errors, the movement of patients is wasteful, is costly, compromises staff as well as patient safety, and fundamentally decreases the overall quality of care.

The fact is, good design always involves the designer in a complex of concerns that are resolved for the given circumstance by a particular specification that is inevitably sub-optimal in some or many regards. The true quality of the design ultimately has to do with the way that it invents new and fruitful paths to the future for the people involved.

An example of this inventive quality within the field of health care architecture can be seen in a project completed nearly 20 years ago. In 1988, St. Joseph Medical Center embarked upon a process of envisioning its future and developed a comprehensive master facility plan in conjunction with this effort. Early in the planning process, the hospital administration considered the way that they admitted patients and executed their pre-testing protocols. Among the ideas that emerged from this assessment process was a Patient Intake Center. Encoded into the master facility plan, it was subsequently built, opening in 1991. This center consolidated the admission process for most of the patients accessing services at the hospital and consolidated several of the pre-testing protocols within the center as well. (St. Joseph Medical Center labeled the center "Admitting" to keep things simple.) Tests such as labwork and EKGs no longer required that patients move to a different location or department in the hospital.

As a result, St. Joseph Medical Center substantially improved patient throughput and patient satisfaction. Cycle times for pre-testing protocols went from a cumbersome average of over 250 minutes to less than 90 minutes, simultaneously reducing staffing requirements for those processes. In fact, the hospital went from financial trouble to financial viability virtually overnight, even though it spent $20 million (in 1990 dollars) to build the project. Today, organizations throughout the country and beyond are developing these centers as a way of streamlining patient services and improving their costs for delivering those services.

This is a simple example of what can happen when the barriers between participants are broken down. Ideas were synthesized from many participants who were asked to collaborate in delivering services together rather than apart. What is important to realize is that this kind of change in care delivery would not be indicated by evidence until *after* it had been accomplished.

I have come to the conclusion that EBD is moving in the direction of actually harming the health care industry and, by association, the professions of architecture and interior design. EBD is diverting our attention from what we should be doing to help the health care industry and is itself doing nothing to help the industry resolve the crisis and systemic mess that it currently faces. EBD in time will become an embarrassment, threatening the credibility of our distinguished tradition and tying design to measures and indicated actions that simply will not stand up to critical scrutiny.

EBD is only one of several current challenges to transforming the health care industry so that it works as effectively as it possibly can to heal patients. Two others that bear noting are regulatory behaviors and the payer model. Like EBD, neither of these set out to be an obstacle for health care, but both, for very different reasons, now threaten the viable evolution of the health care industry.

* * *

Architects, engineers, and regulators are all stakeholders in the health care industry and as such are responsible for its success *or* its failure. Much rides on health care being as successful as it possibly can be. If we do not rise to the challenges of the day, we will deliver far less than what all of us hope for. We must all approach our roles with a clear understanding of the accountability and commitment needed to achieve something far better than what we have been accustomed to delivering.

1. Albert Einstein, See http://www.quotesandpoem.com/quotes/showquotes/ author/albert-einstein/5386.
2. Roger Ulrich, Ph.D., and Craig Zimring, Ph.D., "The Role of the Physical Environment in the Hospital of the 21st Century: A Once-in-a-Lifetime Opportunity," research report for the Center for Health Design (September 2004); summary available at http://www.healthdesign.org/research/reports/ physical_environ.php.
3. Kathryn Montgomery, How Doctors Think: Clinical Judgment and the Practice of Medicine (Oxford, UK, and New York: Oxford University Press, 2006).
4. Ulrich and Zimring.
5. Ibid.
6. Ibid.

Sustaining Improvements
David Munch, MD

Many hospitals and health systems are either implementing Lean improvements or considering doing so. What many are discovering is that the improvements achieved in their Lean activities are short lived. The chaos of the work prevails and eats away at the standard work processes that had been developed, even though initial improvements were quite substantial. When I visit these organizations, I am commonly asked, "How do we sustain our improvements?"

What is ironic is that the answer to this question is in the literature, everywhere, but is usually ignored because it is not the easy part. It involves the adaptive change in people's work and minds—a culture change. True Lean transformation involves change management, which requires observation, questioning, dialogue, design, and coaching at all levels.

Lean must be implemented as a system, not just a set of tools. Engagement must occur at all levels of the organization: executive leadership, management, and staff. Each level has specific roles to play and the connections between them are critically important. It is not the sole responsibility of the kaizen improvement team or the Improvement Department to improve work. This must be owned by Operations and it must define how they work.

To achieve a true transformation, as Steven Covey would advise, let us begin with the end in mind. What do you want to be in the transformed state? What will a successful Lean transformation look like for you and when will you get there? This fundamental question should be asked and answered ideally before you start your Lean journey. If the answer to this question is "Our quality department will have the skills to apply Lean tools and improve our scorecard," you will find the journey very difficult if not impossible because it does not address the responsibilities of frontline staff, your managers, your executive staff, and operations in general. If, on the other hand, your answer to this question is "Every clinical service line and support area will be analyzing, improving, and stabilizing their work on a continuous basis to improve the value we give to our patients and we will achieve this state within the next 5 years," you may very well succeed if you are willing to maintain the focus on this transformation for as long as it takes to get there.

In this future state, what do we see each layer of the organization doing?

■ *Frontline staff* are doing the work as expected, surfacing problems and solving them as close to the work as possible in space and time. This is not the ever so prevalent "workaround." A workaround avoids the deeper problem, does not address root cause, and leaves a broken process with which others will have to suffer. Solving the problem requires knowing the problem deeply enough, analyzing to root cause, implementing countermeasures, and performing a project plan such that others do not experience the same problem in the future.

■ If the preceding is what we need frontline staff to do, that helps define what *managers* need to do. Managers need to support the front line in their responsibilities by knowing the standard work and observing, measuring, and coaching the standard work such that the process is stabilized. This is core management 101 and is understood as a given in almost every other industry. A common problem in healthcare is that we do not give managers the training and skill sets to manage. We commonly assume that since they are good clinicians they will make good managers, but this is not so. Management skills cannot be assumed; they need to be taught, and these people need to be developed intentionally.

Managers also need to coach problem solving and facilitate improvements. Yes, managers need to be facilitating improvements, rather than just members of the quality or Lean department. There is a problem, however. Managers are likely the busiest people in your hospital and will be the first to tell you they do not have time to do these things because they have so much on their plate. They are right. Unless managers' work is intentionally redesigned, failure will be the outcome. What can be taken off their plates? What waste can be eliminated from their current work habits? For example, how many meetings are they attending, how much time is it taking, and what have been the measurable outcomes from these meetings over the past year? Based on this information, what can be eliminated or redesigned?

■ If the preceding is what we need management to do, that helps define what *executive leadership* needs to do. The executive must take an active role in the development and coaching of directors and managers such that they can perform their responsibilities of frontline oversight as defined in the organization's mission, goals, strategies, and plans. The executive, therefore, needs to establish a manageable number of clear organizational goals and align the organization's attention to pursuing them by providing the systems, structures, resources, and coaching necessary. This requires going to where the work is being done regularly, where management can see the work, dialogue with staff, understand the issues, and provide support. It is likely that executives will also need to critically evaluate how staff are currently spending their time and redesign their work such that they have the presence required to lead the transformation. The currency of leadership is presence.

How to Get Started

Learn by doing. You can start anywhere you see a problem. Over the course of time, align your improvement activity to your organizational mission, goals, and strategies. The experience of solving problems and using the Lean tools will provide the means for cultural development. It is easier to act your way into a new way of thinking than to think your way into a new way of acting. Through problem solving and process improvement, you will see what else needs to be addressed. You will gain new perspectives on your work and see things in a new way. It will also help guide you in the skills and practices that your people will need to develop in the (and their) transformation. You can spread your improvement activity throughout your organization as you develop more and more of your people in the skills of Lean. In the end, your success will be determined by your people, your most important asset. Develop them intentionally and you will succeed.

Teach Your People Well

Gary Bergmiller, PhD

When asked about the greatest challenge in teaching American managers the Toyota Way, former North American President of Toyota Atushi (Art) Niimi simply replied, "They want to be managers not teachers." He then explained that every manager at Toyota must be a teacher. This simple yet powerful statement may well be one of the most important and all too often overlooked aspects of becoming a Lean organization.

If you were to observe typical leaders in any industry in America, they would go about their day almost oblivious to the details of how work is performed. They comment dismissively that their people have been through the appropriate training or should have learned what they need to know in school before coming to work here. In addition, they have an arsenal of disciplinary mechanisms at their disposal if associates really screw up. Yet in so doing, they have hit the start button on a ticking time bomb of process variability (V-bomb) and sealed their fate as masters of chaos.

They swoosh through their work areas offering the usual cordialities: "How's everyone doing?" Yet before an answer can be heard, they are at their desks reviewing e-mails and progress reports...tick...tick...tick. They attend committee meetings to figure out why quality is mediocre, productivity is low, and employee moral seems apathetic....tick...tick...tick. They construct elaborate incentive programs to motivate employees to improve performance. They have unwittingly added fuel to the V-bomb by encouraging employees to abandon their standard work processes and take short cuts...tick...tick...tick. Frontline clinical leads spend their day trying to put out fires due to nonstandardized processes of the frontline staff. Employees become disgruntled as solutions are developed by management in committee meetings with no frontline involvement. Committee solutions are passed down as formal policy with the threat of disciplinary action for those who violate these new rules—"Sign here that you understand this new policy and will follow it or risk termination"...tick...tick...tick.

Kaboom! All of a sudden the V-bomb goes off: A patient falls over here, a near-miss happens over there, equipment failure occurs over here, and supplies are missing over there. Everyone scrambles and starts reacting frantically to "fix the problems" while violating every standard protocol along the way: "Just use the Pyxis override and we'll sort it out later." After the usual grilling from the boss about how sloppy everyone was and how "we need to try harder," everyone goes back to business as usual and the start button on the bomb of variability has been reset...tick...tick...tick.

Contrast this to a Lean healthcare organization in which employees are brought together to develop their own standardized work methods based on their own best practices and an educated eye for simplicity through waste elimination. Nothing is taken for granted as the team documents the work using job breakdown sheets to offer details of technique, quality, and safety precautions for each major step of the process. They explain the rationale for performing each step in order to create understanding for those being trained to perform this standard process.

Clinical leads have primary responsibility for assuring that all frontline staff is trained to this standard work using the proven Lean healthcare job instruction method that assures clear understanding and retention of the work detail. They spend their day providing support to the frontline staff and monitoring their ability to perform the standard work in a timely manner. They observe with great compassion, keenly looking for obstacles to safe and efficient operation. They ask supportive questions: Do you understand the steps to your standard work and why they are important to patient safety? Do you have the supplies you need to do your job? Is the equipment available and functioning correctly? They understand that the forces of variability are constantly working against standardization and that it is their primary job to maintain process control. They correct what they can on the spot and also begin to document each obstacle as a team problem-solving opportunity to be addressed at the end of the shift.

Meanwhile, floor managers and directors are touching base with these clinical leads and asking what opportunities for improvement they found today and what they can do to help resolve the problems. Experts in problem solving and the Lean healthcare system teach the team how to determine root cause and implement countermeasures through structured experimentation. They engage support groups such as supply organizations, equipment maintenance, and other departments to collaborate in team problem solving. They help support the revision of standard work by frontline staff and remind them that their continued commitment to following standard work and finding ways to improve it is the most important thing that can be done in this hospital to assure safe, high-quality care for patients.

Committee meetings begin with managers and directors sharing success stories from their staffs' innovations and planning which departments should collaborate to share these best practices across the system. The other half of the meeting involves reviewing where the hospital stands in regard to strategic goals and objectives to help focus staff improvement activities to close performance gaps. Managers and directors return to their staffs to ask for volunteers to work with other departments to share knowledge and standardize best practices throughout the system. They communicate performance gaps in the strategic objectives and challenge them to use their problem-solving skills to come up with innovative ways to assure hospital safety and prosperity.

It seems mysterious to the casual observer how Lean healthcare organizations can simultaneously improve cost, quality, customer service, and employee satisfaction. Yet, when leaders take the time to teach employees how to "make the right work easier to do," the mystery is solved.

Planning for Hospital Renovation or Replacement? Beware of PTSD (Posttraumatic Space Deprivation Disorder)

Teresa Carpenter, RN

As a Lean clinical design consultant with 10 years experience working alongside well meaning hospital employees in the planning and design of numerous building projects, I have come to recognize the signs and symptoms of a very insidious infirmity. I have termed it posttraumatic space deprivation disorder, or PTSD(D). It can dramatically distort reality, lead to improper allocation of square footage, and interfere with project goals such as improving the quality of care and operational efficiency.

Just as in the case of the mainstream mental health affliction, posttraumatic stress disorder, hospital caregivers have endured great difficulty, frustration, and even helplessness in performing their daily responsibilities. They have battled the inefficiencies of aging, antiquated environments with semi-private patient rooms, cluttered work spaces, and distant, small supply closets. When they are called upon to participate in the design of a new work environment, excitement can quickly turn into anxiety. Making decisions about process and space can be overwhelming, even for Lean thinkers.

Even under the most ideal circumstances, such as when an organization is 1–2 years into its Lean transformation, the typical design process focuses on floor plan development by individual departments, which can create work process barriers for today's extremely multidisciplinary treatment model. Left unchecked, PTSD can negatively influence attempts to reduce waste in the new environment and even contribute to the most dastardly budget buster: scope creep.

The symptoms associated with PTSD are remarkably similar to those of its medical counterpart. Early recognition and aggressive treatment are essential in overcoming the negative effects of PTSD. Symptoms of posttraumatic space deprivation include:

- Flashbacks—valiant attempts to recreate a perceived happier time in the past (such as medical school or a previous work situation)
- Bad dreams—exaggerated memories of the rare or occasional occurrences when limited space or capacity caused delays in patient care delivery ("feeling like you must build the church to accommodate the crowd on Easter Sunday")

■ Frightening thoughts—an uncontrollable fear of not having enough storage space, windows, and bathrooms

■ Rationalizing—creating endless logical reasons for maintaining suboptimal or dysfunctional current-state processes (holding onto "the way we do it now")

Steps to overcoming posttraumatic space deprivation include:

■ Get on the Lean path and stick to it! It is never too late to begin transforming culture and process using Lean thinking. One word of caution: Lean design is a little like purchasing a size 6 wedding gown on clearance in January and vowing to lose 50 pounds before your June wedding. There are no refunds on new construction if you have "fallen off the Lean wagon"!

■ Value stream map current-state processes. Pay special attention to understanding how the environment may have shaped process. Identifying existing building barriers will prevent them from being transferred in the new environment.

■ Perform direct observations. There is no substitute for going to the gemba, or where the work is done. It is rare that the reality of direct observation matches how the process is perceived to be working.

■ Utilize 3P (production, preparation, process). Develop ideal future-state processes by focusing on waste elimination in process design. Lean processes can then accurately inform the architectural design.

■ 5S the current-state environment. The exercise will not only give design participants a more accurate picture of how much space is really necessary to accommodate supplies and equipment in the future state, but will also improve efficiency and staff satisfaction with the existing work environment.

PTSD can be overcome through diligent application of basic Lean principles. Design team participants can redirect their natural human tendencies toward more value-added design solutions that focus on healthcare's most important customer: the patient.

The Voice of the Customer
Maureen Sullivan, RN

Over the last decade, significant strides have occurred in eliciting and listening to the expectations of our patient customers in healthcare. In recent weeks, I had the experience of working with a group of caregivers to design a new process and physical space for pre- and postprocedure patient care, followed by an experience of staying with a friend before and after a procedure at a major teaching hospital. Interestingly, the second experience validated the design work of the previous week.

The Lean healthcare team started the event by attempting to understand the voice of the customer from patient and family member stories. Several themes emerged from these stories: Being informed and known by the caregivers, the need for privacy, space to move around for both the staff and the family, and amenities for family members all rose to the surface. The director validated the consistency of these stories with the formal and informal feedback received from patients and their families. Lean healthcare design solutions centered around having the same staff and physical space for patients and staff, privacy provided by fixed walls instead of curtains or cubicles, flexibility with equipment on wheels, and enough space to move easily around the patient.

In particular, the one design concept that stood out for me when I later was sitting with my friend was the need for privacy in pre- and postprocedure areas. Cubicle curtains were worthless in providing privacy to patients. Curtains, by design, have a gap through which to enter the cubicle, and frequently the gap is open at all the wrong times, leaving the patient feeling exposed. Anything said behind the curtain can generally be heard throughout the unit.

This simple example reinforces the need to involve our patients and family members as we use Lean healthcare methodologies to design or improve processes. There are a variety of ways to obtain the voice of the customer when designing new processes, such as patient satisfaction surveys and complaint data, interviews, focus groups, and patients as team participants. The key is to invite the customer's voice into the process, listen to what is being said, and respond by building in value as defined by the customer.

Glossary

3P: Product, Process, Preparation. This model, adapted from the way Toyota designs new equipment quickly, helps teams conceptualize, design and refine work as the project unfolds.

5S: Toyota-based discipline involves Sort; Set in order; Shine; Standardize; Sustain. Workers decide how the building will function and where things will go, in a disciplined and standardized way. (See Workplace Organization.)

A3: helps frontline teams analyze problems to their root causes, envision a better way to work, and devise countermeasures and experiments to get there. It is a one-page, hand-drawn document that relies on observation and teamwork and doubles as both guide to scientific process and as an easy, visual communication tool for consensus building.

A3 Thinking: the scientific method behind the A3, starting with problem statement; working through root causes; proposing experiments to remedy the problem; and measuring results.

ACO: Accountable Care Organization. Within the new 2011 federal healthcare legislation is a provision that provides compensation to organizations that provide a continuum of care, instead of pieces of care.

ASC: Ambulatory Surgery Center

Bidding/documents/construction: Construction phase of the project. Input from staff is complete.

BIM: Building Information Model, advanced real-time architectural software that tracks the model in 3D, and includes every detail across every discipline.

Cath lab: cardiac catheterization laboratory

CNA: certified nursing assistant

CT scanners: computed tomography X-ray system

CV: cardiovascular

Current state value stream map: a map describing the flow of : a) information contained in the request for service, and b) a step-by-step chart showing how the request is carried out. The current state map, based on actual frontline observations, provides graphic evidence of where the process works, and where it breaks down. It points the way to waste that needs to be eliminated.

Design development: Architectural stage where refinements are made, room by room. The plan is already fixed.

DOWNTIME-acronym for eight wastes: Defects; Overproduction; Waiting; Not using talent; Transporting; Inventory; Motion; Excess processing

ED: emergency department

Evaluation Criteria (in 3P, things participants must consider):
– Key assumptions—things that cannot be changed
– Design criteria to examine work flows and pathways
– Organizational criteria, which include the mission, vision and values and make sure that what is being planned aligns with them.

FMEA: failure modes and effects analysis. Typically considers:
1. What is the probability of failure?
2. What is the severity of the effect if a failure does occur?
3. Is a failure detectable or not detectable?

EKG: electrocardiogram

Future state value stream map: a value stream map, based on the current condition, that outlines a better way to work in the future.

Gemba: the place where work is done

GI: gastrointestinal

ICU: intensive care unit

IFD or IPD: Integrated Facility Design or Integrated Project Delivery grants a single contract for all of the major players in a project: architect, engineer, construction trades, etc. Everyone is jointly responsible for the outcome.

Kaizen (rapid improvement event): generally translated as "change for the good." A way to look closely at processes or problems, analyzing how they arose and using the wisdom of the team to quickly devise experiments and improve. Kaizen is done within the existing walls with as little resource as possible.

Kanban: This word translates from Japanese as "signboard." Hospitals think of "par levels," or amounts of things to be kept on hand. Kanban is a way to ensure that the right amounts of the right items are on hand at all times. Kanban can be simple cards, or barcodes, but they signal to the supplier when something is running low and allow items to be replenished "just in time," so inventory does not accumulate. (See Workplace Organization.)

MICU: medical intensive care unit

Move-In/Post-occupancy: At this stage of a lean project, it's time for Workplace Organization, which includes 5S, visual workplace and kanban tracking.

Observation: teams go to the point where work is done ("gemba") to respectfully watch processes in action.

PACU: post anesthesia care unit

PAT: pre-admission testing

Pre-design: early design involving the location of the building site, as well as major blocks of functional areas and adjacencies.

Programming (architectural term):
- Functional program (narrative document)
- Space program (line-by-line spreadsheet of all spaces that will be needed)

"Pull" system: a system that replenishes itself as necessary, rather than stockpiling inventory on-site. The "Pull" system can be used to move equipment from shelves, people through waiting rooms. It is one of the 14 principles of *The Toyota Way* as outlined by Jeffrey Liker.

RFID: Radio frequency identification, usually tags affixed to pieces of hospital equipment to track them.

Rules in Use: Four rules governing Activities, Connections, Pathways and Improvements, devised by Harvard professors Steven Spear and Kent Bowen in their groundbreaking article, "Decoding the DNA of the Toyota Production System," *Harvard Business Review* (September-October 1999

Schematic design: after pre-design, a way to create a more differentiated floor plan.

Seven Service Families: within the Lean-led design model, a way to categorize the hospital functionally, rather than just by department:
1. Patient Access/Intake Services: Business Services
2. Unplanned/Emergency Services
3. Procedural/Invasive Services
4. Imaging/Diagnostic Services
5. Clinical Support Services

6. Operational Support Services (materials mgmt., IT, environmental services)

7. Inpatient Services

Seven Ways: a 3P exercise that helps teams overcome the impulse to design things the way they already are. It's an opportunity to achieve breakthrough thinking.

Takt time: a way to measure the rate of flow through the system. For example, the time available (i.e., a 12-hour shift) divided by the number of people going through the process.

User Group: in traditional architecture, department-by-department groups, usually including leaders only, who view and review architects' plans. Contrast to the 3P group, with multi-departmental, multidisciplinary, cross-hierarchical committees that delve into process before asking for plans from the architect.

Value: Value is created when a good or service delivered to the patient is something the patient and/or customer (i.e., insurance company) would be willing to pay for.

Value diamond™: a matrix against which to assess needs and measure change; in this case, quality, time, satisfaction, and financials.

Value stream map: visual analysis of the flow of information and material during each process.

Value engineering: If project leaders need to reduce costs after the project has begun (but no later than Schematic Design), it will do so through Value Engineering (a euphemism for cost-cutting). Often these are across-the-board cuts, such as 10% smaller rooms, or elimination of a service line, at least for now. A lean design will help target where costs can be safely and rationally cut, avoiding harm to the overall plan.

Virtual space: the reallocation of wasted space that creates more useful space where it's needed.

Visual workplace: Workplace organization principles that give workers an at-a-glance view of what supplies and equipment is there, and what is not. (See Workplace Organization.)

Voice of the customer: considering who the customer is (usually the patient), and working everything in the system or process to pull value to that customer.

Workplace Organization: a term denoting the combination of the disciplines of 5S, kanbn and the Visual Workplace.

Index

"*Lean-Led Hospital Design* is a work we've all been waiting for. The authors do a tremendous job consolidating this relatively new body of knowledge into a practical, applicable application that will impact millions of people—enhancing value delivery by removing non-value added waste from the patient experience."

Mike Orzen, President
Mike Orzen & Associates, Inc
Coauthor, *Lean IT: Enabling & Sustaining Your Lean Transformation*

"High quality care and patient safety are requisites of the health care delivery system. This book is a must for every Lean practitioner with its practical real-time examples of facility improvement that engage frontline staff to remove waste and improve outcomes."

Debra N. Thompson, PhD, RN
Principal, Debra N. Thompson, LLC
Adjunct Faculty, University of Pittsburgh, School of Nursing

"There are many books on Lean management, but this one really sets itself apart in its clarity and readability. Grunden and Hagood offer a thorough discussion of Lean management techniques in building design. They share real-life stories of healthcare leaders and design teams who took the time to analyze their processes and ultimately achieve incredible project and operational savings through facility design. It's written in a compelling tone (once you start, you'll keep reading) providing a clear and actionable path to improved design."

Margaret F. Schulte, DBA
Healthcare Consultant
Author of *Healthcare Delivery in the USA*

"While there are may be many faces of Lean, including process design and facility design, these many faces share one expression—no outcome, no income. Grunden and Hagood have done it! Their latest book points the way, in everyday language, as to how we can achieve an improvement in the quality and outcome of care and save money and reduce error at the same time. This book is a guide for survival under an era of accountability and will drive the 'no outcome, no income' agenda deep into the second decade of the 21st century."

David B. Nash, MD, MBA
Dean, Jefferson School of Population Health
Thomas Jefferson University

"This book by Naida Grunden and Charles Hagood speaks with engaging clarity about how Lean can and should be used as the guiding philosophy for designing hospitals. One compelling feature is its systems perspective that is sensitive to the interrelated roles of people, processes, leadership, and culture in making Lean work. Another is its emphasis on actionable understanding through a great selection of concrete examples, case studies, images, and insights from experienced practitioners. I cannot think of a better primer on Lean-led hospital design."

Rangaraj Ramanujam, Ph.D.
Associate Professor of Management, Owen Graduate School of Management
Vanderbilt University

"Naida Grunden and Charles Hagood have produced a miraculous book integrating smarter and continually improvement management and architectural design. Just practicing the new management which dates back to last mid-century Japan has helped several hundred American hospitals cut costs by 50 percent, get rid of hospital-acquired infections and drastically reduce medication and medical errors saving untold lives. Constructing hospitals with the input of knowledgeable managers, doctors and nurses, who are themselves continually learning, hopefully is the key to solving America's hospital and care delivery crisis. Gruden and Hagood have produced the next leap forward in consciousness and improvement."

Clare Crawford-Mason
Producer, NBC White paper, If Japan Can, Why Can't We?
Co-Author, The Nun and the Bureaucrat,
How they Found an Unlikely Cure for America's Sick Hospitals

"Finally! Proof that Lean—and visual--can do for hospitals what they have already so spectacularly done for industry: improve processes, create dramatic bottom-line results, and align the work culture…and now, while saving lives. Grunden and Hagood make an irrefutable case. Hospital infrastructure in the United States in a disastrous state of decay and insufficiency. The need for new structures—and new paradigms of thinking—is urgent. A beautifully researched and logically delineated book, *Lean-Led Hospital Planning* is a 'must read' for everyone associated with hospital running and planning."

Gwendolyn D. Galsworth, Ph.D.
Visual workplace expert
Author of *Work That Makes Sense & Visual Workplace/Visual Thinking*